ALL GLORY TO ŚRĪ GURU AND GAURĀṄGA

# ŚRĪMAD BHĀGAVATAM

of

KṚṢṆA-DVAIPĀYANA VYĀSA

श्रीगोप्य ऊचुः
**अक्षण्वतां फलमिदं न परं विदामः**
**सख्यः पशूननुविवेशयतोर्वयस्यैः ।**
**वक्त्रं व्रजेशसुतयोरनुवेणुजुष्टं**
**यैर्वा निपीतमनुरक्तकटाक्षमोक्षम् ॥७॥**

*śrī-gopya ūcuḥ*
*akṣaṇvatāṁ phalam idaṁ na paraṁ vidāmaḥ*
*sakhyaḥ paśūn anuviveśayator vayasyaiḥ*
*vaktraṁ vrajeśa-sutayor anuveṇu-juṣṭaṁ*
*yair vā nipītam anurakta-kaṭākṣa-mokṣam*

(p. 6)

## BOOKS by
## His Divine Grace
## A. C. Bhaktivedanta Swami Prabhupāda

Bhagavad-gītā As It Is
Śrīmad-Bhāgavatam, cantos 1–10 (30 vols.)
Śrī Caitanya-caritāmṛta (17 vols.)
Teachings of Lord Caitanya
The Nectar of Devotion
The Nectar of Instruction
Śrī Īśopaniṣad
Easy Journey to Other Planets
Kṛṣṇa Consciousness: The Topmost Yoga System
Kṛṣṇa, The Supreme Personality of Godhead (3 vols.)
Perfect Questions, Perfect Answers
Teachings of Lord Kapila, the Son of Devahūti
Transcendental Teachings of Prahlāda Mahārāja
Teachings of Queen Kuntī
Kṛṣṇa, the Reservoir of Pleasure
The Science of Self-Realization
The Path of Perfection
Search for Liberation
Life Comes from Life
The Perfection of Yoga
Beyond Birth and Death
On the Way to Kṛṣṇa
Geetār-gan (Bengali)
Vairāgya-vidyā (Bengali)
Buddhi-yoga (Bengali)
Bhakti-ratna-bolī (Bengali)
Rāja-vidyā: The King of Knowledge
Elevation to Kṛṣṇa Consciousness
Kṛṣṇa Consciousness: The Matchless Gift
Back to Godhead magazine (founder)

*A complete catalog is available upon request.*

Bhaktivedanta Book Trust
3764 Watseka Avenue
Los Angeles, California 90034

# ŚRĪMAD BHĀGAVATAM

## Tenth Canto

"The Summum Bonum"

## (Part Five—Chapters 21-28)

*With the Original Sanskrit Text,*
*Its Roman Transliteration, Synonyms,*
*Translation and Elaborate Purports*

*The Great Work of*

His Divine Grace
A.C. Bhaktivedanta Swami Prabhupāda
Founder-*Ācārya* of the International Society for Krishna Consciousness

*Continued by*

His Divine Grace
Hridayananda dāsa Goswami Ācāryadeva

*Sanskrit Editing by*

Gopīparāṇadhana dāsa Adhikārī

THE BHAKTIVEDANTA BOOK TRUST
Los Angeles · London · Paris · Bombay · Sydney

Readers interested in the subject matter of this book
are invited by the International Society for Krishna Consciousness
to correspond with its Secretary:

International Society for Krishna Consciousness
3764 Watseka Avenue
Los Angeles, California 90034

First Printing, 1985: 5,000 copies


Printed in West Germany

*Library of Congress Cataloging in Publication Data (Revised)*

Purāṇas. Bhāgavatapurāṇa. English and Sanskrit.
Śrīmad-Bhāgavatam.

Includes bibliographical references and indexes.
Contents: Canto 1. Creation (3 v)— Canto 2. The cosmic manifestation (2 v)— Canto 3. The status quo (4 v)— Canto 4. The creation of the fourth order (4 v)— Canto 5. The creative impetus (2 v)— Canto 6. Prescribed duties for mankind (3 v)— Canto 7. The science of God (3 v)— Canto 8. Withdrawal of the cosmic creations (3 v)— Canto 9. Liberation (3 v)— Canto 10. The summum bonum (14 v)— Canto 11. General history (5 v)— Canto 12. The age of deterioration (2 v)

Cantos 10 (v 4-14), 11 and 12 by Hridayananda Goswami Ācāryadeva, completing the great work of His Divine Grace A. C. Bhaktivedanta Swami Prabhupāda; Sanskrit editing by Gopiparāṇadhana dāsa Adhikārī.

1. Purāṇas. Bhāgavatapurāṇa—Criticism, interpretation, etc. 2. Chaitanya, 1486-1534. 3. Vaishnavites—India—Biography.
I. Bhaktivedanta Swami, A. C., 1896-1977.
II. Hridayananda Goswami, 1948-
III. Gopiparāṇadhana dāsa Adhikārī, 1950-
IV. Title.
BL1140.4.B432E5 1972 294.5'925 73-169353
ISBN 0-89213-139-X (Canto 10, v. 5) AACR2

# Table of Contents

## CHAPTER TWENTY-THREE
# The Brāhmaṇas' Wives Blessed

## CHAPTER TWENTY-FOUR
# Worshiping Govardhana Hill

## CHAPTER TWENTY-FIVE
# Lord Kṛṣṇa Lifts Govardhana Hill

## CHAPTER TWENTY-SIX
# Wonderful Kṛṣṇa

CHAPTER TWENTY-SEVEN
## Lord Indra and Mother Surabhi Offer Prayers



CHAPTER TWENTY-EIGHT
## Kṛṣṇa Rescues Nanda Mahārāja from the Abode of Varuṇa



## Appendixes

# Preface

*nama oṁ viṣṇu-pādāya kṛṣṇa-preṣṭhāya bhū-tale*
*śrīmate bhaktivedānta-svāmin iti nāmine*

I offer my most respectful obeisances at the lotus feet of His Divine Grace A. C. Bhaktivedanta Swami Prabhupāda, who is very dear to Lord Kṛṣṇa on this earth, having taken shelter at His lotus feet.

*namas te sārasvate deve gaura-vāṇī-pracāriṇe*
*nirviśeṣa-śūnyavādi-pāścātya-deśa-tāriṇe*

I offer my most respectful obeisances unto the lotus feet of His Divine Grace A. C. Bhaktivedanta Swami Prabhupāda, who is the disciple of Śrīla Bhaktisiddhānta Sarasvatī Ṭhākura and who is powerfully distributing the message of Caitanya Mahāprabhu and thus saving the fallen Western countries from impersonalism and voidism.

*Śrīmad-Bhāgavatam*, with authorized translation and elaborate purports in the English language, is the great work of His Divine Grace Oṁ Viṣṇupāda Paramahaṁsa Parivrājakācārya Aṣṭottara-śata Śrī Śrīmad A. C. Bhaktivedanta Swami Prabhupāda, our beloved spiritual master. Our present publication is a humble attempt by his servants to complete his most cherished work of *Śrīmad-Bhāgavatam*. Just as one may worship the holy Ganges River by offering Ganges water unto the Ganges, similarly, in our attempt to serve our spiritual master, we are offering to him that which he has given to us.

Śrīla Prabhupāda came to America in 1965 at a critical moment in the history of America and the world in general. The story of Śrīla Prabhupāda's arrival and his specific impact on world civilization, and especially Western civilization, has been brilliantly documented by His Divine Grace Satsvarūpa dāsa Goswami. From Śrīla Satsvarūpa's authorized biography of Śrīla Prabhupāda, called *Śrīla Prabhupāda-līlāmṛta*, the reader can fully understand Śrīla Prabhupāda's purpose, desire and mission in presenting *Śrīmad-Bhāgavatam*. Further, in Śrīla Prabhupāda's own preface to the *Bhāgavatam* (reprinted as the Foreword in this volume), he clearly states that this transcendental literature will provoke a cultural revolution in the world, and that is now underway. I do not wish to be redundant in repeating what Śrīla Prabhupāda has so eloquently stated in his preface, nor that which has been so abundantly documented by Śrīla Satsvarūpa in his authorized biography.

It is necessary to mention, however, that *Śrīmad-Bhāgavatam* is a completely transcendental, liberated sound vibration coming from the spiritual world. And, being absolute, it is not different from the Absolute Truth Himself, Lord Śrī Kṛṣṇa. By understanding *Śrīmad-Bhāgavatam*, consisting of twelve cantos, the reader acquires perfect knowledge, by which he or she may live peacefully and progressively on the earth, attending to all material necessities and simultaneously achieving supreme spiritual liberation. As we have worked to prepare this and other volumes of *Śrīmad-Bhāgavatam*, our intention has been always to serve faithfully the lotus feet of our spiritual master, carefully trying to translate and comment exactly as he would have, thus preserving the unity and spiritual potency of this edition of *Śrīmad-Bhāgavatam*. In other words, by strictly following the disciplic succession, called in Sanskrit *guru-paramparā*, this edition of the *Bhāgavatam* will continue to be throughout its volumes a liberated work, free from material contamination and capable of elevating the reader to the kingdom of God.

The purport is that we have faithfully followed the commentaries of previous *ācāryas* and exercised a calculated selectivity of material based on the example and mood of Śrīla Prabhupāda. One may write transcendental literature only by the mercy of the Supreme Personality of Godhead, Śrī Kṛṣṇa, and the authorized, liberated spiritual masters coming in disciplic succession. Thus, we humbly fall at the lotus feet of the previous *ācāryas*, offering special gratitude to the great commentators on the *Bhāgavatam*, namely Śrīla Śrīdhara Svāmī, Śrīla Jīva Gosvāmī, Śrīla Viśvanātha Cakravartī Ṭhākura and Śrīla Bhaktisiddhānta Sarasvatī Gosvāmī, the spiritual master of Śrīla Prabhupāda. We also offer our obeisances at the lotus feet of Śrīla Vīrarāghavācārya, Śrīla Vijayadhvaja Ṭhākura and Śrīla Vaṁśīdhara Ṭhākura, whose commentaries have also helped in this work. Additionally, we offer our humble obeisances at the lotus feet of the great *ācārya* Śrīla Madhva, who has made innumerable learned comments on *Śrīmad-Bhāgavatam*. We further offer our humble obeisances at the lotus feet of the Supreme Personality of Godhead, Śrī Kṛṣṇa Caitanya Mahāprabhu, and to all of His eternally liberated followers, headed by Śrīla Nityānanda Prabhu, Advaita Prabhu, Gadādhara Prabhu and Śrīvāsa Ṭhākura, and to the six Gosvāmīs, Śrīla Rūpa

Gosvāmī, Śrīla Sanātana Gosvāmī, Śrīla Raghunātha dāsa Gosvāmī, Śrīla Raghunātha Bhaṭṭa Gosvāmī, Śrīla Jīva Gosvāmī and Śrīla Gopāla Bhaṭṭa Gosvāmī. Finally we offer our most respectful obeisances at the lotus feet of the Absolute Truth, Śrī Śrī Rādhā and Kṛṣṇa, and humbly beg for Their mercy so that this great work of *Śrīmad-Bhāgavatam* can be quickly finished. *Śrīmad-Bhāgavatam* is undoubtedly the most important book within the universe, and the sincere readers of *Śrīmad-Bhāgavatam* will undoubtedly achieve the highest perfection of life, Kṛṣṇa consciousness.

In conclusion, I again remind the reader that *Śrīmad-Bhāgavatam* is the great work of His Divine Grace A. C. Bhaktivedanta Swami Prabhupāda, and that the present volume is the humble attempt of his devoted servants.

Hare Kṛṣṇa

Hridayananda dāsa Goswami

# Foreword

We must know the present need of human society. And what is that need? Human society is no longer bounded by geographical limits to particular countries or communities. Human society is broader than in the Middle Ages, and the world tendency is toward one state or one human society. The ideals of spiritual communism, according to *Śrīmad-Bhāgavatam,* are based more or less on the oneness of the entire human society, nay, of the entire energy of living beings. The need is felt by great thinkers to make this a successful ideology. *Śrīmad-Bhāgavatam* will fill this need in human society. It begins, therefore, with an aphorism of Vedānta philosophy, *janmādy asya yataḥ,* to establish the ideal of a common cause.

Human society, at the present moment, is not in the darkness of oblivion. It has made rapid progress in the fields of material comforts, education and economic development throughout the entire world. But there is a pinprick somewhere in the social body at large, and therefore there are large-scale quarrels, even over less important issues. There is need of a clue as to how humanity can become one in peace, friendship and prosperity with a common cause. *Śrīmad-Bhāgavatam* will fill this need, for it is a cultural presentation for the respiritualization of the entire human society.

*Śrīmad-Bhāgavatam* should be introduced also in the schools and colleges, for it is recommended by the great student-devotee Prahlāda Mahārāja in order to change the demoniac face of society.

*kaumāra ācaret prājño*
*dharmān bhāgavatān iha*
*durlabhaṁ mānuṣaṁ janma*
*tad apy adhruvam artha-dam*
(*Bhāg.* 7.6.1)

Disparity in human society is due to lack of principles in a godless civilization. There is God, or the Almighty One, from whom everything emanates, by whom everything is maintained and in whom everything is merged to rest. Material science has tried to find the ultimate source of creation very insufficiently, but it is a fact that there is one ultimate source of everything that be. This ultimate source is explained rationally, authoritatively and systematically in the beautiful *Bhāgavatam*, or *Śrīmad-Bhāgavatam*.

*Śrīmad-Bhāgavatam* is the transcendental science not only for knowing the ultimate source of everything but also for knowing our relation with Him and our duty toward perfection of the human society on the basis of this perfect knowledge. It is powerful reading matter in the Sanskrit language, and it is now rendered into English elaborately so that simply by a careful reading one will know God perfectly well, so much so that the reader will be sufficiently educated to defend himself from the onslaught of atheists. Over and above this, the reader will be able to convert others to accepting God as a concrete principle.

*Śrīmad-Bhāgavatam* begins with the definition of the ultimate source. It is a bona fide commentary on the *Vedānta-sūtra* by the same author, Śrīla Vyāsadeva, and gradually it develops into nine cantos up to the highest state of God realization. The only qualification one needs to study this great book of transcendental knowledge is to proceed step by step cautiously and not jump forward haphazardly as with an ordinary book. It should be gone through chapter by chapter, one after another. The reading matter is so arranged with the original Sanskrit text, its English transliteration, synonyms, translation and purports so that one is sure to become a God-realized soul at the end of finishing the first nine cantos.

The Tenth Canto is distinct from the first nine cantos because it deals directly with the transcendental activities of the Personality of Godhead, Śrī Kṛṣṇa. One will be unable to capture the effects of the Tenth Canto without going through the first nine cantos. The book is complete in twelve cantos, each independent, but it is good for all to read them in small installments one after another.

I must admit my frailties in presenting *Śrīmad-Bhāgavatam*, but still I am hopeful of its good reception by the thinkers and leaders of society on the strength of the following statement of *Śrīmad-Bhāgavatam* (1.5.11):

*tad-vāg-visargo janatāgha-viplavo*
*yasmin prati-ślokam abaddhavaty api*

*nāmāny anantasya yaśo 'ṅkitāni yac*
*chṛṇvanti gāyanti gṛṇanti sādhavaḥ*

"That literature which is full of descriptions of the transcendental glories of the name, fame, form and pastimes of the unlimited Supreme Lord is a transcendental creation meant for bringing about a revolution in the impious life of a misdirected civilization. Such transcendental literature, even though irregularly composed, is heard, sung and accepted by purified men who are thoroughly honest."

*Oṁ tat sat*

A.C. Bhaktivedanta Swami

# Introduction

"This *Bhāgavata Purāṇa* is as brilliant as the sun, and it has arisen just after the departure of Lord Kṛṣṇa to His own abode, accompanied by religion, knowledge, etc. Persons who have lost their vision due to the dense darkness of ignorance in the age of Kali shall get light from this *Purāṇa*." (*Śrīmad-Bhāgavatam* 1.3.43)

The timeless wisdom of India is expressed in the *Vedas*, ancient Sanskrit texts that touch upon all fields of human knowledge. Originally preserved through oral tradition, the *Vedas* were first put into writing five thousand years ago by Śrīla Vyāsadeva, "the literary incarnation of God." After compiling the *Vedas*, Vyāsadeva set forth their essence in the aphorisms known as *Vedānta-sūtras*. *Śrīmad-Bhāgavatam* (*Bhāgavata Purāṇa*) is Vyāsadeva's commentary on his own *Vedānta-sūtras*. It was written in the maturity of his spiritual life under the direction of Nārada Muni, his spiritual master. Referred to as "the ripened fruit of the tree of Vedic literature," *Śrīmad-Bhāgavatam* is the most complete and authoritative exposition of Vedic knowledge.

After compiling the *Bhāgavatam*, Vyāsa imparted the synopsis of it to his son, the sage Śukadeva Gosvāmī. Śukadeva Gosvāmī subsequently recited the entire *Bhāgavatam* to Mahārāja Parīkṣit in an assembly of learned saints on the bank of the Ganges at Hastināpura (now Delhi). Mahārāja Parīkṣit was the emperor of the world and was a great *rājarṣi* (saintly king). Having received a warning that he would die within a week, he renounced his entire kingdom and retired to the bank of the Ganges to fast until death and receive spiritual enlightenment. The *Bhāgavatam* begins with Emperor Parīkṣit's sober inquiry to Śukadeva Gosvāmī: "You are the spiritual master of great saints and devotees. I am therefore begging you to show the way of perfection for all persons, and especially for one who is about to die. Please let me know what a man should hear, chant, remember and worship, and also what he should not do. Please explain all this to me."

Śukadeva Gosvāmī's answer to this question, and numerous other questions posed by Mahārāja Parīkṣit, concerning everything from the nature of the self to the origin of the universe, held the assembled sages in rapt attention continuously for the seven days leading up to the king's death. The sage Sūta Gosvāmī, who was present in that assembly when Śukadeva Gosvāmī first recited *Śrīmad-Bhāgavatam*, later repeated the *Bhāgavatam* before a gathering of sages in the forest of Naimiṣāraṇya. Those sages, concerned about the spiritual welfare of the people in general, had gathered to perform a long, continuous chain of sacrifices to counteract the degrading influence of the incipient age of Kali. In response to the sages' request that he speak the essence of Vedic wisdom, Sūta Gosvāmī repeated from memory the entire eighteen thousand verses of *Śrīmad-Bhāgavatam*, as spoken by Śukadeva Gosvāmī to Mahārāja Parīkṣit.

The reader of *Śrīmad-Bhāgavatam* hears Sūta Gosvāmī relate the questions of Mahārāja Parīkṣit and the answers of Śukadeva Gosvāmī. Also, Sūta Gosvāmī sometimes responds directly to questions put by Śaunaka Ṛṣi, the spokesman for the sages gathered at Naimiṣāraṇya. One therefore simultaneously hears two dialogues: one between Mahārāja Parīkṣit and Śukadeva Gosvāmī on the bank of the Ganges, and another at Naimiṣāraṇya between Sūta Gosvāmī and the sages at Naimiṣāraṇya forest, headed by Śaunaka Ṛṣi. Furthermore, while instructing King Parīkṣit, Śukadeva Gosvāmī often relates historical episodes and gives accounts of lengthy philosophical discussions between such great souls as Nārada Muni and Vasudeva. With this understanding of the history of the *Bhāgavatam*, the reader will easily be able to follow its intermingling of dialogues and events from various sources. Since philosophical wisdom, not chronological order, is most important in the text, one need only be attentive to the subject matter of *Śrīmad-Bhāgavatam* to appreciate fully its profound message.

The translators of this edition compare the *Bhāgavatam* to sugar candy—wherever you taste it, you will find it equally sweet and relishable. Therefore, to taste the sweetness of the *Bhāgavatam*, one may begin by reading any of its volumes. After such an introductory taste, however, the serious reader is best advised to go back to Volume One of the First Canto and then proceed through the *Bhāgavatam*, volume after volume, in its natural order.

This edition of the *Bhāgavatam* is the first complete English translation of this important text with an elaborate commentary, and it is the first widely available to the English-speaking public. The first thirty volumes (Canto One through Canto Ten, Volume Three) are the product of the scholarly and devotional effort of His Divine Grace A. C. Bhaktivedanta Swami Prabhupāda, the world's most distinguished teacher of Indian religious and philosophical thought. His consummate Sanskrit scholarship and intimate familiarity with Vedic culture and thought as well as the modern way of life combine to reveal to the West a magnificent exposition of this important classic. After the departure of Śrīla Prabhupāda from this world in 1977, his monumental work of translating *Śrīmad-Bhāgavatam* has been continued by his disciple His Divine Grace Hridayananda dāsa Goswami Ācāryadeva.

Readers will find this work of value for many reasons. For those interested in the classical roots of Indian civilization, it serves as a vast reservoir of detailed information on virtually every one of its aspects. For students of comparative philosophy and religion, the *Bhāgavatam* offers a penetrating view into the meaning of India's profound spiritual heritage. To sociologists and anthropologists, the *Bhāgavatam* reveals the practical workings of a peaceful and scientifically organized Vedic culture, whose institutions were integrated on the basis of a highly developed spiritual world view. Students of literature will discover the *Bhāgavatam* to be a masterpiece of majestic poetry. For students of psychology, the text provides important perspectives on the nature of consciousness, human behavior and the philosophical study of identity. Finally, to those seeking spiritual insight, the *Bhāgavatam* offers simple and practical guidance for attainment of the highest self-knowledge and realization of the Absolute Truth. The entire multivolume text, presented by the Bhaktivedanta Book Trust, promises to occupy a significant place in the intellectual, cultural and spiritual life of modern man for a long time to come.

—The Publishers

CHAPTER TWENTY-ONE

# The Gopīs Glorify the Song of Kṛṣṇa's Flute

This chapter describes how Lord Śrī Kṛṣṇa entered the enchanting forest of Vṛndāvana upon the arrival of autumn, and the praises the young cowherd girls sang when they heard the vibration of His flute.

As Lord Kṛṣṇa, Lord Balarāma and Their cowherd friends entered the forest to graze the cows, Kṛṣṇa began playing His flute. The *gopīs* heard the enchanting flute-song and understood that Kṛṣṇa was entering the forest. Then they narrated to each other the Lord's various activities.

The *gopīs* declared, "To see Lord Kṛṣṇa playing His flute while taking the cows to pasture is the highest perfection for the eyes. What pious activities has this flute performed that enable him to freely drink the nectar of Śrī Kṛṣṇa's lips—a blessing we cowherd girls find difficult to achieve? Hearing the song of Kṛṣṇa's flute, the peacocks dance, and all the other creatures become stunned when they see them. Demigoddesses traveling through the sky in their airplanes are vexed by Cupid, and their garments become loose. The ears of the cows stand on end as they drink the nectar of this flute-song, and their calves simply stand stunned, the milk they have been drinking from their mothers' udders still in their mouths. The birds take shelter of the branches of the trees and close their eyes, listening to the song of Kṛṣṇa's flute with rapt attention. The flowing rivers become perturbed by conjugal attraction for Kṛṣṇa and, stopping their flow, embrace Kṛṣṇa's lotus feet with the arms of their waves, while the clouds serve as parasols to shade Kṛṣṇa's head from the hot sun. The aborigine women of the Śabara race, seeing the grass stained by the red *kuṅkuma* adorning the Lord's lotus feet, smear this vermilion powder upon their breasts and faces to alleviate the distress created by Cupid. Govardhana Hill offers grass and various kinds of fruits and bulbous roots in worship of Lord Śrī Kṛṣṇa. All the nonmoving living beings take on the characteristics of moving creatures, and the moving living beings become stationary. These things are all very wonderful."

## TEXT 1

श्रीशुक उवाच
इत्थं शरत्स्वच्छजलं पद्माकरसुगन्धिना ।
न्यविशद् वायुना वातं सगोगोपालकोऽच्युतः ॥१॥

*śrī-śuka uvāca*
*itthaṁ śarat-svaccha-jalaṁ*
*padmākara-sugandhinā*
*nyaviśad vāyunā vātaṁ*
*sa-go-gopālako 'cyutaḥ*

*śrī-śukaḥ uvāca*—Śrī Śukadeva Gosvāmī said; *ittham*—in this way; *śarat*—of the fall season; *svaccha*—clear; *jalam*—having water; *padma-ākara*—from the lake filled with lotus flowers; *su-gandhinā*—with the sweet fragrance; *nyaviśat*—He entered; *vāyunā*—by the breeze; *vātam*—ventilated; *sa*—with; *go*—the cows; *gopālakaḥ*—and the cowherd boys; *acyutaḥ*—the infallible Supreme Personality of Godhead.

## TRANSLATION

**Śukadeva Gosvāmī said: Thus the Vṛndāvana forest was filled with transparent autumnal waters and cooled by breezes perfumed with the fragrance of lotus flowers growing in the clear lakes. The infallible Lord, accompanied by His cows and cowherd boyfriends, entered that Vṛndāvana forest.**

## TEXT 2

कुसुमितवनराजिशुष्मिभृंग-
द्विजकुलघुष्टसरःसरिन्महीध्रम् ।
मधुपतिरवगाह्य चारयन् गाः
सहपशुपालबलश्चुकूज वेणुम् ॥२॥

*kusumita-vanarāji-śuṣmi-bhṛṅga-*
*dvija-kula-ghuṣṭa-saraḥ-sarin-mahīdhram*
*madhupatir avagāhya cārayan gāḥ*
*saha-paśu-pāla-balaś cukūja veṇum*

*kusumita*—flowering; *vana-rāji*—among the groups of trees; *śuṣmi*—maddened; *bhṛṅga*—with bees; *dvija*—of birds; *kula*—and flocks; *ghuṣṭa*—resounding; *saraḥ*—its lakes; *sarit*—rivers; *mahīdhram*—and hills; *madhu-patiḥ*—the Lord of Madhu (Kṛṣṇa); *avagāhya*—entering; *cārayan*—while tending; *gāḥ*—the cows; *saha-paśu-pāla-balaḥ*—in the company of the cowherd boys and Lord Balarāma; *cukūja*—vibrated; *veṇum*—His flute.

## TRANSLATION

**The lakes, rivers and hills of Vṛndāvana resounded with the sounds of maddened bees and flocks of birds moving about the flowering trees. In the company of the cowherd boys and Balarāma, Madhupati [Śrī Kṛṣṇa] entered that forest, and while herding the cows He began to vibrate His flute.**

## PURPORT

As suggested by the words *cukūja veṇum*, Lord Kṛṣṇa skillfully blended the sound of His flute with the lovely sounds of Vṛndāvana's multicolored birds. Thus an irresistible, heavenly vibration was created.

## TEXT 3

तद् व्रजस्त्रिय आश्रुत्य वेणुगीतं स्मरोदयम् ।
काश्चित् परोक्षं कृष्णस्य स्वसखीभ्योऽन्ववर्णयन् ॥३॥

*tad vraja-striya āśrutya*
*veṇu-gītaṁ smarodayam*
*kāścit parokṣaṁ kṛṣṇasya*
*sva-sakhībhyo 'nvavarṇayan*

*tat*—that; *vraja-striyaḥ*—the ladies in the cowherd village; *āśrutya*—hearing; *veṇu-gītam*—the song of the flute; *smara-udayam*—which gives rise to the influence of Cupid; *kāścit*—some of them; *parokṣam*—privately; *kṛṣṇasya*—about Kṛṣṇa; *sva-sakhībhyaḥ*—to their intimate companions; *anvavarṇayan*—described.

### TRANSLATION

**When the young ladies in the cowherd village of Vraja heard the song of Kṛṣṇa's flute, which arouses the influence of Cupid, some of them privately began describing Kṛṣṇa's qualities to their intimate friends.**

### TEXT 4

तद् वर्णयितुमारब्धाः स्मरन्त्यः कृष्णचेष्टितम् ।
नाशकन् स्मरवेगेन विक्षिप्तमनसो नृप ॥४॥

*tad varṇayitum ārabdhāḥ*
*smarantyaḥ kṛṣṇa-ceṣṭitam*
*nāśakan smara-vegena*
*vikṣipta-manaso nṛpa*

*tat*—that; *varṇayitum*—to describe; *ārabdhāḥ*—beginning; *smarantyaḥ*—remembering; *kṛṣṇa-ceṣṭitam*—the activities of Kṛṣṇa; *na aśakan*—they were incapable; *smara-vegena*—by the force of Cupid; *vikṣipta*—agitated; *manasaḥ*—whose minds; *nṛpa*—O King Parīkṣit.

### TRANSLATION

**The cowherd girls began to speak about Kṛṣṇa, but when they remembered His activities, O King, the power of Cupid disturbed their minds, and thus they could not speak.**

### TEXT 5

बर्हापीडं नटवरवपुः कर्णयोः कर्णिकारं
बिभ्रद् वासः कनककपिशं वैजयन्तीं च मालाम् ।
रन्ध्रान् वेणोरधरसुधयापूरयन् गोपवृन्दैर्
वृन्दारण्यं स्वपदरमणं प्राविशद् गीतकीर्तिः ॥५॥

*barhāpīḍaṁ naṭa-vara-vapuḥ karṇayoḥ karṇikāraṁ*
*bibhrad vāsaḥ kanaka-kapiśaṁ vaijayantīṁ ca mālām*

*randhrān veṇor adhara-sudhayāpūrayan gopa-vṛndair*
*vṛndāraṇyaṁ sva-pada-ramaṇaṁ prāviśad gīta-kīrtiḥ*

*barha*—a peacock feather; *āpīḍam*—as the decoration of His head; *naṭa-vara*—of the best of dancers; *vapuḥ*—the transcendental body; *karṇayoḥ*—on the ears; *karṇikāram*—a particular kind of blue lotuslike flower; *bibhrat*—wearing; *vāsaḥ*—garments; *kanaka*—like gold; *kapiśam*—yellowish; *vaijayantīm*—named Vaijayantī; *ca*—and; *mālām*—the garland; *randhrān*—the holes; *veṇoḥ*—of His flute; *adhara*—of His lips; *sudhayā*—with the nectar; *āpūrayan*—filling up; *gopa-vṛndaiḥ*—by the cowherd boys; *vṛndā-araṇyam*—the forest of Vṛndāvana; *sva-pada*—because of the marks of His lotus feet; *ramaṇam*—enchanting; *prāviśat*—He entered; *gīta*—being sung; *kīrtiḥ*—His glories.

## TRANSLATION

**Wearing a peacock-feather ornament upon His head, blue *karṇikāra* flowers on His ears, a yellow garment as brilliant as gold, and the Vaijayantī garland, Lord Kṛṣṇa exhibited His transcendental form as the greatest of dancers as He entered the forest of Vṛndāvana, beautifying it with the marks of His footprints. He filled the holes of His flute with the nectar of His lips, and the cowherd boys sang His glories.**

## PURPORT

The *gopīs* remembered all the transcendental qualities of Kṛṣṇa mentioned in this verse. Kṛṣṇa's artful way of dressing and the beautiful blue flowers placed over His ears excited the *gopīs'* romantic desires, and as He poured the nectar of His lips into His flute, they simply lost themselves in ecstatic love for Him.

## TEXT 6

इति वेणुरवं राजन् सर्वभूतमनोहरम् ।
श्रुत्वा व्रजस्त्रियः सर्वा वर्णयन्त्योऽभिरेभिरे ॥६॥

*iti veṇu-ravaṁ rājan*
*sarva-bhūta-manoharam*
*śrutvā vraja-striyaḥ sarvā*
*varṇayantyo 'bhirebhire*

*iti*—thus; *veṇu-ravam*—the vibration of the flute; *rājan*—O King Parīkṣit; *sarva-bhūta*—of all living beings; *manaḥ-haram*—stealing the minds; *śrutvā*—hearing; *vraja-striyaḥ*—the ladies standing in the village of Vraja; *sarvāḥ*—all of them; *varṇayantyaḥ*—engaged in describing; *abhirebhire*—embraced one another.

## TRANSLATION

**O King, when the young ladies in Vraja heard the sound of Kṛṣṇa's flute, which steals the minds of all living beings, they all embraced one another and began describing it.**

## PURPORT

The word *iti* here indicates that after becoming speechless by remembering Kṛṣṇa, the cowherd damsels then regained their composure and were thus able to ecstatically describe the sound of Kṛṣṇa's flute. As a few *gopīs* began to exclaim, and the other *gopīs* realized that they shared the same ecstatic love within their hearts, all of them started embracing one another, overwhelmed with conjugal love for young Kṛṣṇa.

## TEXT 7

श्रीगोप्य ऊचुः
**अक्षण्वतां फलमिदं न परं विदामः**
**सख्यः पशूननुविवेशयतोर्वयस्यैः ।**
**वक्त्रं व्रजेशसुतयोरनुवेणुजुष्टं**
**यैर्वा निपीतमनुरक्तकटाक्षमोक्षम् ॥७॥**

*śrī-gopya ūcuḥ*
*akṣaṇvatāṁ phalam idaṁ na paraṁ vidāmaḥ*
*sakhyaḥ paśūn anuviveśayator vayasyaiḥ*

*vaktraṁ vrajeśa-sutayor anuveṇu-juṣṭaṁ*
*yair vā nipītam anurakta-kaṭākṣa-mokṣam*

*śrī-gopyaḥ ūcuḥ*—the *gopīs* said; *akṣaṇvatām*—of those who have eyes; *phalam*—the fruit; *idam*—this; *na*—not; *param*—other; *vidāmaḥ*—we know; *sakhyaḥ*—O friends; *paśūn*—the cows; *anuviveśayatoḥ*—causing to enter one forest after another; *vayasyaiḥ*—with Their friends of the same age; *vaktram*—the faces; *vraja-īśa*—of Mahārāja Nanda; *sutayoḥ*—of the two sons; *anu-veṇu-juṣṭam*—possessed of flutes; *yaiḥ*—by which; *vā*—or; *nipītam*—imbibed; *anurakta*—loving; *kaṭa-akṣa*—glances; *mokṣam*—giving off.

## TRANSLATION

**The cowherd girls said: O friends, those eyes that see the beautiful faces of the sons of Mahārāja Nanda are certainly fortunate. As these two sons enter the forest, surrounded by Their friends, driving the cows before Them, They hold Their flutes to Their mouths and glance lovingly upon the residents of Vṛndāvana. For those who have eyes, we think there is no greater object of vision.**

## PURPORT

This translation is quoted from Śrīla Prabhupāda's *Caitanya-caritāmṛta* (*Ādi-līlā* 4.155).

Śrīla Viśvanātha Cakravartī Ṭhākura has commented as follows: "The *gopīs* meant to say, 'O friends, if you simply remain in the shackles of family life in this material world, what will you ever get to see? The creator has granted us these eyes, so let us see the most wonderful thing there is to see, Kṛṣṇa.'"

The *gopīs* were aware that their mothers or other elder persons might hear their romantic words and disapprove, and thus they said, *akṣaṇvatāṁ phalam:* "To see Kṛṣṇa is the goal for all persons and not simply ourselves." In other words, the *gopīs* indicated that since Kṛṣṇa is the supreme object of love for everyone, why couldn't they also love Him in spiritual ecstasy?

According to the *ācāryas,* a different *gopī* spoke this and each of the following verses (through Text 19).

## TEXT 8

चूतप्रवालबर्हस्तबकोत्पलाब्ज-
मालानुपृक्तपरिधानविचित्रवेशौ ।
मध्ये विरेजतुरलं पशुपालगोष्ठ्यां
रंगे यथा नटवरौ क्वच गायमानौ ॥८॥

*cūta-pravāla-barha-stabakotpalābja-*
*mālānupṛkta-paridhāna-vicitra-veśau*
*madhye virejatur alaṁ paśu-pāla-goṣṭhyāṁ*
*raṅge yathā naṭa-varau kvaca gāyamānau*

*cūta*—of a mango tree; *pravāla*—with young sprouts; *barha*—peacock feathers; *stabaka*—bunches of flowers; *utpala*—lotuses; *abja*—and lilies; *mālā*—with garlands; *anupṛkta*—touched; *paridhāna*—Their garments; *vicitra*—with great variety; *veśau*—being dressed; *madhye*—in the midst; *virejatuḥ*—the two of Them shone forth; *alam*—magnificently; *paśu-pāla*—of the cowherd boys; *goṣṭhyām*—within the assembly; *raṅge*—upon a stage; *yathā*—just as; *naṭa-varau*—two most excellent dancers; *kvaca*—sometimes; *gāyamānau*—Themselves singing.

## TRANSLATION

**Dressed in a charming variety of garments, upon which Their garlands rest, and decorating Themselves with peacock feathers, lotuses, lilies, newly grown mango sprouts and clusters of flower buds, Kṛṣṇa and Balarāma shine forth magnificently among the assembly of cowherd boys. They look just like the best of dancers appearing on a dramatic stage, and sometimes They sing.**

## PURPORT

The *gopīs* continue singing their ecstatic song as they remember the pastimes of Lord Kṛṣṇa. The *gopīs* wanted to go to the forest where Kṛṣṇa was performing His pastimes and, while remaining concealed, peer through the leaves of the creepers and see the wonder of Kṛṣṇa and Balarāma dancing and singing with Their boyfriends. This was their desire, but because they could not go, they sang this song in ecstatic love.

## TEXT 9

गोप्यः किमाचरदयं कुशलं स्म वेणुर्
दामोदराधरसुधामपि गोपिकानाम् ।
भुंक्ते स्वयं यदवशिष्टरसं ह्रदिन्यो
हृष्यत्त्वचोऽश्रु मुमुचुस्तरवो यथार्याः ॥९॥

*gopyaḥ kim ācarad ayaṁ kuśalaṁ sma veṇur*
*dāmodarādhara-sudhām api gopikānām*
*bhuṅkte svayaṁ yad avaśiṣṭa-rasaṁ hradinyo*
*hṛṣyat-tvaco 'śru mumucus taravo yathāryāḥ*

*gopyaḥ*—O *gopīs; kim*—what; *ācarat*—performed; *ayam*—this; *kuśalam*—auspicious activities; *sma*—certainly; *veṇuḥ*—the flute; *dāmodara*—of Kṛṣṇa; *adhara-sudhām*—the nectar of the lips; *api*—even; *gopikānām*—which is owed to the *gopīs; bhuṅkte*—enjoys; *svayam*—independently; *yat*—from which; *avaśiṣṭa*—remaining; *rasam*—the taste only; *hradinyaḥ*—the rivers; *hṛṣyat*—feeling jubilant; *tvacaḥ*—whose bodies; *aśru*—tears; *mumucuḥ*—shed; *taravaḥ*—the trees; *yathā*—exactly like; *āryāḥ*—old forefathers.

## TRANSLATION

**My dear *gopīs*, what auspicious activities must the flute have performed to enjoy the nectar of Kṛṣṇa's lips independently and leave only a taste for us *gopīs*, for whom that nectar is actually meant! The forefathers of the flute, the bamboo trees, shed tears of pleasure. His mother, the river on whose bank the bamboo was born, feels jubilation, and therefore her blooming lotus flowers are standing like hair on her body.**

## PURPORT

This translation is quoted from Śrīla Prabhupāda's *Caitanya-caritāmṛta* (*Antya* 16.140).

In the guise of releasing flowing sap, the bamboo trees are actually crying tears of ecstasy upon seeing their child become an exalted devotee-flute of the Supreme Personality of Godhead, Śrī Kṛṣṇa.

Sanātana Gosvāmī gives an alternate explanation: The trees are crying because they are unhappy at not being able to play with Kṛṣṇa themselves. One may object that the trees in Vṛndāvana should not lament for that which is impossible for them to obtain, just as a beggar certainly doesn't lament because he is forbidden to meet the king. But the trees are actually just like intelligent persons who suffer when they cannot obtain the goal of life. Thus the trees are crying because they cannot get the nectar of Kṛṣṇa's lips.

## TEXT 10

वृन्दावनं सखि भुवो वितनोति कीर्तिं
यद्देवकीसुतपदाम्बुजलब्धलक्ष्मि ।
गोविन्दवेणुमनु मत्तमयूरनृत्यं
प्रेक्ष्याद्रिसान्ववरतान्यसमस्तसत्त्वम् ॥१०॥

*vṛndāvanaṁ sakhi bhuvo vitanoti kīrtiṁ*
*yad devakī-suta-padāmbuja-labdha-lakṣmi*
*govinda-veṇum anu matta-mayūra-nṛtyaṁ*
*prekṣyādri-sānv-avaratānya-samasta-sattvam*

*vṛndāvanam*—Vṛndāvana; *sakhi*—O friend; *bhuvaḥ*—of the earth; *vitanoti*—spreads; *kīrtim*—the glories; *yat*—because; *devakī-suta*—of the son of Devakī; *pada-ambuja*—from the lotus feet; *labdha*—received; *lakṣmi*—the treasure; *govinda-veṇum*—the flute of Govinda; *anu*—upon hearing; *matta*—maddened; *mayūra*—of the peacocks; *nṛtyam*—in which there is the dancing; *prekṣya*—seeing; *adri-sānu*—upon the peaks of the hills; *avarata*—stunned; *anya*—other; *samasta*—all; *sattvam*—creatures.

## TRANSLATION

**O friend, Vṛndāvana is spreading the glory of the earth, having obtained the treasure of the lotus feet of Kṛṣṇa, the son of Devakī. The peacocks dance madly when they hear Govinda's flute, and when other creatures see them from the hilltops, they all become stunned.**

## PURPORT

Śrīla Śrīdhara Svāmī explains that because activities such as those described in this verse do not occur in any other world, the earth is unique. In fact, the earth's glories are being spread by wonderful Vṛndāvana because it is the place of Kṛṣṇa's pastimes.

The name Devakī also refers to mother Yaśodā, as stated in the *Bṛhad-viṣṇu Purāṇa:*

*dve nāmnī nanda-bhāryāyā*
*yaśodā devakīti ca*
*ataḥ sakhyam abhūt tasyā*
*devakyā śauri-jāyayā*

"The wife of Nanda had two names, Yaśodā and also Devakī. Therefore it was natural that she [the wife of Nanda] develop friendship with Devakī, the wife of Śauri [Vasudeva]."

Śrīla Viśvanātha Cakravartī Ṭhākura explains *kṛṣṇa-līlā* as follows: "In Vṛndāvana, the peacocks request Kṛṣṇa, 'Govinda, please make us dance.' Thus Kṛṣṇa plays His flute, and they surround Him in a circle and dance in time with the rhythm of His melody. And while standing in the midst of their dancing, He also sings and dances. Then those peacocks, who are fully satisfied with His musical performance, out of gratitude offer for His pleasure their own divine feathers. In the usual manner of musical performers, Kṛṣṇa gladly accepts these presentations and places a feather upon the turban atop His head. Gentle animals such as deer and doves greatly relish the transcendental entertainment presented by Kṛṣṇa, and to get a good view they flock to the peaks of hills. Then, as they watch the breathtaking program, they become stunned in ecstasy."

Śrīla Sanātana Gosvāmī comments that because in Vṛndāvana Kṛṣṇa goes barefoot and can thus directly mark the earth with the symbols of His lotus feet, that transcendental land is even more glorious than Vaikuṇṭha, where Viṣṇu wears slippers.

## TEXT 11

धन्याः स्म मूढगतयोऽपि हरिण्य एता
या नन्दनन्दनमुपात्तविचित्रवेशम् ।
आकर्ण्य वेणुरणितं सहकृष्णसाराः
पूजां दधुर्विरचितां प्रणयावलोकैः ॥११॥

*dhanyāḥ sma mūḍha-gatayo 'pi hariṇya etā*
*yā nanda-nandanam upātta-vicitra-veśam*
*ākarṇya veṇu-raṇitaṁ saha-kṛṣṇa-sārāḥ*
*pūjāṁ dadhur viracitāṁ praṇayāvalokaiḥ*

*dhanyāḥ*—fortunate, blessed; *sma*—certainly; *mūḍha-gatayaḥ*—having taken birth in an ignorant animal species; *api*—although; *hariṇyaḥ*—she-deer; *etāḥ*—these; *yāḥ*—who; *nanda-nandanam*—the son of Mahārāja Nanda; *upātta-vicitra-veśam*—dressed very attractively; *ākarṇya*—hearing; *veṇu-raṇitam*—the sound of His flute; *saha-kṛṣṇa-sārāḥ*—accompanied by the black deer (their husbands); *pūjām dadhuḥ*—they worshiped; *viracitām*—performed; *praṇaya-avalokaiḥ*—by their affectionate glances.

## TRANSLATION

**Blessed are all these foolish deer because they have approached Mahārāja Nanda's son, who is gorgeously dressed and is playing on His flute. Indeed, both the doe and the bucks worship the Lord with looks of love and affection.**

## PURPORT

This translation is quoted from Śrīla Prabhupāda's *Caitanya-caritāmṛta* (*Madhya* 17.36).

According to the *ācāryas,* the *gopīs* were thinking as follows: "The female deer can approach Kṛṣṇa along with their husbands because Kṛṣṇa is the ultimate object of affection for the male deer. Because of their affection for Kṛṣṇa, they are encouraged by seeing their wives attracted to Him and thus consider their household lives fortunate. Indeed, they become joyful upon seeing how their wives are searching after Kṛṣṇa, and, following along, they urge their wives to go to the Lord. On the other hand, our husbands are jealous of Kṛṣṇa, and because of their lack of devotion to Him they cannot even stand to smell His fragrance. Therefore what is the use of our lives?"

## TEXT 12

कृष्णं निरीक्ष्य वनितोत्सवरूपशीलं
श्रुत्वा च तत्क्वणितवेणुविविक्तगीतम् ।

देव्यो विमानगतयः स्मरनुन्नसारा
भ्रश्यत्प्रसूनकबरा मुमुहुर्विनीव्यः ॥१२॥

*kṛṣṇaṁ nirīkṣya vanitotsava-rūpa-śīlaṁ*
*śrutvā ca tat-kvaṇita-veṇu-vivikta-gītam*
*devyo vimāna-gatayaḥ smara-nunna-sārā*
*bhraśyat-prasūna-kabarā mumuhur vinīvyaḥ*

*kṛṣṇam*—Lord Kṛṣṇa; *nirīkṣya*—observing; *vanitā*—for all women; *utsava*—a festival; *rūpa*—whose beauty; *śīlam*—and character; *śrutvā*—hearing; *ca*—and; *tat*—by Him; *kvaṇita*—vibrated; *veṇu*—of the flute; *vivikta*—clear; *gītam*—song; *devyaḥ*—the wives of the demigods; *vimāna-gatayaḥ*—traveling in their airplanes; *smara*—by Cupid; *nunna*—agitated; *sārāḥ*—their hearts; *bhraśyat*—slipping; *prasūna-kabarāḥ*—the flowers tied in their hair; *mumuhuḥ*—they became bewildered; *vinīvyaḥ*—their belts loosening.

## TRANSLATION

**Kṛṣṇa's beauty and character create a festival for all women. Indeed, when the demigods' wives flying in airplanes with their husbands catch sight of Him and hear His resonant flute-song, their hearts are shaken by Cupid, and they become so bewildered that the flowers fall out of their hair and their belts loosen.**

## PURPORT

In *Kṛṣṇa, the Supreme Personality of Godhead,* Śrīla Prabhupāda comments: "[This verse indicates] that the transcendental sound of the flute of Kṛṣṇa extended to all corners of the universe. Also, it is significant that the *gopīs* knew about the different kinds of airplanes flying in the sky."

In fact, even while sitting on the laps of their demigod husbands, the demigoddesses became agitated by hearing the sounds of Kṛṣṇa's flute. Thus the *gopīs* thought that they themselves should not be blamed for their ecstatic conjugal attraction for Kṛṣṇa, who after all was a cowherd boy from their own village and thus a natural object of their love. If even demigoddesses became mad after Kṛṣṇa, how could poor, earthly cowherd girls from Kṛṣṇa's own village avoid having their hearts completely conquered by His loving glances and the sounds of His flute?

The *gopīs* also considered that the demigods, although noting their wives' attraction to Kṛṣṇa, did not become envious. The demigods are actually very refined in culture and intelligence, and therefore when flying in their airplanes they regularly take their wives along to see Kṛṣṇa. The *gopīs* thought, "Our husbands, on the other hand, are envious. Therefore even the inferior deer are better off than we, and the demigoddesses are also very fortunate, whereas we poor human beings in an intermediate position are most unfortunate."

## TEXT 13

गावश्च कृष्णमुखनिर्गतवेणुगीत-
पीयूषमुत्तभितकर्णपुटैः पिबन्त्यः ।
शावाः स्नुतस्तनपयःकवलाः स्म तस्थुर्
गोविन्दमात्मनि दृशाश्रुकलाः स्पृशन्त्यः ॥१३॥

*gāvaś ca kṛṣṇa-mukha-nirgata-veṇu-gīta-*
*pīyūṣam uttabhita-karṇa-puṭaiḥ pibantyaḥ*
*śāvāḥ snuta-stana-payaḥ-kavalāḥ sma tasthur*
*govindam ātmani dṛśāśru-kalāḥ spṛśantyaḥ*

*gāvaḥ*—the cows; *ca*—and; *kṛṣṇa-mukha*—from the mouth of Lord Kṛṣṇa; *nirgata*—emitted; *veṇu*—of the flute; *gīta*—of the song; *pīyūṣam*—the nectar; *uttabhita*—raised high; *karṇa*—with their ears; *puṭaiḥ*—which were acting as vessels; *pibantyaḥ*—drinking; *śāvāḥ*—the calves; *snuta*—exuding; *stana*—from their udders; *payaḥ*—the milk; *kavalāḥ*—whose mouthfuls; *sma*—indeed; *tasthuḥ*—stood still; *govindam*—Lord Kṛṣṇa; *ātmani*—within their minds; *dṛśā*—with their vision; *aśru-kalāḥ*—their eyes full of tears; *spṛśantyaḥ*—touching.

## TRANSLATION

**Using their upraised ears as vessels, the cows are drinking the nectar of the flute-song flowing out of Kṛṣṇa's mouth. The calves, their mouths full of milk from their mothers' moist nipples, stand still as they take Govinda within themselves through their tear-filled eyes and embrace Him within their hearts.**

## TEXT 14

प्रायो बताम्ब विहगा मुनयो वनेऽस्मिन्
कृष्णेक्षितं तदुदितं कलवेणुगीतम् ।
आरुह्य ये द्रुमभुजान् रुचिरप्रवालान्
शृण्वन्ति मीलितदृशो विगतान्यवाचः ॥१४॥

*prāyo batāmba vihagā munayo vane 'smin*
*kṛṣṇekṣitaṁ tad-uditaṁ kala-veṇu-gītam*
*āruhya ye druma-bhujān rucira-pravālān*
*śṛṇvanti mīlita-dṛśo vigatānya-vācaḥ*

*prāyaḥ*—almost; *bata*—certainly; *amba*—O mother; *vihagāḥ*—the birds; *munayaḥ*—great sages; *vane*—in the forest; *asmin*—this; *kṛṣṇa-īkṣitam*—in order to see Kṛṣṇa; *tat-uditam*—created by Him; *kala-veṇu-gītam*—sweet vibrations made by playing the flute; *āruhya*—rising; *ye*—who; *druma-bhujān*—to the branches of the trees; *rucira-pravālān*—having beautiful creepers and twigs; *śṛṇvanti*—they hear; *mīlita-dṛśaḥ*—closing their eyes; *vigata-anya-vācaḥ*—stopping all other sounds.

## TRANSLATION

**O mother, in this forest all the birds have risen onto the beautiful branches of the trees to see Kṛṣṇa. With closed eyes they are simply listening in silence to the sweet vibrations of His flute, and they are not attracted by any other sound. Surely these birds are on the same level as great sages.**

## PURPORT

The birds resemble sages because they live in the forest, keep their eyes closed, observe silence and remain motionless. Significantly, it is stated here that even great sages become maddened by the sound of Kṛṣṇa's flute, which is a completely spiritual vibration.

The word *rucira-pravālān* indicates that even the branches of the trees are transformed in ecstasy when struck by the vibration of Kṛṣṇa's flute-song. Indra, Brahmā, Śiva and Viṣṇu, being primordial gods, travel throughout the universe and have extensive knowledge of the science of music, and yet even these great personalities have never heard or composed music like that which emanates from Kṛṣṇa's flute. Indeed, the birds are so moved by the blissful sound that in their ecstasy they close their eyes and cling to the branches to avoid falling off the trees.

Śrīla Viśvanātha Cakravartī Ṭhākura explains that the *gopīs* would sometimes address each other as *amba*, "mother."

## TEXT 15

नद्यस्तदा तदुपधार्य मुकुन्दगीतम्
आवर्तलक्षितमनोभवभग्नवेगाः ।
आलिंगनस्थगितमूर्मिभुजैर्मुरारेर्
गृह्णन्ति पादयुगलं कमलोपहाराः ॥१५॥

*nadyas tadā tad upadhārya mukunda-gītam*
*āvarta-lakṣita-manobhava-bhagna-vegāḥ*
*āliṅgana-sthagitam ūrmi-bhujair murārer*
*gṛhṇanti pāda-yugalaṁ kamalopahārāḥ*

*nadyaḥ*—the rivers; *tadā*—then; *tat*—that; *upadhārya*—perceiving; *mukunda*—of Lord Kṛṣṇa; *gītam*—the song of His flute; *āvarta*—by their whirlpools; *lakṣita*—manifest; *manaḥ-bhava*—by their conjugal desire; *bhagna*—broken; *vegāḥ*—their currents; *āliṅgana*—by their embrace; *sthagitam*—held stationary; *ūrmi-bhujaiḥ*—by the arms of their waves; *murāreḥ*—of Lord Murāri; *gṛhṇanti*—they seize; *pāda-yugalam*—the two lotus feet; *kamala-upahārāḥ*—carrying offerings of lotus flowers.

## TRANSLATION

**When the rivers hear the flute-song of Kṛṣṇa, their minds begin to desire Him, and thus the flow of their currents is broken and their waters are agitated, moving around in whirlpools. Then with the arms of their waves the rivers embrace Murāri's lotus feet and, holding on to them, present offerings of lotus flowers.**

## PURPORT

Even such sacred bodies of water as the Yamunā and the Mānasa-gaṅgā are enchanted by the flute-song, and thus they are disturbed by conjugal attraction for young Kṛṣṇa. The *gopīs* are implying that since many different types of living beings are overwhelmed by conjugal love for Kṛṣṇa, why should the *gopīs* be criticized for their intense desire to serve Kṛṣṇa in the conjugal relationship?

## TEXT 16

दृष्ट्वातपे व्रजपशून् सह रामगोपैः
सञ्चारयन्तमनु वेणुमुदीरयन्तम् ।
प्रेमप्रवृद्ध उदितः कुसुमावलीभिः
सख्युर्व्यधात् स्ववपुषाम्बुद आतपत्रम् ॥१६॥

*dṛṣṭvātape vraja-paśūn saha rāma-gopaiḥ*
*sañcārayantam anu veṇum udīrayantam*
*prema-pravṛddha uditaḥ kusumāvalībhiḥ*
*sakhyur vyadhāt sva-vapuṣāmbuda ātapatram*

*dṛṣṭvā*—seeing; *ātape*—in the full heat of the sun; *vraja-paśūn*—the domestic animals of Vraja; *saha*—together with; *rāma-gopaiḥ*—Lord Balarāma and the cowherd boys; *sañcārayantam*—herding together; *anu*—repeatedly; *veṇum*—His flute; *udīrayantam*—loudly playing; *prema*—out of love; *pravṛddhaḥ*—expanded; *uditaḥ*—rising high; *kusuma-āvalībhiḥ*—(with droplets of water vapor, which are like) groups of flowers; *sakhyuḥ*—for his friend; *vyadhāt*—he constructed; *sva-vapuṣā*—out of his own body; *ambudaḥ*—the cloud; *ātapatram*—an umbrella.

## TRANSLATION

**In the company of Balarāma and the cowherd boys, Lord Kṛṣṇa is continually vibrating His flute as He herds all the animals of Vraja, even under the full heat of the summer sun. Seeing this, the cloud in the sky has expanded himself out of love. He is rising**

**high and constructing out of his own body, with its multitude of flower-like droplets of water, an umbrella for the sake of his friend.**

## PURPORT

Śrīla Prabhupāda states in his *Kṛṣṇa, the Supreme Personality of Godhead:* "The scorching heat of the autumn sunshine was sometimes intolerable, and therefore the clouds in the sky appeared in sympathy above Kṛṣṇa and Balarāma and Their boyfriends while They engaged in blowing Their flutes. The clouds served as a soothing umbrella over Their heads just to make friendship with Kṛṣṇa."

## TEXT 17

पूर्णाः पुलिन्द्य उरुगायपदाब्जराग-
श्रीकुंकुमेन दयितास्तनमण्डितेन ।
तद्दर्शनस्मररुजस्तृणरूषितेन
लिम्पन्त्य आननकुचेषु जहुस्तदाधिम् ॥१७॥

*pūrṇāḥ pulindya urugāya-padābja-rāga-*
*śrī-kuṅkumena dayitā-stana-maṇḍitena*
*tad-darśana-smara-rujas tṛṇa-rūṣitena*
*limpantya ānana-kuceṣu jahus tad-ādhim*

*pūrṇāḥ*—fully satisfied; *pulindyaḥ*—the wives of the Śabara tribe; *urugāya*—of Lord Kṛṣṇa; *pada-abja*—from the lotus feet; *rāga*—of reddish color; *śrī-kuṅkumena*—by the transcendental *kuṅkuma* powder; *dayitā*—of His girlfriends; *stana*—the breasts; *maṇḍitena*—which had decorated; *tat*—of that; *darśana*—by the sight; *smara*—of Cupid; *rujaḥ*—feeling the torment; *tṛṇa*—upon the blades of grass; *rūṣitena*—attached; *limpantyaḥ*—smearing; *ānana*—upon their faces; *kuceṣu*—and breasts; *jahuḥ*—they gave up; *tat*—that; *ādhim*—mental pain.

## TRANSLATION

**The aborigine women of the Vṛndāvana area become disturbed by lust when they see the grass marked with reddish *kuṅkuma***

**powder. Endowed with the color of Kṛṣṇa's lotus feet, this powder originally decorated the breasts of His beloveds, and when the aborigine women smear it on their faces and breasts, they give up all their anxiety.**

## PURPORT

Śrīla Prabhupāda explains this verse as follows: "The wanton aborigine girls also became fully satisfied when they smeared their faces and breasts with the dust of Vṛndāvana, which was reddish from the touch of Kṛṣṇa's lotus feet. The aborigine girls had very full breasts, and they were also very lusty, but when their lovers felt their breasts, they were not very satisfied. When they came out into the midst of the forest, they saw that while Kṛṣṇa was walking, some of the leaves and creepers of Vṛndāvana turned reddish from the *kuṅkuma* powder that fell from His lotus feet. His lotus feet were held by the *gopīs* on their breasts, which were also smeared with *kuṅkuma* powder, but when Kṛṣṇa traveled in the Vṛndāvana forest with Balarāma and His boyfriends, the reddish powder fell on the ground of the Vṛndāvana forest. So the lusty aborigine girls, while looking toward Kṛṣṇa playing His flute, saw the reddish *kuṅkuma* on the ground and immediately took it and smeared it over their faces and breasts. In this way they became fully satisfied, although they were not satisfied when their lovers touched their breasts. All material lusty desires can be immediately satisfied if one comes in contact with Kṛṣṇa consciousness."

## TEXT 18

हन्तायमद्रिरबला हरिदासवर्यो
यद् रामकृष्णचरणस्परशप्रमोदः ।
मानं तनोति सहगोगणयोस्तयोर्यत्
पानीयसूयवसकन्दरकन्दमूलैः ॥१८॥

*hantāyam adrir abalā hari-dāsa-varyo*
*yad rāma-kṛṣṇa-caraṇa-sparaśa-pramodaḥ*
*mānaṁ tanoti saha-go-gaṇayos tayor yat*
*pānīya-sūyavasa-kandara-kandamūlaiḥ*

*hanta*—oh; *ayam*—this; *adriḥ*—hill; *abalāḥ*—O friends; *hari-dāsa-varyaḥ*—the best among the servants of the Lord; *yat*—because; *rāma-kṛṣṇa-caraṇa*—of the lotus feet of Lord Kṛṣṇa and Balarāma; *sparaśa*—by the touch; *pramodaḥ*—jubilant; *mānam*—respect; *tanoti*—offers; *saha*—with; *go-gaṇayoḥ*—the cows, calves and cowherd boys; *tayoḥ*—to Them (Śrī Kṛṣṇa and Balarāma); *yat*—because; *pānīya*—with drinking water; *sūyavasa*—very soft grass; *kandara*—caves; *kanda-mūlaiḥ*—and edible roots.

## TRANSLATION

**Of all the devotees, this Govardhana Hill is the best! O my friends, this hill supplies Kṛṣṇa and Balarāma, along with Their calves, cows and cowherd friends, with all kinds of necessities—water for drinking, very soft grass, caves, fruits, flowers and vegetables. In this way the hill offers respects to the Lord. Being touched by the lotus feet of Kṛṣṇa and Balarāma, Govardhana Hill appears very jubilant.**

## PURPORT

This translation is quoted from Śrīla Prabhupāda's *Caitanya-caritāmṛta* (*Madhya* 18.34).

Śrīla Viśvanātha Cakravartī Ṭhākura explains the opulence of Govardhana Hill as follows: *Pānīya* refers to the fragrant, cool water from the Govardhana waterfalls, which Kṛṣṇa and Balarāma drink and use to wash Their feet and mouths. Govardhana also offers other beverages, such as honey, mango juice and *pīlu* juice. *Sūyavasa* indicates *dūrvā* grass, used to make the religious offering of *arghya.* Govardhana also has grass that is fragrant, soft and conducive to the strong growth of cows and increased production of milk. Thus this grass is used for feeding the transcendental herds. *Kandara* refers to the caves where Kṛṣṇa, Balarāma and Their friends play, sit and lie down. These caves give pleasure when the weather is too hot or too cold, or when it is raining. Govardhana also features soft roots for eating, jewels for ornamenting the body, flat places for sitting, and lamps and mirrors in the form of smooth stones, glistening water and other natural substances.

## TEXT 19

गा गोपकैरनुवनं नयतोरुदार-
वेणुस्वनैः कलपदैस्तनुभृत्सु सख्यः ।
अस्पन्दनं गतिमतां पुलकस्तरूणां
निर्योगपाशकृतलक्षणयोर्विचित्रम् ॥१९॥

*gā gopakair anu-vanaṁ nayator udāra-*
*veṇu-svanaiḥ kala-padais tanu-bhṛtsu sakhyaḥ*
*aspandanaṁ gati-matāṁ pulakas tarūṇāṁ*
*niryoga-pāśa-kṛta-lakṣaṇayor vicitram*

*gāḥ*—the cows; *gopakaiḥ*—with the cowherd boys; *anu-vanam*—to each forest; *nayatoḥ*—leading; *udāra*—very liberal; *veṇu-svanaiḥ*—by the vibrations of the Lord's flute; *kala-padaiḥ*—having sweet tones; *tanu-bhṛtsu*—among the living entities; *sakhyaḥ*—O friends; *aspandanam*—the lack of movement; *gati-matām*—of those living entities that can move; *pulakaḥ*—the ecstatic jubilation; *tarūṇām*—of the otherwise nonmoving trees; *niryoga-pāśa*—the ropes for binding the rear legs of the cows; *kṛta-lakṣaṇayoḥ*—of those two (Kṛṣṇa and Balarāma), who are characterized by; *vicitram*—wonderful.

## TRANSLATION

**My dear friends, as Kṛṣṇa and Balarāma pass through the forest with Their cowherd friends, leading Their cows, They carry ropes to bind the cows' rear legs at the time of milking. When Lord Kṛṣṇa plays on His flute, the sweet music causes the moving living entities to become stunned and the nonmoving trees to tremble with ecstasy. These things are certainly very wonderful.**

## PURPORT

Kṛṣṇa and Balarāma would sometimes wear Their cowherding ropes on Their heads and sometimes carry them on Their shoulders, and thus They were beautifully decorated with all the equipment of cowherd boys.

Śrīla Viśvanātha Cakravartī Ṭhākura explains that the ropes of Kṛṣṇa and Balarāma are made of yellow cloth and have clusters of pearls at both ends. Sometimes They wear these ropes around Their turbans, and the ropes thus become wonderful decorations.

## TEXT 20

**एवंविधा भगवतो या वृन्दावनचारिणः ।**
**वर्णयन्त्यो मिथो गोप्यः क्रीडास्तन्मयतां ययुः ॥२०॥**

*evaṁ-vidhā bhagavato*
*yā vṛndāvana-cāriṇaḥ*
*varṇayantyo mitho gopyaḥ*
*krīḍās tan-mayatāṁ yayuḥ*

*evam-vidhāḥ*—such; *bhagavataḥ*—of the Supreme Personality of Godhead; *yāḥ*—which; *vṛndāvana-cāriṇaḥ*—who was wandering in the Vṛndāvana forest; *varṇayantyaḥ*—engaged in describing; *mithaḥ*—among one another; *gopyaḥ*—the *gopīs; krīḍāḥ*—the pastimes; *tat-mayatām*—fullness in ecstatic meditation upon Him; *yayuḥ*—they attained.

## TRANSLATION

**Thus narrating to one another the playful pastimes of the Supreme Personality of Godhead as He wandered about in the Vṛndāvana forest, the *gopīs* became fully absorbed in thoughts of Him.**

## PURPORT

In this regard Śrīla Prabhupāda comments, "This is the perfect example of Kṛṣṇa consciousness: to somehow or other remain always engrossed in thoughts of Kṛṣṇa. The vivid example is always present in the behavior of the *gopīs;* therefore Lord Caitanya declared that no one can worship the Supreme Lord by any method that is better than the method of the *gopīs.* The *gopīs* were not born in very high *brāhmaṇa* or *kṣatriya* families; they were born in the families of *vaiśyas,* and not in big mercantile communities but in the families of cowherd men. They were not very well educated, although they heard all sorts of knowledge from the *brāhmaṇas,* the authorities of Vedic knowledge. The *gopīs'* only purpose was to remain always absorbed in thoughts of Kṛṣṇa."

*Thus end the purports of the humble servant of His Divine Grace A. C. Bhaktivedanta Swami Prabhupāda to the Tenth Canto, Twenty-first Chapter, of the* Śrīmad-Bhāgavatam, *entitled "The* Gopīs *Glorify the Song of Kṛṣṇa's Flute."*

CHAPTER TWENTY-TWO

# Kṛṣṇa Steals the Garments of the Unmarried Gopīs

This chapter describes how the marriageable daughters of the cowherd men worshiped Kātyāyanī to get Lord Śrī Kṛṣṇa as their husband, and how Kṛṣṇa stole the garments of the young girls and gave the girls benedictions.

During the month of Mārgaśīrṣa, every day early in the morning the young daughters of the cowherds would take one another's hands and, singing of Kṛṣṇa's transcendental qualities, go to the Yamunā to bathe. Desiring to obtain Kṛṣṇa as their husband, they would then worship the goddess Kātyāyanī with incense, flowers and other items.

One day, the young *gopīs* left their garments on the shore as usual and began playing in the water while chanting of Lord Kṛṣṇa's activities. Suddenly Kṛṣṇa Himself came there, took away all the garments and climbed a nearby *kadamba* tree. Wanting to tease the *gopīs*, Kṛṣṇa said, "I understand how fatigued you *gopīs* are from your austerities, so please come onto the shore and take back your clothes."

The *gopīs* then pretended to become angry and said the cold water of the Yamunā was giving them great pain. If Kṛṣṇa did not give them back their garments, they said, they would inform King Kaṁsa of all that had happened. But if He did give the clothes back, they would willingly carry out His orders in the mood of humble servants.

Śrī Kṛṣṇa replied that He had no fear of King Kaṁsa, and that if the girls really intended to follow His command and be His maidservants, they should each immediately come onto the shore and take their respective garments. The girls, trembling from the cold, climbed out of the water with their two hands covering their private parts. Kṛṣṇa, who felt great affection for them, again spoke: "Because while executing a vow you bathed in the water naked, you have committed an offense against the lord of the waters, and to counteract it you should offer obeisances with folded hands. Then your vow of austerity will achieve its full result."

The *gopīs* followed this instruction and, folding their hands in respect, offered obeisances to Śrī Kṛṣṇa. Satisfied, He gave them back their clothing. But the young girls' hearts had become so attracted to Him that they could not leave. Understanding their minds, Kṛṣṇa said that He knew they had worshiped Kātyāyanī to get Him as their husband. Because they had offered their hearts to Him, their desires would never become tainted by the mood of materialistic enjoyment, just as fried barleycorns can no longer grow into shoots. Next autumn, He told them, their most cherished desire would be fulfilled.

Then the *gopīs*, fully satisfied, returned to Vraja, and Śrī Kṛṣṇa and His cowherd friends went off to a distant place to graze the cows.

Sometime later, when the boys felt disturbed by the great heat of summer, they took shelter at the base of a tree that stood just like an umbrella. The Lord then said that the life of a tree is most excellent, for even while feeling pain a tree continues to protect others from heat, rain, snow and so on. With its leaves, flowers, fruits, shade, roots, bark, wood, fragrance, sap, ashes, pulp and sprouts, a tree fulfills the desires of everyone. This kind of life is ideal. Indeed, said Kṛṣṇa, the perfection of life is to act with one's vital energy, wealth, intelligence and words for the benefit of all.

After the Lord had glorified the trees in this way, the entire company went to the Yamunā, where the cowherd boys let the cows drink the sweet water and also drank some themselves.

## TEXT 1

श्रीशुक उवाच
**हेमन्ते प्रथमे मासि नन्दव्रजकुमारिकाः ।**
**चेरुर्हविष्यं भुञ्जानाः कात्यायन्यर्चनव्रतम् ॥१॥**

*śrī-śuka uvāca*
*hemante prathame māsi*
*nanda-vraja-kumārikāḥ*
*cerur haviṣyaṁ bhuñjānāḥ*
*kātyāyany-arcana-vratam*

*śrī-śukaḥ uvāca*—Śrī Śukadeva Gosvāmī said; *hemante*—during the winter; *prathame*—in the first; *māsi*—month; *nanda-vraja*—of the cowherd village of Nanda Mahārāja; *kumārikāḥ*—the unmarried young girls; *ceruḥ*—performed; *haviṣyam*—unseasoned *khichrī; bhuñjānāḥ*—subsisting on; *kātyāyanī*—of the goddess Kātyāyanī; *arcana-vratam*—the vow of worship.

## TRANSLATION

**Śukadeva Gosvāmī said: During the first month of the winter season, the young unmarried girls of Gokula observed the vow of worshiping goddess Kātyāyanī. For the entire month they ate only unspiced *khichrī.***

## PURPORT

The word *hemante* refers to the month of Mārgaśīrṣa—from approximately the middle of November to the middle of December, according to the Western calendar. In Volume One, Chapter Twenty-two, of *Kṛṣṇa, the Supreme Personality of Godhead,* Śrīla Prabhupāda comments that the *gopīs* "first ate *haviṣyānna,* a kind of food prepared by boiling together mung *dāl* and rice without any spices or turmeric. According to Vedic injunction, this kind of food is recommended to purify the body before one enacts a ritualistic ceremony."

## TEXTS 2–3

आप्लुत्याम्भसि कालिन्द्या जलान्ते चोदितेऽरुणे ।
कृत्वा प्रतिकृतिं देवीमानर्चुनृर्प सैकतीम् ॥२॥
गन्धैर्माल्यैः सुरभिभिर्बलिभिर्धूपदीपकैः ।
उच्चावचैश्चोपहारैः प्रवालफलतण्डुलैः ॥३॥

*āplutyāmbhasi kālindyā*
*jalānte codite 'ruṇe*
*kṛtvā pratikṛtiṁ devīm*
*ānarcur nṛpa saikatīm*

*gandhair mālyaiḥ surabhibhir*
*balibhir dhūpa-dīpakaiḥ*
*uccāvacaiś copahāraiḥ*
*pravāla-phala-taṇḍulaiḥ*

*āplutya*—bathing; *ambhasi*—in the water; *kālindyāḥ*—of the Yamunā; *jala-ante*—on the shore of the river; *ca*—and; *udite*—as was arising; *aruṇe*—the dawn; *kṛtvā*—making; *prati-kṛtim*—a deity; *devīm*—the goddess; *ānarcuḥ*—they worshiped; *nṛpa*—O King Parīkṣit; *saikatīm*—made of earth; *gandhaiḥ*—with sandalwood pulp and other fragrant articles; *mālyaiḥ*—with garlands; *surabhibhiḥ*—fragrant; *balibhiḥ*—with gifts; *dhūpa-dīpakaiḥ*—with incense and lamps; *ucca-avacaiḥ*—opulent and also simple; *ca*—and; *upahāraiḥ*—with presentations; *pravāla*—newly grown leaves; *phala*—fruit; *taṇḍulaiḥ*—and betel nuts.

## TRANSLATION

**My dear King, after they had bathed in the water of the Yamunā just as the sun was rising, the *gopīs* made an earthen deity of goddess Durgā on the riverbank. Then they worshiped her with such aromatic substances as sandalwood pulp, along with other items both opulent and simple, including lamps, fruits, betel nuts, newly grown leaves, and fragrant garlands and incense.**

## PURPORT

The word *balibhiḥ* in this verse indicates offerings of clothing, ornaments, food and so on.

## TEXT 4

कात्यायनि महामाये महायोगिन्यधीश्वरि ।
नन्दगोपसुतं देवि पतिं मे कुरु ते नमः ।
इति मन्त्रं जपन्त्यस्ताः पूजां चक्रुः कुमारिकाः ॥४॥

*kātyāyani mahā-māye*
*mahā-yoginy adhīśvari*
*nanda-gopa-sutaṁ devi*
*patiṁ me kuru te namaḥ*
*iti mantraṁ japantyas tāḥ*
*pūjāṁ cakruḥ kumārikāḥ*

*kātyāyani*—O goddess Kātyāyanī; *mahā-māye*—O great potency; *mahā-yogini*—O possessor of great mystic power; *adhīśvari*—O mighty controller; *nanda-gopa-sutam*—the son of Mahārāja Nanda; *devi*—O goddess; *patim*—the husband; *me*—my; *kuru*—please make; *te*—unto you; *namaḥ*—my obeisances; *iti*—with these words; *mantram*—the hymn; *japantyaḥ*—chanting; *tāḥ*—they; *pūjām*—worship; *cakruḥ*—performed; *kumārikāḥ*—the unmarried girls.

## TRANSLATION

**Each of the young unmarried girls performed her worship while chanting the following *mantra:* "O goddess Kātyāyanī, O great potency of the Lord, O possessor of great mystic power and mighty controller of all, please make the son of Nanda Mahārāja my husband. I offer my obeisances unto you."**

## PURPORT

According to various *ācāryas,* the goddess Durgā mentioned in this verse is not the illusory energy of Kṛṣṇa called Māyā but rather the internal potency of the Lord known as Yoga-māyā. The distinction between the internal and external, or illusory, potency of the Lord is described in the *Nārada-pañcarātra,* in the conversation between Śruti and Vidyā:

*jānāty ekāparā kāntaṁ*
*saivā durgā tad-ātmikā*
*yā parā paramā śaktir*
*mahā-viṣṇu-svarūpiṇī*

*yasyā vijñāna-mātreṇa*
*parāṇāṁ paramātmanaḥ*
*muhūrtād deva-devasya*
*prāptir bhavati nānyathā*

*ekeyaṁ prema-sarvasva-*
*svabhāvā gokuleśvarī*
*anayā su-labho jñeya*
*ādi-devo 'khileśvaraḥ*

*asyā āvārika-śaktir*
*mahā-māyākhileśvarī*

*yayā mugdaṁ jagat sarvaṁ*
*sarve dehābhimāninaḥ*

"The Lord's inferior potency, known as Durgā, is dedicated to His loving service. Being the Lord's potency, this inferior energy is nondifferent from Him. There is another, superior potency, whose form is on the same spiritual level as that of God Himself. Simply by scientifically understanding this supreme potency, one can immediately achieve the Supreme Soul of all souls, who is the Lord of all lords. There is no other process to achieve Him. That supreme potency of the Lord is known as Gokuleśvarī, the goddess of Gokula. Her nature is to be completely absorbed in love of God, and through Her one can easily obtain the primeval God, the Lord of all that be. This internal potency of the Lord has a covering potency, known as Mahā-māyā, who rules the material world. In fact she bewilders the entire universe, and thus everyone within the universe falsely identifies himself with the material body."

From the above we can understand that the internal and external, or superior and inferior, potencies of the Supreme Lord are personified as Yoga-māyā and Mahā-māyā, respectively. The name Durgā is sometimes used to refer to the internal, superior potency, as stated in the *Pañcarātra:* "In all *mantras* used to worship Kṛṣṇa, the presiding deity is known as Durgā." Thus in the transcendental sound vibrations glorifying and worshiping the Absolute Truth, Kṛṣṇa, the presiding deity of the particular *mantra* or hymn is called Durgā. The name Durgā therefore refers also to that personality who functions as the internal potency of the Lord and who is thus on the platform of *śuddha-sattva,* pure transcendental existence. This internal potency is understood to be Kṛṣṇa's sister, known also as Ekānaṁśā or Subhadrā. This is the Durgā who was worshiped by the *gopīs* in Vṛndāvana. Several *ācāryas* have pointed out that ordinary people are sometimes bewildered and think that the names Mahā-māyā and Durgā refer exclusively to the external potency of the Lord.

Even if we accept hypothetically that the *gopīs* were worshiping the external Māyā, there is no fault on their part, since in their pastimes of loving Kṛṣṇa they were acting as ordinary members of society. Śrīla Prabhupāda comments in this regard: "The Vaiṣṇavas generally do not worship any demigods. Śrīla Narottama dāsa Ṭhākura has strictly forbidden all worship of the demigods for anyone who wants to advance in pure devotional service. Yet the *gopīs,* who are beyond compare in their affection for Kṛṣṇa, were seen to worship Durgā. The worshipers of demigods also sometimes mention that the *gopīs* also worshiped goddess Durgā, but we must understand the purpose of the *gopīs.* Generally, people worship goddess Durgā for some material benediction. Here, the *gopīs* could adopt any means to satisfy or serve Kṛṣṇa. That was the superexcellent characteristic of the *gopīs.* They worshiped goddess Durgā completely for one month in order to have Kṛṣṇa as their husband. Every day they prayed for Kṛṣṇa, the son of Nanda Mahārāja, to become their husband."

The conclusion is that a sincere devotee of Kṛṣṇa will never imagine any material quality to exist in the transcendental *gopīs,* who are the most exalted devotees of the Lord. The only motivation in all their activities was simply to love and satisfy Kṛṣṇa, and if we foolishly consider their activities to be mundane in any way, it will be impossible for us to understand Kṛṣṇa consciousness.

## TEXT 5

एवं मासं व्रतं चेरुः कुमार्यः कृष्णचेतसः ।
भद्रकालीं समानर्चुर्भूयान्नन्दसुतः पतिः ॥५॥

*evaṁ māsaṁ vrataṁ ceruḥ*
*kumāryaḥ kṛṣṇa-cetasaḥ*
*bhadrakālīṁ samānarcur*
*bhūyān nanda-sutaḥ patiḥ*

*evam*—in this manner; *māsam*—an entire month; *vratam*—their vow; *ceruḥ*—they executed; *kumāryaḥ*—the girls; *kṛṣṇa-cetasaḥ*—their minds absorbed in Kṛṣṇa; *bhadra-kālīm*—the goddess Kātyāyanī; *samānarcuḥ*—they properly worshiped; *bhūyāt*—may He become; *nanda-sutaḥ*—the son of King Nanda; *patiḥ*—my husband.

## TRANSLATION

**Thus for an entire month the girls carried out their vow and properly worshiped the goddess Bhadrakālī, fully absorbing their minds in Kṛṣṇa and meditating upon the following thought: "May the son of King Nanda become my husband."**

## TEXT 6

ऊषस्युत्थाय गोत्रैः स्वैरन्योन्याबद्धबाहवः ।
कृष्णमुच्चैर्जगुर्यान्त्यः कालिन्द्यां स्नातुमन्वहम् ॥६॥

*ūṣasy utthāya gotraiḥ svair*
*anyonyābaddha-bāhavaḥ*
*kṛṣṇam uccair jagur yāntyaḥ*
*kālindyāṁ snātum anvaham*

*ūṣasi*—at dawn; *utthāya*—rising; *gotraiḥ*—by their names; *svaiḥ*—proper; *anyonya*—one with another; *ābaddha*—holding; *bāhavaḥ*—their hands; *kṛṣṇam*—in glorification of Kṛṣṇa; *uccaiḥ*—loudly; *jaguḥ*—they sang; *yāntyaḥ*—while going; *kālindyām*—to the Yamunā; *snātum*—in order to bathe; *anu-aham*—each day.

### TRANSLATION

**Each day they rose at dawn. Calling out to one another by name, they all held hands and loudly sang the glories of Kṛṣṇa while going to the Kālindī to take their bath.**

## TEXT 7

नद्याः कदाचिदागत्य तीरे निक्षिप्य पूर्ववत् ।
वासांसि कृष्णं गायन्त्यो विजह्रुः सलिले मुदा ॥७॥

*nadyāḥ kadācid āgatya*
*tīre nikṣipya pūrva-vat*
*vāsāṁsi kṛṣṇaṁ gāyantyo*
*vijahruḥ salile mudā*

*nadyāḥ*—of the river; *kadācit*—once; *āgatya*—coming; *tīre*—to the shore; *nikṣipya*—throwing down; *pūrva-vat*—as previously; *vāsāṁsi*—their clothing; *kṛṣṇam*—about Kṛṣṇa; *gāyantyaḥ*—singing; *vijahruḥ*—they played; *salile*—in the water; *mudā*—with pleasure.

## TRANSLATION

**One day they came to the riverbank and, putting aside their clothing as they had done before, happily played in the water while singing the glories of Kṛṣṇa.**

## PURPORT

According to Śrīla Viśvanātha Cakravartī Ṭhākura, this incident occurred on the day the young *gopīs* completed their vow, which was a full-moon day. To celebrate the successful completion of their vow, the girls invited young Rādhārāṇī—the daughter of Vṛṣabhānu and the special object of their affection—along with other important *gopīs,* and brought them all to the river to bathe. Their playing in the water was meant to serve as the *avabhṛtha-snāna,* the ceremonial bath taken immediately upon the completion of a Vedic sacrifice.

Śrīla Prabhupāda comments as follows: "It is an old system among Indian girls and women that when they take bath in the river they place their garments on the bank and dip into the water completely naked. The portion of the river where the girls and women take bath was strictly prohibited to any male, and this is still the system. The Supreme Personality of Godhead, knowing the minds of the unmarried young *gopīs,* awarded them their desired objective. They had prayed for Kṛṣṇa to become their husband, and Kṛṣṇa wanted to fulfill their desires."

## TEXT 8

भगवांस्तदभिप्रेत्य कृष्णो योगेश्वरेश्वरः ।
वयस्यैरावृतस्तत्र गतस्तत्कर्मसिद्धये ॥८॥

*bhagavāṁs tad abhipretya*
*kṛṣṇo yogeśvareśvaraḥ*
*vayasyair āvṛtas tatra*
*gatas tat-karma-siddhaye*

*bhagavān*—the Supreme Personality of Godhead; *tat*—that; *abhipretya*—seeing; *kṛṣṇaḥ*—Lord Kṛṣṇa; *yoga-īśvara-īśvaraḥ*—the master of all masters of mystic power; *vayasyaiḥ*—by young companions; *āvṛtaḥ*—surrounded; *tatra*—there; *gataḥ*—went; *tat*—of those girls; *karma*—the ritualistic activities; *siddhaye*—for assuring the result.

## TRANSLATION

**Lord Kṛṣṇa, the Supreme Personality of Godhead and master of all masters of mystic *yoga,* was aware of what the *gopīs* were doing, and thus He went there surrounded by His young companions to award the *gopīs* the perfection of their endeavor.**

## PURPORT

As the master of all masters of mystic power, Lord Kṛṣṇa could easily understand the desires of the *gopīs,* and He could also fulfill them. The *gopīs,* like all young girls from respectable families, considered the embarrassment of appearing naked before a young boy to be worse than giving up their lives. Yet Lord Kṛṣṇa made them come out of the water and bow down to Him. Although the bodily forms of the *gopīs* were all fully developed, and although Kṛṣṇa met them in a secluded place and brought them fully under His control, because the Lord is completely transcendental there was not a trace of material desire in His mind. Lord Kṛṣṇa is the ocean of transcendental bliss, and He wanted to share His bliss with the *gopīs* on the spiritual platform, completely free of ordinary lust.

Śrīla Viśvanātha Cakravartī Ṭhākura explains that the companions of Kṛṣṇa mentioned here were mere toddlers two or three years old. They were completely naked and were unaware of the difference between male and female. When Kṛṣṇa went out to herd the cows, they followed Him because they were so attached to Him that they could not bear to be without His association.

## TEXT 9

तासां वासांस्युपादाय नीपमारुह्य सत्वरः ।
हसद्भिः प्रहसन् बालैः परिहासमुवाच ह ॥९॥

*tāsāṁ vāsāṁsy upādāya*
*nīpam āruhya satvaraḥ*
*hasadbhiḥ prahasan bālaiḥ*
*parihāsam uvāca ha*

*tāsām*—of those girls; *vāsāṁsi*—the garments; *upādāya*—taking; *nīpam*—a *kadamba* tree; *āruhya*—climbing; *satvaraḥ*—quickly; *hasad-bhiḥ*—who were laughing; *prahasan*—Himself laughing loudly; *bālaiḥ*—with the boys; *parihāsam*—joking words; *uvāca ha*—He spoke.

### TRANSLATION

**Taking the girls' garments, He quickly climbed to the top of a *kadamba* tree. Then, as He laughed loudly and His companions also laughed, He addressed the girls jokingly.**

### TEXT 10

अत्रागत्याबलाः कामं स्वं स्वं वासः प्रगृह्यताम् ।
सत्यं ब्रुवाणि नो नर्म यद् यूयं व्रतकर्शिताः ॥१०॥

*atrāgatyābalāḥ kāmaṁ*
*svaṁ svaṁ vāsaḥ pragṛhyatām*
*satyaṁ bruvāṇi no narma*
*yad yūyaṁ vrata-karśitāḥ*

*atra*—here; *āgatya*—coming; *abalāḥ*—O girls; *kāmam*—as you wish; *svam svam*—each your own; *vāsaḥ*—clothing; *pragṛhyatām*—please take; *satyam*—the truth; *bruvāṇi*—I am speaking; *na*—not; *u*—rather; *narma*—jest; *yat*—because; *yūyam*—you; *vrata*—by your vow of austerity; *karśitāḥ*—fatigued.

### TRANSLATION

**My dear girls, you may each come here as you wish and take back your garments. I'm telling you the truth and am not joking with you, since I see you're fatigued from executing austere vows.**

### TEXT 11

न मयोदितपूर्वं वा अनृतं तदिमे विदुः ।
एकैकशः प्रतीच्छध्वं सहैवेति सुमध्यमाः ॥११॥

*na mayodita-pūrvaṁ vā*
*anṛtaṁ tad ime viduḥ*
*ekaikaśaḥ pratīcchadhvaṁ*
*sahaiveti su-madhyamāḥ*

*na*—never; *mayā*—by Me; *udita*—spoken; *pūrvam*—previously; *vai*—definitely; *anṛtam*—anything false; *tat*—that; *ime*—these young boys; *viduḥ*—know; *eka-ekaśaḥ*—one by one; *pratīcchadhvam*—pick out (your garments); *saha*—or all together; *eva*—indeed; *iti*—thus; *su-madhya-māḥ*—O slender-waisted girls.

### TRANSLATION

**I have never before spoken a lie, and these boys know it. Therefore, O slender-waisted girls, please come forward, either one by one or all together, and pick out your clothes.**

## TEXT 12

तस्य तत्क्ष्वेलितं दृष्ट्वा गोप्यः प्रेमपरिप्लुताः ।
व्रीडिताः प्रेक्ष्य चान्योन्यं जातहासा न निर्ययुः ॥१२॥

*tasya tat kṣvelitaṁ dṛṣṭvā*
*gopyaḥ prema-pariplutāḥ*
*vrīḍitāḥ prekṣya cānyonyaṁ*
*jāta-hāsā na niryayuḥ*

*tasya*—His; *tat*—that; *kṣvelitam*—joking behavior; *dṛṣṭvā*—seeing; *gopyaḥ*—the *gopīs; prema-pariplutāḥ*—fully immersed in pure love of Godhead; *vrīḍitāḥ*—embarrassed; *prekṣya*—glancing; *ca*—and; *anyon-yam*—upon one another; *jāta-hāsāḥ*—beginning to laugh; *na niryayuḥ*—they did not come out.

### TRANSLATION

**Seeing how Kṛṣṇa was joking with them, the *gopīs* became fully immersed in love for Him, and as they glanced at each other they began to laugh and joke among themselves, even in their embarrassment. But still they did not come out of the water.**

## PURPORT

Śrīla Viśvanātha Cakravartī Ṭhākura explains this verse as follows:

"The *gopīs* were from most respectable families, and they might have argued with Kṛṣṇa: 'Why don't You simply leave our clothes on the bank of the river and go away?'

"Kṛṣṇa might have replied, 'But there are so many of you that some of the girls might take clothes belonging to another.'

"The *gopīs* would reply, 'We are honest and never steal anything. We never touch another's property.'

"Then Kṛṣṇa would say, 'If that's true, then simply come and get your clothes. What is the difficulty?'

"When the *gopīs* saw Kṛṣṇa's determination, they were filled with loving ecstasy. Although embarrassed, they were overjoyed to receive such attention from Kṛṣṇa. He was joking with them as if they were His wives or girlfriends, and the *gopīs'* only desire was to achieve such a relationship with Him. At the same time, they were embarrassed to be seen naked by Him. But still they could not help laughing at His joking words and even began to joke among themselves, one *gopī* urging another, 'Go ahead, you go first, and let us see if Kṛṣṇa plays any tricks on you. Then we will go later.'"

## TEXT 13

एवं ब्रुवति गोविन्दे नर्मणाक्षिप्तचेतसः ।
आकण्ठमग्नाः शीतोदे वेपमानास्तमब्रुवन् ॥१३॥

*evaṁ bruvati govinde*
*narmaṇākṣipta-cetasaḥ*
*ā-kaṇṭha-magnāḥ śītode*
*vepamānās tam abruvan*

*evam*—thus; *bruvati*—speaking; *govinde*—Lord Govinda; *narmaṇā*—by His joking words; *ākṣipta*—agitated; *cetasaḥ*—their minds; *ā-kaṇṭha*—up to their necks; *magnāḥ*—submerged; *śīta*—cold; *ude*—in the water; *vepamānāḥ*—shivering; *tam*—to Him; *abruvan*—they spoke.

## TRANSLATION

**As Śrī Govinda spoke to the *gopīs* in this way, His joking words completely captivated their minds. Submerged up to their necks**

**in the cold water, they began to shiver. Thus they addressed Him as follows.**

## PURPORT

Śrila Viśvanātha Cakravartī Ṭhākura gives the following example of joking between Kṛṣṇa and the *gopīs.*

*Kṛṣṇa:* O birdlike girls, if you do not come here, then with these garments caught in the branches I will make a swing and a hammock. I need to lie down, since I have spent the entire night awake and am now becoming sleepy.

*Gopīs:* Our dear cowherd boy, Your cows, greedy for grass, have gone into a cave. So You must quickly go there to herd them back on the proper path.

*Kṛṣṇa:* Come now, My dear cowherd girls, you must quickly go from here to Vraja and perform your household duties. Don't become a disturbance to your parents and other elders.

*Gopīs:* Our dear Kṛṣṇa, we will not go home for an entire month, for it is by the order of our parents and other elders that we are executing this vow of fasting, the Kātyāyanī-vrata.

*Kṛṣṇa:* My dear austere ladies, I too, by the strength of seeing you, have now developed a surprising mood of detachment from family life. I wish to stay here for a month and execute the vow of dwelling in the clouds. And if you show mercy to Me, I can come down from here and observe the vow of fasting in your company.

The *gopīs* were completely captivated by Kṛṣṇa's joking words, but out of shyness they submerged themselves in the water up to their necks. Shaking from the cold, they addressed Kṛṣṇa as follows.

## TEXT 14

मानयं भोः कृथास्त्वां तु नन्दगोपसुतं प्रियम् ।
जानीमोऽङग व्रजश्लाघ्यं देहि वासांसि वेपिताः ॥१४॥

*mānayaṁ bhoḥ kṛthās tvāṁ tu*
*nanda-gopa-sutaṁ priyam*
*jānīmo 'ṅga vraja-ślāghyaṁ*
*dehi vāsāṁsi vepitāḥ*

*mā*—do not; *anayam*—injustice; *bhoḥ*—our dear Kṛṣṇa; *kṛthāḥ*—do; *tvām*—You; *tu*—on the other hand; *nanda-gopa*—of Mahārāja Nanda; *sutam*—the son; *priyam*—loved; *jānīmaḥ*—we know; *aṅga*—O dear one; *vraja-ślāghyam*—renowned throughout Vraja; *dehi*—please give; *vāsāṁsi*—our garments; *vepitāḥ*—(to us) who are shivering.

## TRANSLATION

**Dear Kṛṣṇa, don't be unfair! We know that You are the respectable son of Nanda and that You are honored by everyone in Vraja. You are also very dear to us. Please give us back our clothes. We are shivering in the cold water.**

## TEXT 15

श्यामसुन्दर ते दास्यः करवाम तवोदितम् ।
देहि वासांसि धर्मज्ञ नो चेद् राज्ञे ब्रुवाम हे ॥१५॥

*śyāmasundara te dāsyaḥ*
*karavāma tavoditam*
*dehi vāsāṁsi dharma-jña*
*no ced rājñe bruvāma he*

*śyāmasundara*—O Lord Śyāmasundara; *te*—Your; *dāsyaḥ*—maidservants; *karavāma*—we shall do; *tava*—by You; *uditam*—what is spoken; *dehi*—please give; *vāsāṁsi*—our clothing; *dharma-jña*—O knower of religion; *na*—not; *u*—indeed; *cet*—if; *rājñe*—to the king; *bruvāmaḥ*—we shall tell; *he*—O Kṛṣṇa.

## TRANSLATION

**O Śyāmasundara, we are Your maidservants and must do whatever You say. But give us back our clothing. You know what the religious principles are, and if You don't give us our clothes we will have to tell the king. Please!**

## TEXT 16

श्रीभगवानुवाच
भवत्यो यदि मे दास्यो मयोक्तं वा करिष्यथ ।

अत्रागत्य स्ववासांसि प्रतीच्छत शुचिस्मिताः ।
नो चेन्नाहं प्रदास्ये किं क्रुद्धो राजा करिष्यति ॥१६॥

*śrī-bhagavān uvāca*
*bhavatyo yadi me dāsyo*
*mayoktaṁ vā kariṣyatha*
*atrāgatya sva-vāsāṁsi*
*pratīcchata śuci-smitāḥ*
*no cen nāhaṁ pradāsye kiṁ*
*kruddho rājā kariṣyati*

*śrī-bhagavān uvāca*—the Supreme Personality of Godhead said; *bhavatyaḥ*—you; *yadi*—if; *me*—My; *dāsyaḥ*—servants; *mayā*—by Me; *uktam*—what has been spoken; *vā*—or; *kariṣyatha*—you will do; *atra*—here; *āgatya*—coming; *sva-vāsāṁsi*—your own garments; *pratīcchata*—pick out; *śuci*—fresh; *smitāḥ*—whose smiles; *na u*—not; *cet*—if; *na*—not; *aham*—I; *pradāsye*—will give; *kim*—what; *kruddhaḥ*—angry; *rājā*—the king; *kariṣyati*—will be able to do.

## TRANSLATION

**The Supreme Personality of Godhead said: If you girls are actually My maidservants, and if you will really do what I say, then come here with your innocent smiles and let each girl pick out her clothes. If you don't do what I say, I won't give them back to you. And even if the king becomes angry, what can he do?**

## PURPORT

Śrīla Prabhupāda comments, "When the *gopīs* saw that Kṛṣṇa was strong and determined, they had no alternative but to abide by His order."

## TEXT 17

ततो जलाशयात् सर्वा दारिकाः शीतवेपिताः ।
पाणिभ्यां योनिमाच्छाद्य प्रोत्तेरुः शीतकर्शिताः ॥१७॥

*tato jalāśayāt sarvā*
*dārikāḥ śīta-vepitāḥ*
*pāṇibhyāṁ yonim ācchādya*
*protteruḥ śīta-karśitāḥ*

*tataḥ*—then; *jala-āśayāt*—out of the river; *sarvāḥ*—all; *dārikāḥ*—the young girls; *śīta-vepitāḥ*—shivering from the cold; *pāṇibhyām*—with their hands; *yonim*—their pubic area; *ācchādya*—covering; *protteruḥ*—they came up; *śīta-karśitāḥ*—pained by the cold.

## TRANSLATION

**Then, shivering from the painful cold, all the young girls rose up out of the water, covering their pubic area with their hands.**

## PURPORT

The *gopīs* had assured Kṛṣṇa that they were His eternal servants and would do whatever He said, and thus they were now defeated by their own words. If they delayed any longer, they thought, some other man might come along, and this would be unbearable for them. The *gopīs* loved Kṛṣṇa so much that even in that awkward situation their attachment to Him was increasing more and more, and they were very eager to stay in His company. Thus they did not even consider drowning themselves in the river because of the embarrassing situation.

They concluded that they could do nothing but go forward to their beloved Kṛṣṇa, putting aside their embarrassment. Thus the *gopīs* assured each other that there was no alternative and rose up out of the water to meet Him.

## TEXT 18

भगवानाहता वीक्ष्य शुद्धभावप्रसादितः ।
स्कन्धे निधाय वासांसि प्रीतः प्रोवाच सस्मितम् ॥१८॥

*bhagavān āhatā vīkṣya*
*śuddha-bhāva-prasāditaḥ*
*skandhe nidhāya vāsāṁsi*
*prītaḥ provāca sa-smitam*

*bhagavān*—the Supreme Lord; *āhatāḥ*—struck; *vīkṣya*—seeing; *śuddha*—pure; *bhāva*—by their loving affection; *prasāditaḥ*—satisfied; *skandhe*—upon His shoulder; *nidhāya*—placing; *vāsāṁsi*—their garments; *prītaḥ*—lovingly; *provāca*—spoke; *sa-smitam*—while smiling.

## TRANSLATION

**When the Supreme Lord saw how the *gopīs* were struck with embarrassment, He was satisfied by their pure loving affection. Putting their clothes on His shoulder, the Lord smiled and spoke to them with affection.**

## PURPORT

Śrīla Prabhupāda comments, "The *gopīs'* simple presentation was so pure that Lord Kṛṣṇa immediately became pleased with them. All the unmarried *gopīs* who prayed to Kātyāyanī to have Kṛṣṇa as their husband were thus satisfied. A woman cannot be naked before any male except her husband. The unmarried *gopīs* desired Kṛṣṇa as their husband, and He fulfilled their desire in this way."

For aristocratic girls like the *gopīs*, standing naked before a young boy was worse than death, and yet they decided to give up everything for the pleasure of Lord Kṛṣṇa. He wanted to see the power of their love for Him, and He was completely satisfied by their unalloyed devotion.

## TEXT 19

यूयं विवस्त्रा यदपो धृतव्रता
व्यगाहतैतत्तदु देवहेलनम् ।
बद्ध्वाञ्जलिं मूर्ध्न्यपनुत्तयेऽंहसः
कृत्वा नमोऽधोवसनं प्रगृह्यताम् ॥१९॥

*yūyaṁ vivastrā yad apo dhṛta-vratā*
*vyagāhataitat tad u deva-helanam*
*baddhvāñjaliṁ mūrdhny apanuttaye 'ṁhasaḥ*
*kṛtvā namo 'dho-vasanaṁ pragṛhyatām*

*yūyam*—you; *vivastrāḥ*—naked; *yat*—because; *apaḥ*—in the water; *dhṛta-vratāḥ*—while executing a Vedic ritualistic vow; *vyagāhata*—bathed; *etat tat*—this; *u*—indeed; *deva-helanam*—an offense against Varuṇa and the other gods; *baddhvā añjalim*—with hands folded together; *mūrdhni*—upon your heads; *apanuttaye*—for counteracting; *aṁhasaḥ*—your sinful action; *kṛtvā namaḥ*—paying obeisances; *adhaḥ-vasanam*—your lower garments; *pragṛhyatām*—please take back.

## TRANSLATION

**You girls bathed naked while executing your vow, and that is certainly an offense against the demigods. To counteract your sin you should offer obeisances while placing your folded hands above your heads. Then you should take back your lower garments.**

## PURPORT

Kṛṣṇa wanted to see the full surrender of the *gopīs,* and thus He ordered them to offer obeisances with their hands folded above their heads. In other words, the *gopīs* could no longer cover their bodies. We should not foolishly think that Lord Kṛṣṇa is an ordinary lusty boy enjoying the naked beauty of the *gopīs.* Kṛṣṇa is the Supreme Absolute Truth, and He was acting to fulfill the loving desire of the young cowherd girls of Vṛndāvana. In this world we would certainly become lusty in a situation like this. But to compare ourselves to God is a great offense, and because of this offense we will not be able to understand Kṛṣṇa's transcendental position, for we will wrongly take Him to be materially conditioned like ourselves. To lose transcendental sight of Kṛṣṇa is certainly a great disaster for one trying to relish the bliss of the Absolute Truth.

## TEXT 20

इत्यच्युतेनाभिहितं व्रजाबला
मत्वा विवस्त्राप्लवनं व्रतच्युतिम् ।
तत्पूर्तिकामास्तदशेषकर्मणां
साक्षात्कृतं नेमुरवद्यमृग् यतः ॥२०॥

*ity acyutenābhihitaṁ vrajābalā*
*matvā vivastrāplavanaṁ vrata-cyutim*
*tat-pūrti-kāmās tad-aśeṣa-karmaṇāṁ*
*sākṣāt-kṛtaṁ nemur avadya-mṛg yataḥ*

*iti*—in these words; *acyutena*—by the infallible Supreme Lord; *abhihitam*—indicated; *vraja-abalāḥ*—the girls of Vraja; *matvā*—considering; *vivastra*—naked; *āplavanam*—the bathing; *vraja-cyutim*—a falldown from their vow; *tat-pūrti*—the successful completion of that; *kāmāḥ*—intently desiring; *tat*—of that performance; *aśeṣa-karmaṇām*—and of unlimited other pious activities; *sākṣāt-kṛtam*—to the directly manifest fruit; *nemuḥ*—they offered their obeisances; *avadya-mṛk*—the cleanser of all sins; *yataḥ*—because.

## TRANSLATION

**Thus the young girls of Vṛndāvana, considering what Lord Acyuta had told them, accepted that they had suffered a falldown from their vow by bathing naked in the river. But they still desired to successfully complete their vow, and since Lord Kṛṣṇa is Himself the ultimate result of all pious activities, they offered their obeisances to Him to cleanse away all their sins.**

## PURPORT

The transcendental position of Kṛṣṇa consciousness is clearly described here. The *gopīs* decided that it was better to renounce their so-called family tradition and traditional morality and simply surrender unto the Supreme Lord Kṛṣṇa. This does not mean that the Kṛṣṇa consciousness movement advocates immoral activities. In fact, the devotees of ISKCON practice the highest standard of restraint and morality, but at the same time we recognize the transcendental position of Kṛṣṇa. Lord Kṛṣṇa is God and therefore has no material desire to enjoy young girls in sexual affairs. As will be seen in this chapter, Lord Kṛṣṇa was not at all attracted to enjoying the *gopīs;* rather He was attracted to their love and wanted to satisfy them.

The greatest offense is to imitate the activities of Lord Kṛṣṇa. In India there is a group called *prākṛta-sahajiyā,* who imitate these affairs of Kṛṣṇa and try to enjoy naked young girls in the name of worshiping Kṛṣṇa. The

ISKCON movement sternly rejects this mockery of religion, because the greatest offense is for a human being to ludicrously imitate the Supreme Personality of Godhead. In the ISKCON movement there are no cheap incarnations, and it is not possible for a devotee of this movement to promote himself to the position of Kṛṣṇa.

Five hundred years ago Kṛṣṇa appeared as Lord Caitanya Mahāprabhu, who practiced strict celibacy throughout His student life and at the age of twenty-four took *sannyāsa,* a lifelong vow of celibacy. Caitanya Mahāprabhu rigidly avoided contact with women in order to carry out His vow of loving service to Kṛṣṇa. When Kṛṣṇa personally appeared five thousand years ago, He exhibited these wonderful pastimes, which attract our attention. We should not become envious or shocked when we hear that God can perform such pastimes. Our shock is due to our ignorance, because if we tried to perform these activities our bodies would be afflicted by lust. Lord Kṛṣṇa, however, is the Supreme Absolute Truth and is therefore never disturbed by any material desire whatsoever. Thus, this incident—in which the *gopīs* gave up normal standards of morality and, raising their hands to their head, bowed down in compliance with Kṛṣṇa's order—is an example of pure devotional surrender and not a discrepancy in religious principles.

In fact, the *gopīs'* surrender is the perfection of all religion, as Śrīla Prabhupāda describes in *Kṛṣṇa, the Supreme Personality of Godhead:* "The *gopīs* were all simple souls, and whatever Kṛṣṇa said, they took to be true. In order to be freed from the wrath of Varuṇadeva, as well as to fulfill the desired end of their vows and ultimately to please their worshipable Lord, Kṛṣṇa, they immediately abided by His order. Thus they became the greatest lovers of Kṛṣṇa, and His most obedient servitors.

"Nothing can compare to the Kṛṣṇa consciousness of the *gopīs.* Actually the *gopīs* did not care for Varuṇa or any other demigod; they only wanted to satisfy Kṛṣṇa."

## TEXT 21

तास्तथावनता दृष्ट्वा भगवान् देवकीसुतः ।
वासांसि ताभ्यः प्रायच्छत्करुणस्तेन तोषितः ॥२१॥

*tās tathāvanatā dṛṣṭvā*
*bhagavān devakī-sutaḥ*

*vāsāṁsi tābhyaḥ prāyacchat*
*karuṇas tena toṣitaḥ*

*tāḥ*—then; *tathā*—thus; *avanatāḥ*—bowed down; *dṛṣṭvā*—seeing; *bhagavān*—the Supreme Personality of Godhead; *devakī-sutaḥ*—Kṛṣṇa, the son of Devakī; *vāsāṁsi*—the garments; *tābhyaḥ*—to them; *prāyacchat*—He returned; *karuṇaḥ*—compassionate; *tena*—by that act; *toṣitaḥ*—satisfied.

### TRANSLATION

**Seeing them bow down like that, the Supreme Personality of Godhead, the son of Devakī, gave them back their garments, feeling compassionate toward them and satisfied by their act.**

### TEXT 22

दृढं प्रलब्धास्त्रपया च हापिताः
प्रस्तोभिताः क्रीडनवच्च कारिताः ।
वस्त्राणि चैवापहृतान्यथाप्यमुं
ता नाभ्यसूयन् प्रियसंगनिर्वृताः ॥२२॥

*dṛḍhaṁ pralabdhās trapayā ca hāpitāḥ*
*prastobhitāḥ krīḍana-vac ca kāritāḥ*
*vastrāṇi caivāpahṛtāny athāpy amuṁ*
*tā nābhyasūyan priya-saṅga-nirvṛtāḥ*

*dṛḍham*—thoroughly; *pralabdhāḥ*—cheated; *trapayā*—of their shame; *ca*—and; *hāpitāḥ*—deprived; *prastobhitāḥ*—laughed at; *krīḍana-vat*—just like toy dolls; *ca*—and; *kāritāḥ*—made to act; *vastrāṇi*—their clothing; *ca*—and; *eva*—indeed; *apahṛtāni*—stolen; *atha api*—nevertheless; *amum*—toward Him; *tāḥ*—they; *na abhyasūyan*—did not feel inimical; *priya*—of their beloved; *saṅga*—by the association; *nirvṛtāḥ*—joyful.

### TRANSLATION

**Although the *gopīs* had been thoroughly cheated, deprived of their modesty, ridiculed and made to act just like toy dolls, and although their clothing had been stolen, they did not feel at all**

**inimical toward Śrī Kṛṣṇa. Rather, they were simply joyful to have this opportunity to associate with their beloved.**

## PURPORT

Śrīla Prabhupāda comments, "This attitude of the *gopīs* is described by Lord Caitanya Mahāprabhu when he prays, 'My dear Lord Kṛṣṇa, You may embrace Me or trample Me under Your feet, or You may make Me brokenhearted by never being present before Me. Whatever You like, You can do, because You have complete freedom to act. But in spite of all of Your dealings, You are My Lord eternally, and I have no other worshipable object.' This is the attitude of the *gopīs* toward Kṛṣṇa."

## TEXT 23

परिधाय स्ववासांसि प्रेष्ठसंगमसज्जिताः ।
गृहीतचित्ता नो चेलुस्तस्मिन् लज्जायितेक्षणाः ॥२३॥

*paridhāya sva-vāsāṁsi*
*preṣṭha-saṅgama-sajjitāḥ*
*gṛhīta-cittā no celus*
*tasmin lajjāyitekṣaṇāḥ*

*paridhāya*—putting on; *sva-vāsāṁsi*—their own garments; *preṣṭha*—of their beloved; *saṅgama*—by this association; *sajjitāḥ*—becoming completely attached to Him; *gṛhīta*—taken away; *cittāḥ*—whose minds; *na*—could not; *u*—indeed; *celuḥ*—move; *tasmin*—upon Him; *lajjāyita*—full of shyness; *īkṣaṇāḥ*—whose glances.

## TRANSLATION

**The *gopīs* were addicted to associating with their beloved Kṛṣṇa, and thus they became captivated by Him. Thus, even after putting their clothes on they did not move. They simply remained where they were, shyly glancing at Him.**

## PURPORT

By association with their beloved Kṛṣṇa, the *gopīs* had become more attached to Him than ever. Just as Kṛṣṇa had stolen their clothes, He had also stolen their minds and their love. The *gopīs* interpreted the whole incident as proof that Kṛṣṇa was also attached to them. Otherwise, why would He have gone to the trouble of playing with them in this way? Because they thought that Kṛṣṇa was now attached to them, they glanced at Him with shyness, and being stunned by the rising of their ecstatic love, they could not move from where they stood. Kṛṣṇa had overcome their shyness and forced them to come out of the water naked, but now, having dressed properly, they again became shy in His presence. In fact, this incident increased their humbleness before Kṛṣṇa. They did not want Kṛṣṇa to see them staring at Him, but they cautiously took the opportunity to glance at the Lord.

## TEXT 24

तासां विज्ञाय भगवान् स्वपादस्पर्शकाम्यया ।
धृतव्रतानां संकल्पमाह दामोदरोऽबलाः ॥२४॥

*tāsāṁ vijñāya bhagavān*
*sva-pāda-sparśa-kāmyayā*
*dhṛta-vratānāṁ saṅkalpam*
*āha dāmodaro 'balāḥ*

*tāsām*—of these girls; *vijñāya*—understanding; *bhagavān*—the Supreme Personality of Godhead; *sva-pāda*—of His own feet; *sparśa*—for the touch; *kāmyayā*—with the desire; *dhṛta-vratānām*—who had taken their vow; *saṅkalpam*—the motivation; *āha*—spoke; *dāmodaraḥ*—Lord Dāmodara; *abalāḥ*—to the girls.

## TRANSLATION

**The Supreme Lord understood the determination of the *gopīs* in executing their strict vow. The Lord also knew that the girls desired to touch His lotus feet, and thus Lord Dāmodara, Kṛṣṇa, spoke to them as follows.**

## TEXT 25

संकल्पो विदितः साध्व्यो भवतीनां मदर्चनम् ।
मयानुमोदितः सोऽसौ सत्यो भवितुमर्हति ॥२५॥

*saṅkalpo viditaḥ sādhvyo*
*bhavatīnāṁ mad-arcanam*
*mayānumoditaḥ so 'sau*
*satyo bhavitum arhati*

*saṅkalpaḥ*—the motivation; *viditaḥ*—understood; *sādhvyaḥ*—O pious girls; *bhavatīnām*—your; *mat-arcanam*—worship of Me; *mayā*—by Me; *anumoditaḥ*—approved of; *saḥ asau*—that; *satyaḥ*—true; *bhavitum*—to become; *arhati*—must.

## TRANSLATION

**O saintly girls, I understand that your real motive in this austerity has been to worship Me. That intent of yours is approved of by Me, and indeed it must come to pass.**

## PURPORT

Just as Kṛṣṇa is free of all impure desire, so are the *gopīs*. Their attempt to gain Kṛṣṇa as their husband was therefore motivated not by a desire for personal sense gratification but by their overwhelming desire to serve Kṛṣṇa and to please Him. Because of their intense love, the *gopīs* did not see Kṛṣṇa as God but rather as the most wonderful boy in all creation, and being beautiful young girls, they desired only to please Him by loving service. Lord Kṛṣṇa understood the pure desire of the *gopīs* and was thus satisfied. The Lord could certainly not be satisfied by ordinary lust, but He was moved by the intense loving devotion of the cowherd girls of Vṛndāvana.

## TEXT 26

**न मय्यावेशितधियां कामः कामाय कल्पते ।**
**भर्जिता क्वथिता धानाः प्रायो बीजाय नेशते ॥२६॥**

*na mayy āveśita-dhiyāṁ*
*kāmaḥ kāmāya kalpate*
*bharjitā kvathitā dhānāḥ*
*prāyo bījāya neśate*

*na*—not; *mayi*—in Me; *āveśita*—fully absorbed; *dhiyām*—of those whose consciousness; *kāmaḥ*—desire; *kāmāya*—to material lust; *kalpate*—leads; *bharjitāḥ*—burned; *kvathitāḥ*—cooked; *dhānāḥ*—grains; *prāyaḥ*—for the most part; *bījāya*—new growth; *na iṣyate*—are not capable of causing.

## TRANSLATION

**The desire of those who fix their minds on Me does not lead to material desire for sense gratification, just as barleycorns burned by the sun and then cooked can no longer grow into new sprouts.**

## PURPORT

The words *mayy āveśita-dhiyām* are very significant here. Unless one has achieved an advanced degree of devotion, one cannot fix the mind and intelligence on Kṛṣṇa, since Kṛṣṇa is pure spiritual existence. Self-realization is a state not of desirelessness but rather of purified desire, wherein one desires only the pleasure of Lord Kṛṣṇa. The *gopīs* were certainly attracted to Kṛṣṇa in a mood of conjugal love, and yet, having fixed their minds and indeed their entire existence completely on Kṛṣṇa, their conjugal desire could never manifest as material lust; rather, it became the most exalted form of love of Godhead ever seen within the universe.

## TEXT 27

याताबला व्रजं सिद्धा मयेमा रंस्यथ क्षपाः ।
यदुद्दिश्य व्रतमिदं चेरुरार्यार्चनं सतीः ॥२७॥

*yātābalā vrajaṁ siddhā*
*mayemā raṁsyatha kṣapāḥ*
*yad uddiśya vratam idaṁ*
*cerur āryārcanaṁ satīḥ*

*yāta*—go now; *abalāḥ*—My dear girls; *vrajam*—to Vraja; *siddhāḥ*—having achieved your desire; *mayā*—with Me; *imāḥ*—these; *raṁsyatha*—you will enjoy; *kṣapāḥ*—the nights; *yat*—which; *uddiśya*—having in mind; *vratam*—vow; *idam*—this; *ceruḥ*—you executed; *āryā*—of goddess Kātyāyanī; *arcanam*—the worship; *satīḥ*—being pure.

## TRANSLATION

**Go now, girls, and return to Vraja. Your desire is fulfilled, for in My company you will enjoy the coming nights. After all, this was the purpose of your vow to worship goddess Kātyāyanī, O pure-hearted ones.**

## TEXT 28

श्रीशुक उवाच
इत्यादिष्टा भगवता लब्धकामाः कुमारिकाः ।
ध्यायन्त्यस्तत्पदाम्भोजं कृच्छ्रान्निर्विविशुर्व्रजम् ॥२८॥

*śrī-śuka uvāca*
*ity ādiṣṭā bhagavatā*
*labdha-kāmāḥ kumārikāḥ*
*dhyāyantyas tat-padāmbhojaṁ*
*kṛcchrān nirviviśur vrajam*

*śrī-śukaḥ uvāca*—Śrī Śukadeva Gosvāmī said; *iti*—thus; *ādiṣṭāḥ*—instructed; *bhagavatā*—by the Supreme Personality of Godhead; *labdha*—having obtained; *kāmāḥ*—their desire; *kumārikāḥ*—the young girls; *dhyāyantyaḥ*—meditating; *tat*—His; *pada-ambhojam*—upon the lotus feet; *kṛcchrāt*—with difficulty; *nirviviśuḥ*—they returned; *vrajam*—to the cowherd village.

## TRANSLATION

**Śukadeva Gosvāmī said: Thus instructed by the Supreme Personality of Godhead, the young girls, their desire now fulfilled, could bring themselves only with great difficulty to return to the village of Vraja, meditating all the while upon His lotus feet.**

## PURPORT

The *gopīs'* desire was fulfilled because Lord Kṛṣṇa had agreed to act as their husband. A young girl can never spend the night with any man except her husband, and thus when Kṛṣṇa agreed to engage the girls in the nocturnal *rāsa* dance during the coming autumn season, in effect He was agreeing to reciprocate their love for Him in the role of a husband.

## TEXT 29

**अथ गोपैः परिवृतो भगवान् देवकीसुतः ।**
**वृन्दावनाद् गतो दूरं चारयन् गाः सहाग्रजः ॥२९॥**

*atha gopaiḥ parivṛto*
*bhagavān devakī-sutaḥ*
*vṛndāvanād gato dūraṁ*
*cārayan gāḥ sahāgrajaḥ*

*atha*—some time later; *gopaiḥ*—by the cowherd boys; *parivṛtaḥ*—surrounded; *bhagavān*—the Supreme Lord; *devakī-sutaḥ*—the son of Devakī; *vṛndāvanāt*—from Vṛndāvana; *gataḥ*—He went; *dūram*—a distance; *cārayan*—grazing; *gāḥ*—the cows; *saha-agrajaḥ*—together with His brother Balarāma.

## TRANSLATION

**Some time later Lord Kṛṣṇa, the son of Devakī, surrounded by His cowherd friends and accompanied by His elder brother, Balarāma, went a good distance away from Vṛndāvana, herding the cows.**

## PURPORT

Having described how Lord Kṛṣṇa stole the garments of the young *gopīs*, Śukadeva Gosvāmī now begins introducing the description of Lord Kṛṣṇa's blessings upon the wives of some ritualistic *brāhmaṇas*.

## TEXT 30

**निदाघार्कातपे तिग्मे छायाभिः स्वाभिरात्मनः ।**
**आतपत्रायितान् वीक्ष्य द्रुमानाह व्रजौकसः ॥३०॥**

*nidāghārkātape tigme*
*chāyābhiḥ svābhir ātmanaḥ*
*ātapatrāyitān vīkṣya*
*drumān āha vrajaukasaḥ*

*nidāgha*—of the hot season; *arka*—of the sun; *ātape*—in the heat; *tigme*—fierce; *chāyābhiḥ*—with the shade; *svābhiḥ*—their own; *āt-manaḥ*—for Himself; *ātapatrāyitān*—serving as umbrellas; *vīkṣya*—observing; *drumān*—the trees; *āha*—He said; *vraja-okasaḥ*—to the boys of Vraja.

## TRANSLATION

**When the sun's heat became intense, Lord Kṛṣṇa saw that the trees were acting as umbrellas by shading Him, and thus He spoke as follows to His boyfriends.**

## TEXTS 31–32

हे स्तोककृष्ण हे अंशो श्रीदामन् सुबलार्जुन ।
विशाल वृषभौजस्विन् देवप्रस्थ वरूथप ॥३१॥
पश्यतैतान्महाभागान् परार्थैकान्तजीवितान् ।
वातवर्षातपहिमान् सहन्तो वारयन्ति नः ॥३२॥

*he stoka-kṛṣṇa he aṁśo*
*śrīdāman subalārjuna*
*viśāla vṛṣabhaujasvin*
*devaprastha varūthapa*

*paśyataitān mahā-bhāgān*
*parārthaikānta-jīvitān*
*vāta-varṣātapa-himān*
*sahanto vārayanti naḥ*

*he stoka-kṛṣṇa*—O Stoka Kṛṣṇa; *he aṁśo*—O Aṁśu; *śrīdāman subala arjuna*—O Śrīdāmā, Subala and Arjuna; *viśāla vṛṣabha ojasvin*—O Viśāla, Vṛṣabha and Ojasvī; *devaprastha varūthapa*—O Devaprastha and Varūthapa; *paśyata*—just see; *etān*—these; *mahā-bhāgān*—most fortunate; *para-artha*—for the benefit of others; *ekānta*—exclusively; *jīvitān*—whose life; *vāta*—the wind; *varṣa*—rain; *ātapa*—heat of the sun; *himān*—and snow; *sahantaḥ*—tolerating; *vārayanti*—keep off; *naḥ*—for us.

## TRANSLATION

**Lord Kṛṣṇa said: O Stoka Kṛṣṇa and Aṁśu, O Śrīdāmā, Subala and Arjuna, O Vṛṣabha, Ojasvī, Devaprastha and Varūthapa, just see these greatly fortunate trees, whose lives are completely dedicated to the benefit of others. Even while tolerating the wind, rain, heat and snow, they protect us from these elements.**

## PURPORT

Lord Kṛṣṇa was preparing to bestow His mercy on the wives of the hard-hearted ritualistic *brāhmaṇas*, and in these verses the Lord indicates that even trees who are dedicated to the welfare of others are superior to *brāhmaṇas* who are not. Certainly the members of the Kṛṣṇa consciousness movement should soberly study this point.

## TEXT 33

अहो एषां वरं जन्म सर्वप्राण्युपजीवनम् ।
सुजनस्येव येषां वै विमुखा यान्ति नार्थिनः ॥३३॥

*aho eṣāṁ varaṁ janma*
*sarva-prāṇy-upajīvanam*
*su-janasyeva yeṣāṁ vai*
*vimukhā yānti nārthinaḥ*

*aho*—oh, just see; *eṣām*—of these trees; *varam*—superior; *janma*—birth; *sarva*—for all; *prāṇi*—living entities; *upajīvinam*—who provide maintenance; *su-janasya iva*—like a great personality; *yeṣām*—from whom; *vai*—certainly; *vimukhāḥ*—disappointed; *yānti*—go away; *na*—never; *arthinaḥ*—those who are asking for something.

## TRANSLATION

**Just see how these trees are maintaining every living entity! Their birth is successful. Their behavior is just like that of great personalities, for anyone who asks anything from a tree never goes away disappointed.**

## PURPORT

This translation is quoted from Śrīla Prabhupāda's *Caitanya-caritāmṛta* (*Ādi* 9.46).

## TEXT 34

पत्रपुष्पफलच्छायामूलवल्कलदारुभिः ।
गन्धनिर्यासभस्मास्थितोक्मैः कामान् वितन्वते ॥३४॥

*patra-puṣpa-phala-cchāyā-*
*mūla-valkala-dārubhiḥ*
*gandha-niryāsa-bhasmāsthi-*
*tokmaiḥ kāmān vitanvate*

*patra*—by their leaves; *puṣpa*—flowers; *phala*—fruits; *chāyā*—shade; *mūla*—roots; *valkala*—bark; *dārubhiḥ*—and wood; *gandha*—by their fragrance; *niryāsa*—sap; *bhasma*—ashes; *asthi*—pulp; *tokmaiḥ*—and young shoots; *kāmān*—desirable things; *vitanvate*—they award.

## TRANSLATION

**These trees fulfill one's desires with their leaves, flowers and fruits, their shade, roots, bark and wood, and also with their fragrance, sap, ashes, pulp and shoots.**

## TEXT 35

एतावज्जन्मसाफल्यं देहिनामिह देहिषु ।
प्राणैरर्थैर्धिया वाचा श्रेयआचरणं सदा ॥३५॥

*etāvaj janma-sāphalyaṁ*
*dehinām iha dehiṣu*
*prāṇair arthair dhiyā vācā*
*śreya-ācaraṇaṁ sadā*

*etāvat*—up to this; *janma*—of birth; *sāphalyam*—perfection; *dehinām*—of every living being; *iha*—in this world; *dehiṣu*—toward those who are embodied; *prāṇaiḥ*—by life; *arthaiḥ*—by wealth; *dhiyā*—by intelligence; *vācā*—by words; *śreyaḥ*—eternal good fortune; *ācaraṇam*—acting practically; *sadā*—always.

### TRANSLATION

**It is the duty of every living being to perform welfare activities for the benefit of others with his life, wealth, intelligence and words.**

### PURPORT

This translation is quoted from Śrīla Prabhupāda's *Caitanya-caritāmṛta* (*Ādi* 9.42).

### TEXT 36

इति प्रवालस्तबकफलपुष्पदलोत्करैः ।
तरूणां नम्रशाखानां मध्यतो यमुनां गतः ॥३६॥

*iti pravāla-stabaka-*
*phala-puṣpa-dalotkaraiḥ*
*tarūṇāṁ namra-śākhānāṁ*
*madhyato yamunāṁ gataḥ*

*iti*—thus speaking; *pravāla*—of new branches; *stabaka*—by the clusters; *phala*—of fruit; *puṣpa*—flowers; *dala*—and leaves; *utkaraiḥ*—by the abundance; *tarūṇām*—of the trees; *namra*—bowed down; *śākhānām*—whose branches; *madhyataḥ*—from within the midst; *yamunām*—the Yamunā River; *gataḥ*—He came upon.

### TRANSLATION

**Thus moving among the trees, whose branches were bent low by their abundance of twigs, fruits, flowers and leaves, Lord Kṛṣṇa came to the Yamunā River.**

### TEXT 37

तत्र गाः पाययित्वापः सुमृष्टाः शीतलाः शिवाः ।
ततो नृप स्वयं गोपाः कामं स्वादु पपुर्जलम् ॥३७॥

*tatra gāḥ pāyayitvāpaḥ*
*su-mṛṣṭāḥ śītalāḥ śivāḥ*
*tato nṛpa svayaṁ gopāḥ*
*kāmaṁ svādu papur jalam*

*tatra*—there; *gāḥ*—the cows; *pāyayitvā*—making drink; *apaḥ*—the water; *su-mṛṣṭāḥ*—very clear; *śītalāḥ*—cool; *śivāḥ*—wholesome; *tataḥ*—then; *nṛpa*—O King Parīkṣit; *svayam*—themselves; *gopāḥ*—the cowherd boys; *kāmam*—freely; *svādu*—sweet-tasting; *papuḥ*—they drank; *jalam*—the water.

### TRANSLATION

**The cowherd boys let the cows drink the clear, cool and wholesome water of the Yamunā. O King Parīkṣit, the cowherd boys themselves also drank that sweet water to their full satisfaction.**

### TEXT 38

तस्या उपवने कामं चारयन्तः पशून्नृप ।
कृष्णरामावुपागम्य क्षुधार्ता इदमब्रुवन् ॥३८॥

*tasyā upavane kāmaṁ*
*cārayantaḥ paśūn nṛpa*
*kṛṣṇa-rāmāv upāgamya*
*kṣudh-ārtā idam abruvan*

*tasyāḥ*—along the Yamunā; *upavane*—within a small forest; *kāmam*—here and there, as they wished; *cārayantaḥ*—tending; *paśūn*—the animals; *nṛpa*—O King; *kṛṣṇa-rāmau*—Lord Kṛṣṇa and Lord Rāma; *upāgamya*—approaching; *kṣut-ārtāḥ*—disturbed by hunger; *idam*—this; *abruvan*—they (the cowherd boys) said.

### TRANSLATION

**Then, O King, the cowherd boys began herding the animals in a leisurely way within a small forest along the Yamunā. But soon they became afflicted by hunger and, approaching Kṛṣṇa and Balarāma, spoke as follows.**

## PURPORT

Śrīla Jīva Gosvāmī explains that the cowherd boys were concerned that Kṛṣṇa would be hungry, and thus they feigned their own hunger so that Kṛṣṇa and Balarāma would make suitable arrangements to eat.

*Thus end the purports of the humble servant of His Divine Grace A. C. Bhaktivedanta Swami Prabhupāda to the Tenth Canto, Twenty-second Chapter, of the* Śrīmad-Bhāgavatam, *entitled "Kṛṣṇa Steals the Garments of the Unmarried* Gopīs."

## CHAPTER TWENTY-THREE

# The Brāhmaṇas' Wives Blessed

This chapter describes how Lord Śrī Kṛṣṇa, after inducing the cowherd boys to beg for food, showed mercy to the wives of some *brāhmaṇas* performing a sacrifice and made the *brāhmaṇas* themselves feel remorse.

When the cowherd boys became very hungry, they asked Śrī Kṛṣṇa about obtaining food, and He sent them to beg some from a group of *brāhmaṇas* who were performing a sacrifice nearby. But these *brāhmaṇas* ignored the boys, thinking Śrī Kṛṣṇa an ordinary human being. The boys returned disappointed, but the Lord sent them off again, advising them to ask the *brāhmaṇas*' wives for the food. These ladies had heard of Kṛṣṇa's transcendental qualities and were very much attached to Him. Thus as soon as they learned He was nearby, they went to Him in great haste, bringing all four varieties of food. In this way they offered themselves to Śrī Kṛṣṇa.

Kṛṣṇa told the women that while one can develop transcendental love for Him by seeing His Deity form in the temple, meditating upon Him and chanting His glories, one cannot achieve this result simply by being in His physical presence. He advised them that since they were housewives, their particular duty was to help their husbands perform sacrifices. He therefore instructed them to return to their homes.

When the ladies went back home, their *brāhmaṇa* husbands at once felt remorse, and they lamented, "For anyone inimical to Kṛṣṇa, his three births—seminal, brahminical and sacrificial—are all condemned. On the other hand, these womenfolk, who have not undergone the purificatory processes of the brahminical class or performed any austerity or pious rituals, have through devotion for Kṛṣṇa easily cut off the bondage of death.

"Since Lord Kṛṣṇa's every desire is completely fulfilled, His begging for food was simply an act of mercy toward us *brāhmaṇas*. All the fruits of Vedic sacrifice—and indeed all things on earth—are His opulences, yet out of ignorance we could not appreciate this fact."

Having spoken thus, all the *brāhmaṇas* offered their obeisances to Lord

Śrī Kṛṣṇa, hoping to counteract their offense. Nonetheless, out of fear of King Kaṁsa they did not go to see the Lord in person.

### TEXT 1

श्रीगोपा ऊचुः
**राम राम महाबाहो कृष्ण दुष्टनिबर्हण ।**
**एषा वै बाधते क्षुन्नस्तच्छान्तिं कर्तुमर्हथः ॥१॥**

*śrī-gopā ūcuḥ*
*rāma rāma mahā-bāho*
*kṛṣṇa duṣṭa-nibarhaṇa*
*eṣā vai bādhate kṣun nas*
*tac-chāntiṁ kartum arhathaḥ*

*śrī-gopāḥ ūcuḥ*—the cowherd boys said; *rāma rāma*—O Lord Rāma, Lord Rāma; *mahā-bāho*—O mighty-armed one; *kṛṣṇa*—O Lord Kṛṣṇa; *duṣṭa*—of the wicked; *nibarhaṇa*—O destroyer; *eṣā*—this; *vai*—indeed; *bādhate*—is causing distress; *kṣut*—hunger; *naḥ*—to us; *tat-śāntim*—its counteraction; *kartum arhathaḥ*—You ought to do.

### TRANSLATION

**The cowherd boys said: O Rāma, Rāma, mighty-armed one! O Kṛṣṇa, chastiser of the wicked! We are being harassed by hunger, and You should do something about it.**

### PURPORT

The cowherd boys jokingly implied that since Śrī Kṛṣṇa is the subduer of all bad things, the Lord should subdue their hunger by arranging for them to eat. In this statement by the cowherd boys, we observe the intimate loving friendship they enjoyed with the Supreme Personality of Godhead.

### TEXT 2

श्रीशुक उवाच
**इति विज्ञापितो गोपैर्भगवान् देवकीसुतः ।**
**भक्ताया विप्रभार्यायाः प्रसीदन्निदमब्रवीत् ॥२॥**

*śrī-śuka uvāca*
*iti vijñāpito gopair*
*bhagavān devakī-sutaḥ*
*bhaktāyā vipra-bhāryāyāḥ*
*prasīdann idam abravīt*

*śrī-śukaḥ uvāca*—Śrī Śukadeva Gosvāmī said; *iti*—thus; *vijñāpitaḥ*—informed; *gopaiḥ*—by the cowherd boys; *bhagavān*—the Supreme Personality of Godhead; *devakī-sutaḥ*—the son of Devakī; *bhaktāyāḥ*—His devotees; *vipra-bhāryāyāḥ*—the wives of the *brāhmaṇas; prasīdan*—desiring to satisfy; *idam*—this; *abravīt*—He spoke.

## TRANSLATION

**Śukadeva Gosvāmī said: Thus entreated by the cowherd boys, the Supreme Personality of Godhead, the son of Devakī, replied as follows, desiring to please certain of His devotees who were *brāhmaṇas'* wives.**

## TEXT 3

प्रयात देवयजनं ब्राह्मणा ब्रह्मवादिनः ।
सत्रमाङ्गिरसं नाम ह्यासते स्वर्गकाम्यया ॥३॥

*prayāta deva-yajanaṁ*
*brāhmaṇā brahma-vādinaḥ*
*satram āṅgirasaṁ nāma*
*hy āsate svarga-kāmyayā*

*prayāta*—please go; *deva-yajanam*—to the sacrificial arena; *brāhmaṇāḥ*—*brāhmaṇas; brahma-vādinaḥ*—followers of the Vedic injunctions; *satram*—a sacrifice; *āṅgirasam nāma*—known as Āṅgirasa; *hi*—indeed; *āsate*—they are now performing; *svarga-kāmyayā*—with the motive of promotion to heaven.

## TRANSLATION

**Please go to the sacrificial arena where a group of *brāhmaṇas*, learned in the Vedic injunctions, are now performing the Āṅgirasa sacrifice to gain promotion to heaven.**

## TEXT 4

तत्र गत्वौदनं गोपा याचतास्मद्विसर्जिताः ।
कीर्तयन्तो भगवत आर्यस्य मम चाभिधाम् ॥४॥

*tatra gatvaudanaṁ gopā*
*yācatāsmad-visarjitāḥ*
*kīrtayanto bhagavata*
*āryasya mama cābhidhām*

*tatra*—there; *gatvā*—going; *odanam*—food; *gopāḥ*—My dear cowherd boys; *yācata*—just request; *asmat*—by Us; *visarjitāḥ*—dispatched; *kīrtayantaḥ*—announcing; *bhagavataḥ*—of the Supreme Lord; *āryasya*—the elder; *mama*—My; *ca*—also; *abhidhām*—name.

## TRANSLATION

**When you go there, My dear cowherd boys, simply request some food. Declare to them the name of My elder brother, the Supreme Lord Balarāma, and also My name, and explain that you have been sent by Us.**

## PURPORT

Lord Kṛṣṇa encouraged His boyfriends to request charity without being embarrassed. In case the boys felt they had no right to personally approach such respectable *brāhmaṇas*, the Lord told them to mention the names of Balarāma and Kṛṣṇa, the holy names of God.

## TEXT 5

इत्यादिष्टा भगवता गत्वायाचन्त ते तथा ।
कृताञ्जलिपुटा विप्रान् दण्डवत् पतिता भुवि ॥५॥

*ity ādiṣṭā bhagavatā*
*gatvā yācanta te tathā*
*kṛtāñjali-puṭā viprān*
*daṇḍa-vat patitā bhuvi*

*iti*—in these words; *ādiṣṭāḥ*—ordered; *bhagavatā*—by the Supreme Lord Kṛṣṇa; *gatvā*—going; *yācanta*—begged; *te*—they; *tathā*—in that manner; *kṛta-añjali-puṭāḥ*—folding their hands in humble supplication; *viprān*—to the *brāhmaṇas; daṇḍa-vat*—like sticks; *patitāḥ*—falling; *bhuvi*—upon the ground.

## TRANSLATION

**Thus instructed by the Supreme Personality of Godhead, the cowherd boys went there and submitted their request. They stood before the *brāhmaṇas* with hands folded in supplication and then fell flat on the ground to offer respect.**

## TEXT 6

हे भूमिदेवाः शृणुत कृष्णस्यादेशकारिणः ।
प्राप्ताञ्जानीत भद्रं वो गोपान्नो रामचोदितान् ॥६॥

*he bhūmi-devāḥ śṛṇuta*
*kṛṣṇasyādeśa-kāriṇaḥ*
*prāptāñ jānīta bhadraṁ vo*
*gopān no rāma-coditān*

*he bhūmi-devāḥ*—O earthly gods; *śṛṇuta*—please hear us; *kṛṣṇasya ādeśa*—of the order of Kṛṣṇa; *kāriṇaḥ*—the executors; *prāptān*—arrived; *jānīta*—please recognize; *bhadram*—all good; *vaḥ*—unto you; *gopān*—cowherd boys; *naḥ*—us; *rāma-coditān*—sent by Lord Rāma.

## TRANSLATION

**O earthly gods, please hear us. We cowherd boys are executing the orders of Kṛṣṇa, and we have been sent here by Balarāma. We wish all good for you. Please acknowledge our arrival.**

## PURPORT

The term *bhūmi-devāḥ*, "gods on earth," refers here to the *brāhmaṇas*, who are supposed to closely represent the will of the Supreme Lord. The philosophy of Kṛṣṇa consciousness is not a primitive polytheistic doctrine holding that human beings on the earth are gods. Rather, it is a science that traces the descent of authority from the Absolute Truth Himself, Śrī Kṛṣṇa. The authority and power of God naturally extend along with the extension of His creation, and on the earth the Lord's will and authority are represented by purified, enlightened men called *brāhmaṇas.*

This account will illustrate that the ritualistic *brāhmaṇas* approached by the cowherd boys were not at all properly enlightened and thus could not appreciate the position of Kṛṣṇa and Balarāma or that of Their intimate associates. In fact, this pastime exposes the pretentious position of so-called *brāhmaṇas* who are not faithful devotees of the Supreme Lord.

## TEXT 7

**गाश्चारयन्तावविदूर ओदनं**
**रामाच्युतौ वो लषतो बुभुक्षितौ ।**
**तयोर्द्विजा ओदनमर्थिनोर्यदि**
**श्रद्धा च वो यच्छत धर्मवित्तमाः ॥७॥**

*gāś cārayantāv avidūra odanaṁ*
*rāmācyutau vo laṣato bubhukṣitau*
*tayor dvijā odanam arthinor yadi*
*śraddhā ca vo yacchata dharma-vittamāḥ*

*gāḥ*—Their cows; *cārayantau*—grazing; *avidūre*—not far away; *odanam*—food; *rāma-acyutau*—Lord Rāma and Lord Acyuta; *vaḥ*—from you; *laṣataḥ*—are desiring; *bubhukṣitau*—being hungry; *tayoḥ*—for Them; *dvijāḥ*—O *brāhmaṇas; odanam*—food; *arthinoḥ*—begging; *yadi*—if; *śraddhā*—any faith; *ca*—and; *vaḥ*—on your part; *yacchata*—please give; *dharma-vit-tamāḥ*—O best knowers of the principles of religion.

## TRANSLATION

**Lord Rāma and Lord Acyuta are tending Their cows not far from here. They are hungry and want you to give Them some of your food. Therefore, O *brāhmaṇas,* O best of the knowers of religion, if you have faith please give some food to Them.**

## PURPORT

The cowherd boys doubted the generosity of the *brāhmaṇas,* and thus they used the word *bubhukṣitau,* meaning that Kṛṣṇa and Balarāma were hungry. The boys expected the *brāhmaṇas* to know the Vedic injunction *annasya kṣuditaṁ pātram:* "Anyone who is hungry is a fit candidate for receiving food in charity." But if the *brāhmaṇas* would not recognize the authority of Kṛṣṇa and Balarāma, their title *dvija* would be taken to mean merely "born from two parents" (*dvi*—from two, *ja*—born) rather than "twice-born." When the *brāhmaṇas* did not respond to the cowherd boys' initial request, the boys addressed the *brāhmaṇas,* with a slight trace of sarcasm, as *dharma-vit-tamāḥ,* "O best of the knowers of religion."

## TEXT 8

दीक्षायाः पशुसंस्थायाः सौत्रामण्याश्च सत्तमाः ।
अन्यत्र दीक्षितस्यापि नान्नमश्नन् हि दुष्यति ॥८॥

*dīkṣāyāḥ paśu-saṁsthāyāḥ*
*sautrāmaṇyāś ca sattamāḥ*
*anyatra dīkṣitasyāpi*
*nānnam aśnan hi duṣyati*

*dīkṣāyāḥ*—beginning with the initiation for a sacrifice; *paśu-saṁsthāyāḥ*—until sacrificing the animal; *sautrāmaṇyāḥ*—outside of the sacrifice known as Sautrāmaṇi; *ca*—and; *sat-tamāḥ*—O purest ones; *anyatra*—elsewhere; *dīkṣitasya*—of one who has been initiated for the sacrifice; *api*—even; *na*—not; *annam*—food; *aśnan*—eating; *hi*—indeed; *duṣyati*—creates offense.

## TRANSLATION

**Except during the interval between the initiation of the performer of a sacrifice and the actual sacrifice of the animal, O most pure *brāhmaṇas,* it is not contaminating for even the initiated to partake of food, at least in sacrifices other than the Sautrāmaṇi.**

## PURPORT

The cowherd boys anticipated the possible objection from the *brāhmaṇas* that they couldn't give the boys any food because they themselves had not yet eaten, and that a priest initiated to perform a sacrifice should not eat. Therefore the boys humbly informed the *brāhmaṇas* about various technicalities of ritualistic sacrifice. The cowherd boys were not unaware of the formalities of Vedic culture, but their real intention was simply to render loving service to Lord Kṛṣṇa.

## TEXT 9

इति ते भगवद्याच्ञां शृण्वन्तोऽपि न शुश्रुवुः ।
क्षुद्राशा भूरिकर्माणो बालिशा वृद्धमानिनः ॥९॥

*iti te bhagavad-yācñāṁ*
*śṛṇvanto 'pi na śuśruvuḥ*
*kṣudrāśā bhūri-karmāṇo*
*bāliśā vṛddha-māninaḥ*

*iti*—thus; *te*—they, the *brāhmaṇas; bhagavat*—of the Supreme Personality of Godhead; *yācñām*—the supplication; *śṛṇvantaḥ*—hearing; *api*—although; *na śuśruvuḥ*—they did not hear; *kṣudra-āśāḥ*—full of petty desire; *bhūri-karmāṇaḥ*—entangled in elaborate ritualistic activities; *bāliśāḥ*—childish fools; *vṛddha-māninaḥ*—presuming themselves to be wise men.

## TRANSLATION

**The *brāhmaṇas* heard this supplication from the Supreme Personality of Godhead, yet they refused to pay heed. Indeed, they were full of petty desires and entangled in elaborate rituals. Though presuming themselves advanced in Vedic learning, they were actually inexperienced fools.**

## PURPORT

These childish *brāhmaṇas* were full of petty desires, such as the desire to attain to material heaven, and therefore they could not recognize the golden transcendental opportunity offered them by the arrival of Kṛṣṇa's personal boyfriends. Presently, throughout the world, people are madly pursuing material advancement and thus cannot hear the message of the

Supreme Lord Kṛṣṇa that is being broadcast through the missionary activities of the Kṛṣṇa consciousness movement. Times have hardly changed, and proud, materialistic priests are still prevalent on the earth.

## TEXTS 10–11

देशः कालः पृथग् द्रव्यं मन्त्रतन्त्रर्त्विजोऽग्नयः ।
देवता यजमानश्च क्रतुर्धर्मश्च यन्मयः ॥१०॥
तं ब्रह्म परमं साक्षाद् भगवन्तमधोक्षजम् ।
मनुष्यदृष्ट्या दुष्प्रज्ञा मर्त्यात्मानो न मेनिरे ॥११॥

*deśaḥ kālaḥ pṛthag dravyaṁ*
*mantra-tantrartvijo 'gnayaḥ*
*devatā yajamānaś ca*
*kratur dharmaś ca yan-mayaḥ*

*taṁ brahma paramaṁ sākṣād*
*bhagavantam adhokṣajam*
*manuṣya-dṛṣṭyā duṣprajñā*
*martyātmāno na menire*

*deśaḥ*—the place; *kālaḥ*—time; *pṛthak dravyam*—particular items of paraphernalia; *mantra*—Vedic hymns; *tantra*—prescribed rituals; *ṛtvijaḥ*—priests; *agnayaḥ*—sacrificial fires; *devatāḥ*—the presiding demigods; *yajamānaḥ*—the performer of the sacrifice; *ca*—and; *kratuḥ*—the offering; *dharmaḥ*—the invisible power of fruitive results; *ca*—and; *yat*—whom; *mayaḥ*—constituting; *tam*—Him; *brahma paramam*—the Supreme Absolute Truth; *sākṣāt*—directly manifest; *bhagavantam*—the Personality of Godhead; *adhokṣajam*—who is transcendental to material senses; *manuṣya-dṛṣṭyā*—seeing Him as an ordinary man; *duṣprajñāḥ*—perverted in their intelligence; *martya-ātmānaḥ*—falsely identifying themselves with the material body; *na menire*—they did not properly honor.

## TRANSLATION

**Although the ingredients of sacrificial performance—the place, time, particular paraphernalia, *mantras*, rituals, priests, fires,**

**demigods, performer, offering and the as yet unseen beneficial results—are all simply aspects of His opulences, the *brāhmaṇas* saw Lord Kṛṣṇa as an ordinary human because of their perverted intelligence. They failed to recognize that He is the Supreme Absolute Truth, the directly manifest Personality of Godhead, whom the material senses cannot ordinarily perceive. Thus bewildered by their false identification with the mortal body, they did not show Him proper respect.**

## PURPORT

The ritualistic *brāhmaṇas* could not understand why the sacrificial food should be offered to Lord Kṛṣṇa, whom they considered an ordinary human being. Just as a person with rose-colored glasses sees the entire world as rose-colored, a conditioned soul with mundane vision sees even God Himself as mundane and thus loses the opportunity to go back home, back to Godhead.

## TEXT 12

न ते यदोमिति प्रोचुर्न नेति च परन्तप ।
गोपा निराशाः प्रत्येत्य तथोचुः कृष्णरामयोः ॥१२॥

*na te yad om iti procur*
*na neti ca parantapa*
*gopā nirāśāḥ pratyetya*
*tathocuḥ kṛṣṇa-rāmayoḥ*

*na*—not; *te*—they; *yat*—when; *om*—"so be it"; *iti*—thus; *procuḥ*—did speak; *na*—not; *na*—"no"; *iti*—thus; *ca*—either; *parantapa*—O chastiser of the enemies, Parīkṣit Mahārāja; *gopāḥ*—the cowherd boys; *nirāśāḥ*—discouraged; *pratyetya*—returning; *tathā*—thus; *ūcuḥ*—described; *kṛṣṇa-rāmayoḥ*—to Lord Kṛṣṇa and Lord Rāma.

## TRANSLATION

**When the *brāhmaṇas* failed to reply even with a simple yes or**

**no, O chastiser of the enemy [Parīkṣit], the cowherd boys returned disappointed to Kṛṣṇa and Rāma and reported this to Them.**

## TEXT 13

तदुपाकर्ण्य भगवान् प्रहस्य जगदीश्वरः ।
व्याजहार पुनर्गोपान् दर्शयन् लौकिकीं गतिम् ॥१३॥

*tad upākarṇya bhagavān*
*prahasya jagad-īśvaraḥ*
*vyājahāra punar gopān*
*darśayan laukikīṁ gatim*

*tat*—that; *upākarṇya*—hearing; *bhagavān*—the Supreme Lord; *prahasya*—laughing; *jagat-īśvaraḥ*—the controller of the entire universe; *vyājahāra*—addressed; *punaḥ*—again; *gopān*—the cowherd boys; *darśayan*—showing; *laukikīm*—of the ordinary world; *gatim*—the way.

## TRANSLATION

**Hearing what had happened, the Supreme Personality of Godhead, the Lord of the universe, simply laughed. Then He again addressed the cowherd boys, showing them the way men act in this world.**

## PURPORT

By laughing, Lord Kṛṣṇa indicated to the cowherd boys that they need not be angry at the ritualistic *brāhmaṇas* but should understand that one who begs will often be refused.

## TEXT 14

मां ज्ञापयत पत्नीभ्यः ससंकर्षणमागतम् ।
दास्यन्ति काममन्नं वः स्निग्धा मय्युषिता धिया ॥१४॥

*māṁ jñāpayata patnībhyaḥ*
*sa-saṅkarṣaṇam āgatam*

*dāsyanti kāmam annaṁ vaḥ*
*snigdhā mayy uṣitā dhiyā*

*mām*—Me; *jñāpayata*—please announce; *patnībhyaḥ*—to the wives; *sa-saṅkarṣaṇam*—together with Lord Balarāma; *āgatam*—arrived; *dāsyanti*—they will give; *kāmam*—as much as you desire; *annam*—food; *vaḥ*—to you; *snigdhāḥ*—affectionate; *mayi*—in Me; *uṣitāḥ*—residing; *dhiyā*—with their intelligence.

## TRANSLATION

**Tell the wives of the *brāhmaṇas* that I have come here with Lord Saṅkarṣaṇa. They will certainly give you all the food you want, for they are most affectionate toward Me and, indeed, with their intelligence reside in Me alone.**

## PURPORT

While physically the wives of the *brāhmaṇas* remained at home, within their minds they resided in the Supreme Lord Kṛṣṇa because of intense affection for Him. Śrīla Viśvanātha Cakravartī Ṭhākura explains that the reason Lord Kṛṣṇa did not have the cowherd boys tell the *brāhmaṇas'* wives He was hungry is that He knew this would severely distress these devoted ladies. Simply out of affection for Lord Kṛṣṇa, however, the wives would be happy to give all the food requested of them. They would not heed their husbands' prohibitions, since they resided within the Lord through their transcendental intelligence.

## TEXT 15

गत्वाथ पत्नीशालायां दृष्ट्वासीनाः स्वलंकृताः ।
नत्वा द्विजसतीर्गोपाः प्रश्रिता इदमब्रुवन् ॥१५॥

*gatvātha patnī-śālāyāṁ*
*dṛṣṭvāsīnāḥ sv-alaṅkṛtāḥ*
*natvā dvija-satīr gopāḥ*
*praśritā idam abruvan*

*gatvā*—going; *atha*—then; *patnī-śālāyām*—in the house of the wives of the *brāhmaṇas; dṛṣṭvā*—seeing them; *āsīnāḥ*—sitting; *su-alaṅkṛtāḥ*—nicely ornamented; *natvā*—bowing down to offer obeisances; *dvija-satīḥ*—to the chaste wives of the *brāhmaṇas; gopāḥ*—the cowherd boys; *praśritāḥ*—humbly; *idam*—this; *abruvan*—spoke.

### TRANSLATION

**The cowherd boys then went to the house where the *brāhmaṇas'* wives were staying. There the boys saw those chaste ladies sitting, nicely decorated with fine ornaments. Bowing down to the *brāhmaṇa* ladies, the boys addressed them in all humility.**

### TEXT 16

नमो वो विप्रपत्नीभ्यो निबोधत वचांसि नः ।
इतोऽविदूरे चरता कृष्णेनेहेषिता वयम् ॥१६॥

*namo vo vipra-patnībhyo*
*nibodhata vacāṁsi naḥ*
*ito 'vidūre caratā*
*kṛṣṇenehesitā vayam*

*namaḥ*—obeisances; *vaḥ*—unto you; *vipra-patnībhyaḥ*—the wives of the *brāhmaṇas; nibodhata*—please hear; *vacāṁsi*—words; *naḥ*—our; *itaḥ*—from here; *avidūre*—not distant; *caratā*—who is going; *kṛṣṇena*—by Lord Kṛṣṇa; *iha*—here; *iṣitāḥ*—sent; *vayam*—we.

### TRANSLATION

**Obeisances unto you, O wives of the learned *brāhmaṇas.* Kindly hear our words. We have been sent here by Lord Kṛṣṇa, who is passing by not far from here.**

### TEXT 17

गाश्चारयन् स गोपालैः सरामो दूरमागतः ।
बुभुक्षितस्य तस्यान्नं सानुगस्य प्रदीयताम् ॥१७॥

*gāś cārayan sa gopālaiḥ*
*sa-rāmo dūram āgataḥ*
*bubhukṣitasya tasyānnaṁ*
*sānugasya pradīyatām*

*gāḥ*—the cows; *cārayan*—tending; *saḥ*—He; *gopālaiḥ*—in the company of the cowherd boys; *sa-rāmaḥ*—together with Lord Balarāma; *dūram*—from far away; *āgataḥ*—has come; *bubhukṣitasya*—who is hungry; *tasya*—for Him; *annam*—food; *sa-anugasya*—together with His companions; *pradīyatām*—should be given.

### TRANSLATION

**He has come a long way with the cowherd boys and Lord Balarāma, tending the cows. Now He is hungry, so some food should be given for Him and His companions.**

### TEXT 18

श्रुत्वाच्युतमुपायातं नित्यं तद्दर्शनोत्सुकाः ।
तत्कथाक्षिप्तमनसो बभूवुर्जातसम्भ्रमाः ॥१८॥

*śrutvācyutam upāyātaṁ*
*nityaṁ tad-darśanotsukāḥ*
*tat-kathākṣipta-manaso*
*babhūvur jāta-sambhramāḥ*

*śrutvā*—hearing; *acyutam*—Lord Kṛṣṇa; *upāyātam*—come nearby; *nityam*—constantly; *tat-darśana*—for the sight of Him; *utsukāḥ*—eager; *tat-kathā*—by descriptions of Him; *ākṣpita*—enchanted; *manasaḥ*—their minds; *babhūvuḥ*—they became; *jāta-sambhramāḥ*—excited.

### TRANSLATION

**The wives of the *brāhmaṇas* were always eager to see Kṛṣṇa, for their minds had been enchanted by descriptions of Him. Thus as soon as they heard that He had come, they became very excited.**

## TEXT 19

चतुर्विधं बहुगुणमन्नमादाय भाजनैः ।
अभिसस्रुः प्रियं सर्वाः समुद्रमिव निम्नगाः ॥१९॥

*catur-vidhaṁ bahu-guṇam*
*annam ādāya bhājanaiḥ*
*abhisasruḥ priyaṁ sarvāḥ*
*samudram iva nimnagāḥ*

*catuḥ-vidham*—of the four varieties (that which is chewed, that which is swallowed, that which is licked and that which is sucked); *bahu-guṇam*—endowed with many rich tastes and fragrances; *annam*—food; *ādāya*—bringing; *bhājanaiḥ*—in large vessels; *abhisasruḥ*—they went forward; *priyam*—to their beloved; *sarvāḥ*—all of them; *samudram*—to the ocean; *iva*—just as; *nimna-gāḥ*—the rivers.

## TRANSLATION

**Taking along in large vessels the four kinds of foods, full of fine tastes and aromas, all the ladies went forth to meet their beloved, just as rivers flow toward the sea.**

## PURPORT

Śrīla Viśvanātha Cakravartī Ṭhākura explains that the wives of the *brāhmaṇas* experienced conjugal feelings toward Kṛṣṇa, as if He were their paramour; thus they could not be checked as they rushed to see Him.

## TEXTS 20–21

निषिध्यमानाः पतिभिर्भ्रातृभिर्बन्धुभिः सुतैः ।
भगवत्युत्तमश्लोके दीर्घश्रुतधृताशयाः ॥२०॥
यमुनोपवनेऽशोकनवपल्लवमण्डिते ।
विचरन्तं वृतं गोपैः साग्रजं ददृशुः स्त्रियः ॥२१॥

*niṣidhyamānāḥ patibhir*
*bhrātṛbhir bandhubhiḥ sutaiḥ*
*bhagavaty uttama-śloke*
*dīrgha-śruta-dhṛtāśayāḥ*

*yamunopavane 'śoka-*
*nava-pallava-maṇḍite*
*vicarantaṁ vṛtaṁ gopaiḥ*
*sāgrajaṁ dadṛśuḥ striyaḥ*

*niṣidhyamānāḥ*—being forbidden; *patibhiḥ*—by their husbands; *bhrātṛbhiḥ*—by their brothers; *bandhubhiḥ*—by other relatives; *sutaiḥ*—and by their sons; *bhagavati*—directed toward the Supreme Personality of Godhead; *uttama-śloke*—who is praised with transcendental hymns; *dīrgha*—for a long time; *śruta*—because of hearing; *dhṛta*—acquired; *āśayāḥ*—whose expectations; *yamunā-upavane*—in a garden along the river Yamunā; *aśoka-nava-pallava*—by the buds of the *aśoka* trees; *maṇḍite*—decorated; *vicarantam*—wandering; *vṛtam*—surrounded; *gopaiḥ*—by the cowherd boys; *sa-agrajam*—together with His elder brother; *dadṛśuḥ*—they saw; *striyaḥ*—the ladies.

## TRANSLATION

**Although their husbands, brothers, sons and other relatives tried to forbid them from going, their hope of seeing Kṛṣṇa, cultivated by extensive hearing of His transcendental qualities, won out. Along the river Yamunā, within a garden decorated with buds of *aśoka* trees, they caught sight of Him strolling along in the company of the cowherd boys and His elder brother, Balarāma.**

## TEXT 22

श्यामं हिरण्यपरिधिं वनमाल्यबर्ह-
धातुप्रवालनटवेषमनुव्रतांसे ।
विन्यस्तहस्तमितरेण धुनानमब्जं
कर्णोत्पलालककपोलमुखाब्जहासम् ॥२२॥

*śyāmaṁ hiraṇya-paridhiṁ vanamālya-barha-*
*dhātu-pravāla-naṭa-veṣam anuvratāṁse*
*vinyasta-hastam itareṇa dhunānam abjaṁ*
*karṇotpalālaka-kapola-mukhābja-hāsam*

*śyāmam*—dark blue in complexion; *hiraṇya*—golden; *paridhim*—whose garment; *vana-mālya*—with a forest garland; *barha*—peacock feather; *dhātu*—colored minerals; *pravāla*—and sprigs of buds; *naṭa*—like a dancer upon the stage; *veṣam*—dressed; *anuvrata*—of a friend; *aṁse*—upon the shoulder; *vinyasta*—placed; *hastam*—His hand; *itareṇa*—with the other; *dhunānam*—twirling; *abjam*—a lotus; *karṇa*—upon His ears; *utpala*—lilies; *alaka-kapola*—with hair extending over His cheeks; *mukha-abja*—upon His lotuslike face; *hāsam*—having a smile.

## TRANSLATION

**His complexion was dark blue and His garment golden. Wearing a peacock feather, colored minerals, sprigs of flower buds, and a garland of forest flowers and leaves, He was dressed just like a dramatic dancer. He rested one hand upon the shoulder of a friend and with the other twirled a lotus. Lilies graced His ears, His hair hung down over His cheeks, and His lotuslike face was smiling.**

## TEXT 23

प्रायःश्रुतप्रियतमोदयकर्णपूरैर्
यस्मिन्निमग्नमनसस्तमथाक्षिरन्ध्रैः ।
अन्तः प्रवेश्य सुचिरं परिरभ्य तापं
प्राज्ञं यथाभिमतयो विजहुर्नरेन्द्र ॥२३॥

*prāyaḥ-śruta-priyatamodaya-karṇa-pūrair*
*yasmin nimagna-manasas tam athākṣi-randhraiḥ*
*antaḥ praveśya su-ciraṁ parirabhya tāpaṁ*
*prājñaṁ yathābhimatayo vijahur narendra*

*prāyaḥ*—repeatedly; *śruta*—heard; *priya-tama*—of their dearmost; *udaya*—the glories; *karṇa-pūraiḥ*—which were the ornaments of their ears; *yasmin*—in whom; *nimagna*—submerged; *manasaḥ*—their minds; *tam*—Him; *atha*—then; *akṣi-randhraiḥ*—through the apertures of their eyes; *antaḥ*—within; *praveśya*—making enter; *su-ciram*—for a long time; *parirabhya*—embracing; *tāpam*—their distress; *prājñam*—the inner consciousness; *yathā*—as; *abhimatayaḥ*—the functions of false ego; *vijahuḥ*—they gave up; *nara-indra*—O ruler of men.

## TRANSLATION

**O ruler of men, for a long time those *brāhmaṇa* ladies had heard about Kṛṣṇa, their beloved, and His glories had become the constant ornaments of their ears. Indeed, their minds were always absorbed in Him. Through the apertures of their eyes they now forced Him to enter within their hearts, and then they embraced Him within for a long time. In this way they finally gave up the pain of separation from Him, just as sages give up the anxiety of false ego by embracing their innermost consciousness.**

## TEXT 24

तास्तथा त्यक्तसर्वाशाः प्राप्ता आत्मदिदृक्षया ।
विज्ञायाखिलदृग्द्रष्टा प्राह प्रहसिताननः ॥२४॥

*tās tathā tyakta-sarvāśāḥ*
*prāptā ātma-didṛkṣayā*
*vijñāyākhila-dṛg-draṣṭā*
*prāha prahasitānanaḥ*

*tāḥ*—those ladies; *tathā*—in such a state; *tyakta-sarva-āśāḥ*—having given up all material desires; *prāptāḥ*—arrived; *ātma-didṛkṣayā*—with the desire of seeing Himself; *vijñāya*—understanding; *akhila-dṛk*—of the vision of all creatures; *draṣṭā*—the seer; *prāha*—He spoke; *prahasita-ānanah*—with a smile upon His face.

## TRANSLATION

**Lord Kṛṣṇa, who witnesses the thoughts of all creatures, understood how those ladies had abandoned all worldly hopes and come there simply to see Him. Thus He addressed them as follows with a smile upon His face.**

## TEXT 25

स्वागतं वो महाभागा आस्यतां करवाम किम् ।
यन्नो दिदृक्षया प्राप्ता उपपन्नमिदं हि वः ॥२५॥

*svāgataṁ vo mahā-bhāgā*
*āsyatāṁ karavāma kim*
*yan no didṛkṣayā prāptā*
*upapannam idaṁ hi vaḥ*

*su-āgatam*—auspicious welcome; *vaḥ*—for you; *mahā-bhāgāḥ*—O fortunate ladies; *āsyatām*—please come sit; *karavāma*—I can do; *kim*—what; *yat*—because; *naḥ*—Us; *didṛkṣayā*—with the desire of seeing; *prāptāḥ*—you have come; *upapannam*—fitting; *idam*—this; *hi*—certainly; *vaḥ*—on your part.

## TRANSLATION

**Welcome, O most fortunate ladies. Please sit down and make yourselves comfortable. What can I do for you? That you have come here to see Me is most appropriate.**

## PURPORT

Just as Śrī Kṛṣṇa welcomed the *gopīs* who came to dance with Him at night, He similarly welcomed the *brāhmaṇas'* wives, whose pure love for Him was proved by their overcoming many hindrances to see the Lord. The word *upapannam* indicates that although these ladies had rejected their husbands' orders, their behavior was not at all inappropriate, since their husbands had obviously tried to obstruct their loving service to Lord Kṛṣṇa.

## TEXT 26

नन्वद्धा मयि कुर्वन्ति कुशलाः स्वार्थदर्शिनः ।
अहैतुक्यव्यवहितां भक्तिमात्मप्रिये यथा ॥२६॥

*nanv addhā mayi kurvanti*
*kuśalāḥ svārtha-darśinaḥ*
*ahaituky avyavahitāṁ*
*bhaktim ātma-priye yathā*

*nanu*—certainly; *addhā*—directly; *mayi*—unto Me; *kurvanti*—they perform; *kuśalāḥ*—those who are expert; *sva-artha*—their own true benefit; *darśinaḥ*—who perceive; *ahaitukī*—unmotivated; *avyavahitām*—uninterrupted; *bhaktim*—devotional service; *ātma*—to the soul; *priye*—who am most dear; *yathā*—properly.

## TRANSLATION

**Certainly expert personalities, who can see their own true interest, render unmotivated and uninterrupted devotional service directly unto Me, for I am most dear to the soul.**

## PURPORT

The Supreme Lord informed the *brāhmaṇas'* wives that not only they but all people who recognize their true self-interest take to the spiritual process of loving service to the Lord. Lord Kṛṣṇa is *ātma-priya,* the real object of love for everyone. Although each individual has his own taste and freedom, ultimately every living being is a spiritual spark of the Supreme Personality of Godhead; thus everyone's primary loving attraction is constitutionally meant for Lord Śrī Kṛṣṇa. Loving service to the Lord should be *ahaitukī,* without personal motive, and *avyavahitā,* unobstructed by mental speculation, selfish desire or any quirk of time and circumstance.

## TEXT 27

प्राणबुद्धिमनःस्वात्मदारापत्यधनादयः ।
यत्सम्पर्कात् प्रिया आसंस्ततः कोऽन्वपरः प्रियः ॥२७॥

*prāṇa-buddhi-manaḥ-svātma-*
*dārāpatya-dhanādayaḥ*
*yat-samparkāt priyā āsaṁs*
*tataḥ ko nv aparaḥ priyaḥ*

*prāṇa*—one's vital force; *buddhi*—intelligence; *manaḥ*—mind; *sva*—relatives; *ātma*—body; *dāra*—wife; *apatya*—children; *dhana*—wealth; *ādayaḥ*—and so forth; *yat*—with which (self); *samparkāt*—because of contact; *priyāḥ*—dear; *āsan*—have become; *tataḥ*—than that; *kaḥ*—what; *nu*—indeed; *aparaḥ*—other; *priyaḥ*—dear object.

## TRANSLATION

**It is only by contact with the self that one's vital breath, intelligence, mind, friends, body, wife, children, wealth and so on are dear. Therefore what object can possibly be more dear than one's own self?**

## PURPORT

The word *yat-samparkāt* in this verse refers to contact with the individual self and ultimately with the Supreme Self, the Lord, who is the origin of the individual living being. By developing Kṛṣṇa consciousness, one automatically becomes self-realized, and thus one's vital strength, intelligence, mind, relatives, body, family and wealth all become enhanced and brilliant by the central influence of Kṛṣṇa consciousness. This happens because Kṛṣṇa consciousness is the optimum efficient conjunction of the individual self, who is pure consciousness, with the Supreme Self and supreme consciousness, Kṛṣṇa.

## TEXT 28

तद् यात देवयजनं पतयो वो द्विजातयः ।
स्वसत्रं पारयिष्यन्ति युष्माभिर्गृहमेधिनः ॥२८॥

*tad yāta deva-yajanaṁ*
*patayo vo dvijātayaḥ*
*sva-satraṁ pārayiṣyanti*
*yuṣmābhir gṛha-medhinaḥ*

*tat*—therefore; *yāta*—go; *deva-yajanam*—to the sacrificial arena; *patayaḥ*—the husbands; *vaḥ*—your; *dvi-jātayaḥ*—the *brāhmaṇas; sva-satram*—their own sacrifices; *pārayiṣyanti*—will be able to finish; *yuṣmābhiḥ*—together with you; *gṛha-medhinaḥ*—the householders.

### TRANSLATION

**You should thus return to the sacrificial arena, because your husbands, the learned *brāhmaṇas*, are householders and need your assistance to finish their respective sacrifices.**

### TEXT 29

श्रीपत्न्य ऊचुः
मैवं विभोऽर्हति भवान् गदितुं नृशंसं
सत्यं कुरुष्व निगमं तव पादमूलम् ।
प्राप्ता वयं तुलसिदाम पदावसृष्टं
केशैर्निवोढुमतिलंघ्य समस्तबन्धून् ॥२९॥

*śrī-patnya ūcuḥ*
*maivaṁ vibho 'rhati bhavān gadituṁ nṛ-śaṁsaṁ*
*satyaṁ kuruṣva nigamaṁ tava pāda-mūlam*
*prāptā vayaṁ tulasi-dāma padāvasṛṣṭaṁ*
*keśair nivoḍhum atilaṅghya samasta-bandhūn*

*śrī-patnyaḥ ūcuḥ*—the wives of the *brāhmaṇas* said; *mā*—not; *evam*—like this; *vibho*—O almighty Lord; *arhati*—ought; *bhavān*—You; *gaditum*—to speak; *nṛ-śaṁsam*—harshly; *satyam*—true; *kuruṣva*—please make; *nigamam*—the promise given in the revealed scripture; *tava*—Your; *pāda-mūlam*—the base of the lotus feet; *prāptāḥ*—having obtained; *vayam*—we; *tulasi-dāma*—the garland of *tulasī* leaves; *padā*—by Your foot; *avasṛṣṭam*—neglectfully kicked away; *keśaiḥ*—upon our hair; *nivoḍhum*—in order to carry; *atilaṅghya*—rejecting; *samasta*—all; *bandhūn*—relations.

### TRANSLATION

**The wives of the *brāhmaṇas* replied: O almighty one, please do not speak such cruel words. Rather, You should fulfill Your**

**promise that You always reciprocate with Your devotees in kind. Now that we have attained Your lotus feet, we simply wish to remain here in the forest so we may carry upon our heads the garlands of *tulasī* leaves You may neglectfully kick away with Your lotus feet. We are ready to give up all material relationships.**

## PURPORT

Here the *brāhmaṇas'* wives are saying something similar to what the *gopīs* say at the beginning of the *rāsa* dance (*Bhāg.* 10.29.31), when Lord Kṛṣṇa tells them to go home as well. Like this verse, the *gopīs'* statement begins with the words *maivaṁ vibho 'rhati bhavān gadituṁ nṛ-śaṁsam.*

*Nigama* refers to the Vedic literature, which states that one who surrenders at the lotus feet of the Lord does not return to this material world. Thus the *brāhmaṇas'* wives appealed to the Lord that since they had surrendered to Him, it was unfair for Him to order them to return to their materialistic husbands.

According to Śrīla Viśvanātha Cakravartī Ṭhākura, Lord Kṛṣṇa might have pointed out to the *brāhmaṇas'* wives, "You young ladies are members of the aristocratic *brāhmaṇa* community, so how can you surrender at the feet of a mere cowherd boy?"

To this the ladies might have replied, "Since we have already surrendered at Your lotus feet, and since we desire to become Your servants, we are obviously not maintaining a false identification as members of the so-called *brāhmaṇa* community. You can easily ascertain this from our words."

Lord Kṛṣṇa might have replied, "I am a cowherd boy, and My proper maidservants and girlfriends are the cowherd girls, the *gopīs.*"

The wives might have answered, "True, let them be so. Let them shine forth if You are embarrassed in front of Your relatives to make *brāhmaṇa* ladies Your maidservants. We certainly don't want to embarrass You. We will not go to Your village but will rather remain in Vṛndāvana, like presiding deities of the forest. We simply desire to perfect our lives by even a slight trace of connection with You."

Thus by the spiritual insight of Śrīla Viśvanātha Cakravartī Ṭhākura, we learn that the *brāhmaṇas'* wives offered to remain at a distance and simply take the *tulasī* leaves that would fall from the lotus feet of Kṛṣṇa or be crushed by the feet of His girlfriends when He would embrace them.

The ladies offered to carry these *tulasī* leaves upon their heads. Thus renouncing the desire to become Kṛṣṇa's intimate girlfriends or maidservants (a position they knew was difficult to achieve), the young *brāhmaṇa* ladies begged to remain in Vṛndāvana forest. If the Lord had then asked, "Then what will your family members say?" they would have replied, "We have already transcended our so-called relatives because we are seeing You, the Supreme Lord, face to face."

## TEXT 30

गृह्णन्ति नो न पतयः पितरौ सुता वा
न भ्रातृबन्धुसुहृदः कुत एव चान्ये ।
तस्माद् भवत्प्रपदयोः पतितात्मनां नो
नान्या भवेद् गतिररिन्दम तद् विधेहि ॥३०॥

*gṛhṇanti no na patayaḥ pitarau sutā vā*
*na bhrātṛ-bandhu-suhṛdaḥ kuta eva cānye*
*tasmād bhavat-prapadayoḥ patitātmanāṁ no*
*nānyā bhaved gatir arindama tad vidhehi*

*gṛhṇanti*—they will accept; *naḥ*—us; *na*—not; *patayaḥ*—our husbands; *pitarau*—fathers; *sutāḥ*—sons; *vā*—or; *na*—not; *bhrātṛ*—brothers; *bandhu*—other relatives; *suhṛdaḥ*—and friends; *kutaḥ*—how then; *eva*—indeed; *ca*—and; *anye*—other people; *tasmāt*—therefore; *bhavat*—Your; *prapadayoḥ*—at the tips of the lotus feet; *patita*—fallen; *ātmanām*—whose bodies; *naḥ*—for us; *na*—not; *anyā*—any other; *bhavet*—there can be; *gatiḥ*—destination; *arim-dama*—O chastiser of enemies; *tat*—that; *vidhehi*—kindly bestow upon us.

## TRANSLATION

**Our husbands, fathers, sons, brothers, other relatives and friends will no longer take us back, and how could anyone else be willing to give us shelter? Therefore, since we have thrown ourselves at Your lotus feet and have no other destination, please, O chastiser of enemies, grant our desire.**

## PURPORT

Śrīla Viśvanātha Cakravartī Ṭhākura comments as follows: "From their very youth the *brāhmaṇas'* wives had heard about Lord Kṛṣṇa's beauty, qualities and sweetness from the womenfolk of Vṛndāvana village, and also from the flower ladies, the betel-nut sellers and others. Consequently they always felt ecstatic love for Kṛṣṇa and were indifferent to their household duties. Their husbands, seeing them as deviant, doubted them and avoided dealing with them as far as possible. Now the wives of the *brāhmaṇas* were ready to formally reject their so-called families and neighbors, and out of great agitation they were crying and placing their heads upon Lord Kṛṣṇa's lotus feet, offering obeisances. In this way, with choking voices, they spoke the above verse. They begged that Lord Kṛṣṇa bestow upon them the benediction that He be their only destination, that He, the chastiser of enemies, subdue all *their* enemies—those difficulties obstructing them from attaining the Lord."

The wives of the *brāhmaṇas* simply wanted to serve Lord Kṛṣṇa, and this is pure Kṛṣṇa consciousness in ecstatic love of Godhead.

## TEXT 31

श्रीभगवानुवाच
पतयो नाभ्यसूयेरन् पितृभ्रातृसुतादयः ।
लोकाश्च वो मयोपेता देवा अप्यनुमन्वते ॥३१॥

*śrī-bhagavān uvāca*
*patayo nābhyasūyeran*
*pitṛ-bhrātṛ-sutādayaḥ*
*lokāś ca vo mayopetā*
*devā apy anumanvate*

*śrī-bhagavān uvāca*—the Supreme Personality of Godhead said; *patayaḥ*—your husbands; *na abhyasūyeran*—will not feel inimical; *pitṛ-bhrātṛ-suta-ādayaḥ*—your fathers, brothers, sons and others; *lokāḥ*—the general populace; *ca*—also; *vaḥ*—toward you; *mayā*—by Me; *upetāḥ*—advised; *devāḥ*—the demigods; *api*—even; *anumanvate*—regard favorably.

## TRANSLATION

**The Supreme Personality of Godhead replied: Rest assured that your husbands will not be inimical toward you, nor will your fathers, brothers, sons, other relatives or the general populace. I will personally advise them of the situation. Indeed, even the demigods will express their approval.**

## TEXT 32

न प्रीतयेऽनुरागाय ह्यंगसंगो नृणामिह ।
तन्मनो मयि युञ्जाना अचिरान्मामवाप्स्यथ ॥३२॥

*na prītaye 'nurāgāya*
*hy aṅga-saṅgo nṛṇām iha*
*tan mano mayi yuñjānā*
*acirān mām avāpsyatha*

*na*—not; *prītaye*—for satisfaction; *anurāgāya*—for loving attraction; *hi*—certainly; *aṅga-saṅgaḥ*—physical association; *nṛṇām*—for people; *iha*—in this world; *tat*—therefore; *manaḥ*—your minds; *mayi*—upon Me; *yuñjānāḥ*—fixing; *acirāt*—very quickly; *mām*—Me; *avāpsyatha*—you will achieve.

## TRANSLATION

**For you to remain in My bodily association would certainly not please people in this world, nor would it be the best way for you to increase your love for Me. Rather, you should fix your minds on Me, and very soon you will achieve Me.**

## PURPORT

The Lord pointed out that people in general would not appreciate a loving affair between Lord Kṛṣṇa, who superficially was appearing as a cowherd boy, and the wives from the *brāhmaṇa* community. Also, the *brāhmaṇa* ladies' own devotion and love would increase most efficiently in separation. In other words, it would be best all around if they continued to fix their minds on Lord Kṛṣṇa and thus went on with the process they had been practicing throughout their lives. The Lord and

His bona fide representative, the spiritual master, expertly engage the Lord's devotees in different types of service so that all of them can quickly return to His lotus feet.

## TEXT 33

श्रवणाद्दर्शनाद् ध्यानान्मयि भावोऽनुकीर्तनात् ।
न तथा सन्निकर्षेण प्रतियात ततो गृहान् ॥३३॥

*śravaṇād darśanād dhyānān*
*mayi bhāvo 'nukīrtanāt*
*na tathā sannikarṣeṇa*
*pratiyāta tato gṛhān*

*śravaṇāt*—by hearing; *darśanāt*—by seeing the Deity form; *dhyānāt*—by meditation; *mayi*—for Me; *bhāvaḥ*—love; *anukīrtanāt*—by chanting My names and qualities; *na*—not; *tathā*—in the same way; *sannikarṣeṇa*—by literal proximity; *pratiyāta*—return; *tataḥ*—therefore; *gṛhān*—to your homes.

### TRANSLATION

**It is by hearing about Me, seeing My Deity form, meditating upon Me and chanting My names and glories that love for Me develops, not by physical proximity. Therefore please go back to your homes.**

## TEXT 34

श्रीशुक उवाच
इत्युक्ता द्विजपत्न्यस्ता यज्ञवाटं पुनर्गताः ।
ते चानसूयवस्ताभिः स्त्रीभिः सत्रमपारयन् ॥३४॥

*śrī-śuka uvāca*
*ity uktā dvija-patnyas tā*
*yajña-vāṭaṁ punar gatāḥ*
*te cānasūyavas tābhiḥ*
*strībhiḥ satram apārayan*

*śrī-śukaḥ uvāca*—Śrī Śukadeva Gosvāmī said; *iti*—with these words; *uktāḥ*—spoken to; *dvija-patnyaḥ*—the wives of the *brāhmaṇas; tāḥ*—they; *yajña-vāṭam*—to the place of sacrifice; *punaḥ*—again; *gatāḥ*—went; *te*—they, their husbands; *ca*—and; *anasūyavaḥ*—not inimical; *tābhiḥ*—together with them; *strībhiḥ*—their wives; *satram*—the sacrificial performance; *apārayan*—they completed.

## TRANSLATION

**Śrīla Śukadeva Gosvāmī said: Thus instructed, the wives of the *brāhmaṇas* returned to the place of sacrifice. The *brāhmaṇas* did not find any fault with their wives, and together with them they finished the sacrifice.**

## PURPORT

The wives of the *brāhmaṇas* obeyed Lord Kṛṣṇa's order and returned to the sacrificial arena of their husbands, whereas the *gopīs*, although ordered by Kṛṣṇa to go home, remained in the forest to dance with Him through the full-moon night. Both the *gopīs* and the *brāhmaṇas'* wives achieved pure love of Godhead.

## TEXT 35

तत्रैका विधृता भर्त्रा भगवन्तं यथाश्रुतम् ।
हृदोपगुह्य विजहौ देहं कर्मानुबन्धनम् ॥३५॥

*tatraikā vidhṛtā bhartrā*
*bhagavantaṁ yathā-śrutam*
*hṛdopaguhya vijahau*
*dehaṁ karmānubandhanam*

*tatra*—there; *ekā*—one of them; *vidhṛtā*—held back by force; *bhartrā*—by her husband; *bhagavantam*—the Supreme Lord, Śrī Kṛṣṇa; *yathā-śrutam*—as she heard about Him from the others; *hṛdā*—within her heart; *upaguhya*—embracing; *vijahau*—she gave up; *deham*—her material body; *karma-anubandhanam*—which is simply the basis of bondage to material activity.

### TRANSLATION

**One of the ladies had been forcibly kept back by her husband. When she heard the others describe the Supreme Lord Kṛṣṇa, she embraced Him within her heart and gave up her material body, the basis of bondage to material activity.**

### PURPORT

The lady described here was especially devoted to Lord Kṛṣṇa. Upon giving up her material body, she immediately attained a spiritual body and left the sacrificial arena to join the Supreme Personality of Godhead.

### TEXT 36

**भगवानपि गोविन्दस्तेनैवान्नेन गोपकान् ।**
**चतुर्विधेनाशयित्वा स्वयं च बुभुजे प्रभुः ॥३६॥**

*bhagavān api govindas*
*tenaivānnena gopakān*
*catur-vidhenāśayitvā*
*svayaṁ ca bubhuje prabhuḥ*

*bhagavān*—the Supreme Personality of Godhead; *api*—moreover; *govindaḥ*—Lord Govinda; *tena*—with that; *eva*—very same; *annena*—food; *gopakān*—the cowherd boys; *catuḥ-vidhena*—of four varieties; *aśayitvā*—feeding; *svayam*—Himself; *ca*—and; *bubhuje*—partook; *prabhuḥ*—the Almighty.

### TRANSLATION

**Govinda, the Supreme Personality of Godhead, fed the cowherd boys with that food of four varieties. Then the all-powerful Lord Himself partook of the preparations.**

### TEXT 37

**एवं लीलानरवपुर्नृलोकमनुशीलयन् ।**
**रेमे गोगोपगोपीनां रमयन् रूपवाक्कृतैः ॥३७॥**

*evaṁ līlā-nara-vapur*
*nṛ-lokam anuśīlayan*
*reme go-gopa-gopīnāṁ*
*ramayan rūpa-vāk-kṛtaiḥ*

*evam*—in this manner; *līlā*—for pastimes; *nara*—appearing as a human being; *vapuḥ*—whose transcendental body; *nṛ-lokam*—human society; *anuśīlayan*—imitating; *reme*—He took pleasure; *go*—the cows; *gopa*—cowherd boys; *gopīnām*—the cowherd girls; *ramayan*—pleasing; *rūpa*—with His beauty; *vāk*—words; *kṛtaiḥ*—and actions.

## TRANSLATION

**Thus the Supreme Lord, appearing like a human being to perform His pastimes, imitated the ways of human society. He enjoyed pleasing His cows, cowherd boyfriends and cowherd girlfriends with His beauty, words and actions.**

## TEXT 38

अथानुस्मृत्य विप्रास्ते अन्वतप्यन् कृतागसः ।
यद् विश्वेश्वरयोर्याच्ञामहन्म नृविडम्बयोः ॥३८॥

*athānusmṛtya viprās te*
*anvatapyan kṛtāgasaḥ*
*yad viśveśvarayor yācñām*
*ahanma nṛ-viḍambayoḥ*

*atha*—then; *anusmṛtya*—coming to their senses; *viprāḥ*—the *brāhmaṇas; te*—they; *anvatapyan*—felt great remorse; *kṛta-agasaḥ*—having committed sinful offenses; *yat*—because; *viśva-īśvarayoḥ*—of the two Lords of the universe, Kṛṣṇa and Balarāma; *yācñām*—the humble supplication; *ahanma*—we transgressed; *nṛ-viḍambayoḥ*—of those who were deceptively appearing as human beings.

## TRANSLATION

**The *brāhmaṇas* then came to their senses and began to feel great remorse. They thought, "We have sinned, for we have denied**

**the request of the two Lords of the universe, who deceptively appeared as ordinary human beings."**

## PURPORT

Lord Kṛṣṇa and Lord Balarāma did not try to deceive the *brāhmaṇas:* They straightforwardly requested food from them. Rather, the *brāhmaṇas* deceived themselves, as indicated by the Sanskrit word *nṛ-viḍambayoḥ,* which means that Kṛṣṇa and Balarāma are bewildering for an ordinary human being who considers Them also to be human. Still, because the wives of the *brāhmaṇas* were great devotees of the Lord, the foolish *brāhmaṇas* received spiritual benefit and finally came to their senses.

## TEXT 39

दृष्ट्वा स्त्रीणां भगवति कृष्णे भक्तिमलौकिकीम् ।
आत्मानं च तया हीनमनुतप्ता व्यगर्हयन् ॥३९॥

*dṛṣṭvā strīṇāṁ bhagavati*
*kṛṣṇe bhaktim alaukikīm*
*ātmānaṁ ca tayā hīnam*
*anutaptā vyagarhayan*

*dṛṣṭvā*—observing; *strīṇām*—of their wives; *bhagavati*—for the Supreme Personality of Godhead; *kṛṣṇe*—Śrī Kṛṣṇa; *bhaktim*—the pure devotion; *alaukikīm*—transcendental to this world; *ātmānam*—themselves; *ca*—and; *tayā*—of that; *hīnam*—devoid; *anutaptāḥ*—lamenting; *vyagarhayan*—they condemned.

## TRANSLATION

**Taking note of their wives' pure, transcendental devotion for Lord Kṛṣṇa, the Supreme Personality of Godhead, and seeing their own lack of devotion, the *brāhmaṇas* felt most sorrowful and began to condemn themselves.**

## TEXT 40

धिग् जन्म नस्त्रिवृद् यत्तद्धिग् व्रतं धिग् बहुज्ञताम् ।
धिक्कुलं धिक्क्रियादाक्ष्यं विमुखा ये त्वधोक्षजे ॥४०॥

*dhig janma nas tri-vṛd yat tad*
*dhig vrataṁ dhig bahu-jñatām*
*dhik kulaṁ dhik kriyā-dākṣyaṁ*
*vimukhā ye tv adhokṣaje*

*dhik*—to hell; *janma*—with the birth; *naḥ*—our; *tri-vṛt*—threefold (the first from the physical parents, the second at the time of brahminical initiation, and the third at the time of initiation into the performances of Vedic sacrifice); *yat tat*—whatever; *dhik*—to hell; *vratam*—with our vow (of celibacy); *dhik*—to hell; *bahu-jñatām*—with our extensive knowledge; *dhik*—to hell; *kulam*—with our aristocratic lineage; *dhik*—to hell; *kriyā-dākṣyam*—with our expertise in ritualistic activities; *vimukhāḥ*—inimical; *ye*—who; *tu*—however; *adhokṣaje*—to the transcendental Personality of Godhead.

## TRANSLATION

**To hell with our threefold birth, our vow of celibacy and our extensive learning! To hell with our aristocratic background and our expertise in the rituals of sacrifice! These are all condemned because we were inimical to the transcendental Personality of Godhead.**

## PURPORT

As explained in the definitions above, the words *tri-vṛd janma*, or "threefold birth," refer to 1) physical birth, 2) brahminical initiation, and 3) initiation into the performance of Vedic sacrifice. Everything is useless if one is ignorant of the Absolute Truth, the Supreme Lord Kṛṣṇa.

## TEXT 41

नूनं भगवतो माया योगिनामपि मोहिनी ।
यद् वयं गुरवो नृणां स्वार्थे मुह्यामहे द्विजाः ॥४१॥

*nūnaṁ bhagavato māyā*
*yoginām api mohinī*
*yad vayaṁ guravo nṛṇāṁ*
*svārthe muhyāmahe dvijāḥ*

*nūnam*—indeed; *bhagavataḥ*—of the Supreme Lord; *māyā*—the illusory potency; *yoginām*—for great mystics; *api*—even; *mohinī*—is bewildering; *yat*—since; *vayam*—we; *guravaḥ*—the spiritual masters; *nṝṇām*—of society in general; *sva-arthe*—about our own real interest; *muhyāmahe*—have become bewildered; *dvijāḥ*—*brāhmaṇas.*

## TRANSLATION

**The illusory potency of the Supreme Lord certainly bewilders even the great mystics, what to speak of us. As *brāhmaṇas* we are supposed to be the spiritual masters of all classes of men, yet we have been bewildered about our own real interest.**

## TEXT 42

**अहो पश्यत नारीणामपि कृष्णे जगद्गुरौ ।**
**दुरन्तभावं योऽविध्यन्मृत्युपाशान् गृहाभिधान् ॥४२॥**

*aho paśyata nārīṇām*
*api kṛṣṇe jagad-gurau*
*duranta-bhāvaṁ yo 'vidhyan*
*mṛtyu-pāśān gṛhābhidhān*

*aho paśyata*—just see; *nārīṇām*—of these women; *api*—even; *kṛṣṇe*—for Lord Kṛṣṇa; *jagat-gurau*—the spiritual master of the entire universe; *duranta*—unlimited; *bhāvam*—the devotion; *yaḥ*—which; *avidhyat*—has broken; *mṛtyu*—of death; *pāśān*—the bonds; *gṛha-abhidhān*—known as family life.

## TRANSLATION

**Just see the unlimited love these women have developed for Lord Kṛṣṇa, the spiritual master of the entire universe! This love has broken for them the very bonds of death—their attachment to family life.**

## PURPORT

Superficially, the husbands, fathers, fathers-in-law and so on were the ladies' *gurus,* or teachers. Yet the women had become perfect in Kṛṣṇa consciousness, whereas the men had fallen into the darkness of ignorance.

According to Śrīla Viśvanātha Cakravartī Ṭhākura, upon returning home the ladies showed transcendental ecstatic symptoms, such as trembling of the body, shedding of tears, standing of the bodily hairs on end, discoloration of the complexion, crying out "O pleasure of my life, O Kṛṣṇa!" with faltering words, and so forth.

Śrīla Viśvanātha Cakravartī goes on to state that while one may object that it is not fitting for a woman to love anyone other than her husband, here the husbands themselves point out that they are *gurus* only in imitation of the Supreme Lord, who is *jagad-guru*, the universal teacher and spiritual master. The husbands noted that the women, having perfected their transcendental attachment for Kṛṣṇa, did not have even a trace of attachment left for home, husband, children and so forth. Therefore from that day on the husbands accepted those ladies as their worshipable spiritual masters and no longer thought of them as their wives or property.

## TEXTS 43–44

**नासां द्विजातिसंस्कारो न निवासो गुरावपि ।**
**न तपो नात्ममीमांसा न शौचं न क्रियाः शुभाः ॥४३॥**
**तथापि ह्युत्तमःश्लोके कृष्णे योगेश्वरेश्वरे ।**
**भक्तिर्दृढा न चास्माकं संस्कारादिमतामपि ॥४४॥**

*nāsāṁ dvijāti-saṁskāro*
*na nivāso gurāv api*
*na tapo nātma-mīmāṁsā*
*na śaucaṁ na kriyāḥ śubhāḥ*

*tathāpi hy uttamaḥ-śloke*
*kṛṣṇe yogeśvareśvare*
*bhaktir dṛḍhā na cāsmākaṁ*
*saṁskārādimatām api*

*na*—there is not; *āsām*—on their part; *dvijāti-saṁskāraḥ*—the purificatory rituals pertaining to the twice-born classes of society; *na*—nor;

*nivāsaḥ*—residence; *gurau*—in the *āśrama* of a spiritual master (that is, training as a *brahmacārī*); *api*—even; *na*—no; *tapaḥ*—execution of austerities; *na*—no; *ātma-mīmāṁsā*—philosophical inquiry into the reality of the self; *na*—no; *śaucam*—rituals of cleanliness; *na*—no; *kriyāḥ*—ritualistic activities; *śubhāḥ*—pious; *tathā api*—nevertheless; *hi*—indeed; *uttamaḥ-śloke*—whose glories are chanted by the exalted *mantras* of the *Vedas; kṛṣṇe*—for Lord Kṛṣṇa; *yoga-īśvara-īśvare*—the supreme master of all masters of mystic power; *bhaktiḥ*—pure devotional service; *dṛḍhā*—firm; *na*—not; *ca*—on the other hand; *asmākam*—of us; *saṁskāra-ādi-matām*—who possess such purification and so forth; *api*—even though.

## TRANSLATION

**These women have never undergone the purificatory rites of the twice-born classes, nor have they lived as *brahmacārīs* in the *āśrama* of a spiritual master, nor have they executed austerities, speculated on the nature of the self, followed the formalities of cleanliness or engaged in pious rituals. Nevertheless, they have firm devotion for Lord Kṛṣṇa, whose glories are chanted by the exalted hymns of the *Vedas* and who is the supreme master of all masters of mystic power. We, on the other hand, have no such devotion for the Lord, although we have executed all these processes.**

## PURPORT

According to Śrīla Śrīdhara Svāmī, the husbands were not aware that their wives had occasionally associated with residents of Vṛndāvana, such as the flower ladies, and had heard about the beauty and qualities of Kṛṣṇa. The *brāhmaṇas* were astonished at their wives' loving devotion for Lord Kṛṣṇa, not realizing that this devotion had developed as a result of hearing and chanting about the Lord in the association of His pure devotees.

## TEXT 45

ननु स्वार्थविमूढानां प्रमत्तानां गृहेहया ।
अहो नः स्मारयामास गोपवाक्यैः सतां गतिः ॥४५॥

*nanu svārtha-vimūḍhānāṁ*
*pramattānāṁ gṛhehayā*
*aho naḥ smārayām āsa*
*gopa-vākyaiḥ satāṁ gatiḥ*

*nanu*—indeed; *sva-artha*—about their own true benefit; *vimūḍhānām*—who were bewildered; *pramattānām*—who were intoxicated; *gṛha-īhayā*—with their household endeavors; *aho*—ah; *naḥ*—us; *smārayām āsa*—He reminded about; *gopa-vākyaiḥ*—by the words of cowherds; *satām*—of the transcendental souls; *gatiḥ*—the ultimate destination.

### TRANSLATION

**Indeed, infatuated as we are with our household affairs, we have deviated completely from the real aim of our life. But now just see how the Lord, through the words of these simple cowherd boys, has reminded us of the ultimate destination of all true transcendentalists.**

### TEXT 46

अन्यथा पूर्णकामस्य कैवल्याद्याशिषां पतेः ।
ईशितव्यैः किमस्माभिरीशस्यैतद् विडम्बनम् ॥४६॥

*anyathā pūrṇa-kāmasya*
*kaivalyādy-āśiṣāṁ pateḥ*
*īśitavyaiḥ kim asmābhir*
*īśasyaitad viḍambanam*

*anyathā*—otherwise; *pūrṇa-kāmasya*—of Him whose every possible desire is fulfilled; *kaivalya*—of liberation; *ādi*—and others; *āśiṣām*—benedictions; *pateḥ*—the master; *īśitavyaiḥ*—with those who are meant to be controlled; *kim*—what; *asmābhiḥ*—with us; *īśasya*—of Him who is the absolute controller; *etat*—this; *viḍambanam*—pretense.

### TRANSLATION

**Otherwise, why would the supreme controller—whose every desire is already fulfilled and who is the master of liberation and**

**all other transcendental benedictions—enact this pretense with us, who are always to be controlled by Him?**

## PURPORT

Although Lord Kṛṣṇa is the Absolute Truth, He humbly sent His cowherd boyfriends to beg food from the *brāhmaṇas*. In so doing, He exposed the *brāhmaṇas'* foolish arrogance and established the glories of His own transcendental beauty by attracting their very wives to surrender at His lotus feet.

## TEXT 47

हित्वान्यान् भजते यं श्रीः पादस्पर्शाशयासकृत् ।
स्वात्मदोषापवर्गेण तद्याच्ञा जनमोहिनी ॥४७॥

*hitvānyān bhajate yaṁ śrīḥ*
*pāda-sparśāśayāsakṛt*
*svātma-doṣāpavargeṇa*
*tad-yācñā jana-mohinī*

*hitvā*—giving up; *anyān*—others; *bhajate*—worships; *yam*—which Lord; *śrīḥ*—the goddess of fortune; *pāda-sparśa*—for the touch of His lotus feet; *āśayā*—with the desire; *asakṛt*—constantly; *sva-ātma*—of herself; *doṣa*—the faults (of fickleness and pride); *apavargeṇa*—putting aside; *tat*—His; *yācñā*—begging; *jana*—ordinary humans; *mohinī*—bewildering.

## TRANSLATION

**Hoping for the touch of His lotus feet, the goddess of fortune perpetually worships Him alone, leaving aside all others and renouncing her pride and fickleness. That He begs is certainly astonishing to everyone.**

## PURPORT

The supreme master of the goddess of fortune herself obviously does not have to beg for food, as pointed out here by the *brāhmaṇas*, who are finally manifesting real spiritual intelligence.

## TEXTS 48–49

देशः कालः पृथग् द्रव्यं मन्त्रतन्त्रर्त्विजोऽग्नयः ।
देवता यजमानश्च क्रतुर्धर्मश्च यन्मयः ॥४८॥
स एव भगवान् साक्षाद् विष्णुर्योगेश्वरेश्वरः ।
जातो यदुष्वित्याशृण्म ह्यपि मूढा न विद्महे ॥४९॥

*deśaḥ kālaḥ pṛthag dravyaṁ*
*mantra-tantrartvijo 'gnayaḥ*
*devatā yajamānaś ca*
*kratur dharmaś ca yan-mayaḥ*

*sa eva bhagavān sākṣād*
*viṣṇur yogeśvareśvaraḥ*
*jāto yaduṣv ity āśṛṇma*
*hy api mūḍhā na vidmahe*

*deśaḥ*—the place; *kālaḥ*—time; *pṛthak dravyam*—particular items of paraphernalia; *mantra*—Vedic hymns; *tantra*—prescribed rituals; *ṛtvijaḥ*—priests; *agnayaḥ*—and the sacrificial fires; *devatā*—the presiding demigods; *yajamānaḥ*—the performer; *ca*—and; *kratuḥ*—the offering; *dharmaḥ*—the pious reaction; *ca*—and; *yat*—whom; *mayaḥ*—constituting; *saḥ*—He; *eva*—indeed; *bhagavān*—the Supreme Personality of Godhead; *sākṣāt*—directly; *viṣṇuḥ*—Lord Viṣṇu; *yoga-īśvara-īśvaraḥ*—the Lord of all mystic controllers; *jātaḥ*—taken birth; *yaduṣu*—among the Yadu dynasty; *iti*—thus; *āśṛṇma*—we have heard; *hi*—certainly; *api*—nevertheless; *mūḍhāḥ*—foolish; *na vidmahe*—we could not understand.

## TRANSLATION

**All the aspects of sacrifice—the auspicious place and time, the various items of paraphernalia, the Vedic hymns, the prescribed rituals, the priests and sacrificial fires, the demigods, the patron of the sacrifice, the sacrificial offering and the pious results obtained—all are simply manifestations of His opulences. Yet even though we had heard that the Supreme Personality of Godhead, Viṣṇu, the Lord of all mystic controllers, had taken birth in**

**the Yadu dynasty, we were so foolish that we could not recognize Śrī Kṛṣṇa to be none other than Him.**

## TEXT 50

तस्मै नमो भगवते कृष्णायाकुण्ठमेधसे ।
यन्मायामोहितधियो भ्रमामः कर्मवर्त्मसु ॥५०॥

*tasmai namo bhagavate*
*kṛṣṇāyākuṇṭha-medhase*
*yan-māyā-mohita-dhiyo*
*bhramāmaḥ karma-vartmasu*

*tasmai*—unto Him; *namaḥ*—obeisances; *bhagavate*—unto the Supreme Personality of Godhead; *kṛṣṇāya*—Lord Kṛṣṇa; *akuṇṭha-medhase*—whose intelligence is never restricted; *yat-māyā*—by whose illusory potency; *mohita*—bewildered; *dhiyaḥ*—whose minds; *bhramāmaḥ*—we are wandering; *karma-vartmasu*—upon the paths of fruitive activity.

## TRANSLATION

**Let us offer our obeisances unto Lord Kṛṣṇa, the Supreme Personality of Godhead. His intelligence is never bewildered, whereas we, confused by His power of illusion, are simply wandering about on the paths of fruitive work.**

## TEXT 51

स वै न आद्यः पुरुषः स्वमायामोहितात्मनाम् ।
अविज्ञातानुभावानां क्षन्तुमर्हत्यतिक्रमम् ॥५१॥

*sa vai na ādyaḥ puruṣaḥ*
*sva-māyā-mohitātmanām*
*avijñātānubhāvānāṁ*
*kṣantum arhaty atikramam*

*saḥ*—He; *vai*—indeed; *naḥ*—our; *ādyaḥ*—the primeval Lord; *puruṣaḥ*—the Supreme Personality of Godhead; *sva-māyā-mohita-ātmanām*—of those whose minds have been bewildered by His illusory potency; *avijñāta*—who did not understand; *anubhāvānām*—His influence; *kṣantum*—to forgive; *arhati*—should; *atikramam*—the offense.

## TRANSLATION

**We were bewildered by Lord Kṛṣṇa's illusory potency and thus could not understand His influence as the original Personality of Godhead. Now we hope He will kindly forgive our offense.**

## TEXT 52

इति स्वाघमनुस्मृत्य कृष्णे ते कृतहेलनाः ।
दिदृक्षवो व्रजमथ कंसाद् भीता न चाचलन् ॥५२॥

*iti svāgham anusmṛtya*
*kṛṣṇe te kṛta-helanāḥ*
*didṛkṣavo vrajam atha*
*kaṁsād bhītā na cācalan*

*iti*—thus; *sva-agham*—their own offense; *anusmṛtya*—thinking back upon; *kṛṣṇe*—against Lord Kṛṣṇa; *te*—they; *kṛta-helanāḥ*—having shown contempt; *didṛkṣavaḥ*—wishing to see; *vrajam*—to the village of Nanda Mahārāja; *atha*—then; *kaṁsāt*—of Kaṁsa; *bhītāḥ*—afraid; *na*—not; *ca*—and; *acalan*—they went.

## TRANSLATION

**Thus reflecting on the sin they had committed by neglecting Lord Kṛṣṇa, they became very eager to see Him. But being afraid of King Kaṁsa, they did not dare go to Vraja.**

## PURPORT

Realizing their offense against Lord Kṛṣṇa, and finally appreciating His almighty position, the *brāhmaṇas* naturally wanted to rush to Vraja and surrender at the lotus feet of the Lord. But they were afraid that Kaṁsa would certainly kill them when his spies reported that they had gone to Kṛṣṇa. The *brāhmaṇas'* wives were absorbed in ecstatic Kṛṣṇa consciousness and thus went to Kṛṣṇa anyway, just as the *gopīs*, simply to dance with the Lord, traveled in the dead of night through a forest inhabited by wild animals. But the *brāhmaṇas* were not on such an advanced platform of Kṛṣṇa consciousness and thus, overcome by fear of Kaṁsa, could not see the Lord face to face.

*Thus end the purports of the humble servant of His Divine Grace A. C. Bhaktivedanta Swami Prabhupāda to the Tenth Canto, Twenty-third Chapter, of the* Śrīmad-Bhāgavatam, *entitled "The* Brāhmaṇas' *Wives Blessed."*

CHAPTER TWENTY-FOUR

# Worshiping Govardhana Hill

In this chapter Lord Śrī Kṛṣṇa crushes the pride of Indra by prohibiting a sacrifice intended for him and initiating a substitute sacrifice in worship of Govardhana Hill.

When Śrī Kṛṣṇa saw the cowherd men busily preparing for a sacrifice to Indra, He inquired about it from their king, Nanda. Nanda explained that the rain given by Indra enables all living entities to maintain their lives, and therefore this sacrifice would be executed to satisfy him. Kṛṣṇa responded that it is because of *karma* alone that living entities take their birth in a certain body, experience varieties of happiness and suffering in that body, and then give it up as the *karma* pertaining to it runs out. Thus it is *karma* alone that is our enemy, our friend, our *guru* and our lord, and Indra can do nothing to alter the happiness and distress of anyone, for everyone is tightly bound by his karmic reactions. The material modes of goodness, passion and ignorance bring about the creation, maintenance and destruction of this world. The clouds give forth rain when they are impelled by the mode of passion, and cowherds prosper by protecting the cows. Furthermore, the cowherds' proper residence is in the forest and on the hills. Therefore they should offer worship to the cows, the *brāhmaṇas* and Govardhana Hill.

After Kṛṣṇa spoke thus, He arranged for the cowherd men to worship Govardhana with the paraphernalia collected for the sacrifice to Indra. He then assumed a huge, unprecedented transcendental form and devoured all the food and other offerings presented to Govardhana. As He did so He proclaimed to the cowherd community that although they had worshiped Indra for so long, he had never appeared in person, whereas Govardhana himself had now manifested before their eyes and eaten their offerings of foodstuffs. Therefore they should all now offer obeisances to Govardhana Hill. Then Lord Kṛṣṇa joined the cowherds in offering obeisances to His own newly assumed form.

## TEXT 1

श्रीशुक उवाच
भगवानपि तत्रैव बलदेवेन संयुतः ।
अपश्यन्निवसन् गोपानिन्द्रयागकृतोद्यमान् ॥१॥

*śrī-śuka uvāca*
*bhagavān api tatraiva*
*baladevena saṁyutaḥ*
*apaśyan nivasan gopān*
*indra-yāga-kṛtodyamān*

*śrī-śukaḥ uvāca*—Śrī Śukadeva Gosvāmī said; *bhagavān*—the Supreme Personality of Godhead; *api*—also; *tatra eva*—in that same place; *bala-devena*—by Lord Balarāma; *saṁyutaḥ*—joined; *apaśyat*—saw; *nivasan*—staying; *gopān*—the cowherd men; *indra*—for Indra, the King of heaven; *yāga*—for the sake of a sacrifice; *kṛta*—making; *udyamān*—great endeavor.

## TRANSLATION

**Śukadeva Gosvāmī said: While staying in that very place with His brother Baladeva, Lord Kṛṣṇa happened to see the cowherd men busily arranging for a sacrifice to Indra.**

## PURPORT

According to Śrīla Śrīdhara Svāmī and other *ācāryas,* the words *tatra eva* in this verse indicate that Lord Kṛṣṇa stayed in the village of the *brāhmaṇas* whose wives had satisfied Him by their devotion. Thus He gave His mercy to those *brāhmaṇas* as well as to their chaste wives, who had no one to associate with except their husbands. In that place the cowherd men, headed by Lord Kṛṣṇa's father, Nanda Mahārāja, were somehow or other preparing an elaborate sacrifice to Lord Indra, and Lord Kṛṣṇa reacted as follows.

## TEXT 2

तदभिज्ञोऽपि भगवान् सर्वात्मा सर्वदर्शनः ।
प्रश्रयावनतोऽपृच्छद् वृद्धान्नन्दपुरोगमान् ॥२॥

*tad-abhijño 'pi bhagavān*
*sarvātmā sarva-darśanaḥ*
*praśrayāvanato 'pṛcchad*
*vṛddhān nanda-purogamān*

*tat-abhijñaḥ*—being in full knowledge about it; *api*—although; *bhagavān*—the Supreme Lord; *sarva-ātmā*—the Supersoul within everyone's heart; *sarva-darśanaḥ*—the omniscient Personality of Godhead; *praśraya-avanataḥ*—bowing down humbly; *apṛcchat*—He inquired; *vṛddhān*—from the elders; *nanda-puraḥ-gamān*—headed by Mahārāja Nanda.

## TRANSLATION

**Being the omniscient Supersoul, the Supreme Lord Kṛṣṇa already understood the situation, yet He still humbly inquired from the elders, headed by His father, Nanda Mahārāja.**

## PURPORT

Lord Kṛṣṇa was eager to enact His pastime of lifting Govardhana Hill and defeating the false pride of Indra, and thus He cleverly inquired from His father about the imminent sacrifice.

## TEXT 3

कथ्यतां मे पितः कोऽयं सम्भ्रमो व उपागतः ।
किं फलं कस्य वोद्देशः केन वा साध्यते मखः ॥३॥

*kathyatāṁ me pitaḥ ko 'yaṁ*
*sambhramo va upāgataḥ*
*kiṁ phalaṁ kasya voddeśaḥ*
*kena vā sādhyate makhaḥ*

*kathyatām*—let it be explained; *me*—to Me; *pitaḥ*—My dear father; *kaḥ*—what; *ayam*—this; *sambhramaḥ*—flurry of activity; *vaḥ*—upon you; *upāgataḥ*—come; *kim*—what; *phalam*—the consequence; *kasya*—for whose; *vā*—and; *uddeśaḥ*—sake; *kena*—by what means; *vā*—and; *sādhyate*—is to be accomplished; *makhaḥ*—this sacrifice.

## TRANSLATION

**My dear father, kindly explain to Me what this great endeavor of yours is all about. What is it meant to accomplish? If this is a ritual sacrifice, then for whose satisfaction is it intended and by what means is it going to be executed?**

## TEXT 4

एतद् ब्रूहि महान् कामो मह्यं शुश्रूषवे पितः ।
न हि गोप्यं हि साधूनां कृत्यं सर्वात्मनामिह ।
अस्त्यस्वपरदृष्टीनाममित्रोदास्तविद्विषाम् ॥४॥

*etad brūhi mahān kāmo*
*mahyaṁ śuśrūṣave pitaḥ*
*na hi gopyaṁ hi sādhūnāṁ*
*kṛtyaṁ sarvātmanām iha*
*asty asva-para-dṛṣṭīnām*
*amitrodāsta-vidviṣām*

*etat*—this; *brūhi*—please speak; *mahān*—great; *kāmaḥ*—desire; *mahyam*—to Me; *śuśrūṣave*—who am ready to hear faithfully; *pitaḥ*—O father; *na*—not; *hi*—indeed; *gopyam*—to be kept secret; *hi*—certainly; *sādhūnām*—of saintly persons; *kṛtyam*—the activities; *sarva-ātmanām*—who see everyone as equal to themselves; *iha*—in this world; *asti*—there is; *asva-para-dṛṣṭīnām*—who do not distinguish between what is their own and what is another's; *amitra-udāsta-vidviṣām*—who do not distinguish between friends, neutral parties and enemies.

## TRANSLATION

**Please tell Me about it, O father. I have a great desire to know and am ready to hear in good faith. Certainly, no secrets are to be kept by saintly personalities, who see all others as equal to themselves, who have no conception of "mine" or "another's" and who do not consider who is a friend, who is an enemy and who is neutral.**

## PURPORT

Lord Kṛṣṇa's father might have thought that his son was a mere child and thus could not properly question the validity of a Vedic sacrifice. But the Lord's clever statement here would certainly have convinced Nanda that Śrī Kṛṣṇa was making a serious, not a whimsical, inquiry and that a serious answer should thus be given.

## TEXT 5

उदासीनोऽरिवद् वर्ज्य आत्मवत् सुहृदुच्यते ॥५॥

*udāsīno 'ri-vad varjya*
*ātma-vat suhṛd ucyate*

*udāsīnaḥ*—one who is indifferent; *ari-vat*—just like an enemy; *varjyaḥ*—is to be avoided; *ātma-vat*—like one's own self; *suhṛt*—a friend; *ucyate*—is said to be.

## TRANSLATION

**One who is neutral may be avoided like an enemy, but a friend should be considered like one's own self.**

## PURPORT

Even if Nanda Mahārāja did not see friends, enemies and neutral parties as entirely equal, Lord Kṛṣṇa, being Nanda Mahārāja's son, was certainly a most trustworthy friend and should therefore not be left out of intimate discussions. In other words, Nanda Mahārāja might have thought that as a householder he could not act on the highest saintly platform, and thus Lord Kṛṣṇa furnished additional reasons why His father should trust Him and reveal the entire purpose of the sacrifice.

According to Śrīla Jīva Gosvāmī, Nanda Mahārāja stood silent, doubting his position of parental aloofness, since Garga Muni had predicted that his son would be "equal to Nārāyaṇa in His qualities," and the young boy had already conquered and killed many powerful demons.

## TEXT 6

ज्ञात्वाज्ञात्वा च कर्माणि जनोऽयमनुतिष्ठति ।
विदुषः कर्मसिद्धिः स्याद्यथा नाविदुषो भवेत् ॥६॥

*jñātvājñātvā ca karmāṇi*
*jano 'yam anutiṣṭhati*
*viduṣaḥ karma-siddhiḥ syād*
*yathā nāviduṣo bhavet*

*jñātvā*—understanding; *ajñātvā*—not understanding; *ca*—also; *karmāṇi*—activities; *janaḥ*—the common people; *ayam*—these; *anutiṣṭhati*—perform; *viduṣaḥ*—for one who is wise; *karma-siddhiḥ*—achievement of the intended goal of activity; *syāt*—arises; *yathā*—as; *na*—not; *aviduṣaḥ*—for one who is foolish; *bhavet*—occurs.

## TRANSLATION

**When people in this world perform activities, sometimes they understand what they are doing and sometimes they don't. Those who know what they are doing achieve success in their work, whereas ignorant people do not.**

## PURPORT

The Lord here informs His father that people should perform a particular ceremony or activity only after thoroughly understanding it through discussion with friends. We should not be blind followers of tradition. If a person doesn't even know what he's doing, how can he be successful in his work? This, essentially, is the Lord's argument in this verse. Since Śrī Kṛṣṇa, as the young child of Nanda, would naturally be expected to show enthusiasm for His father's religious activities, it was the father's duty to give the son a thorough explanation of the ceremony.

## TEXT 7

**तत्र तावत् क्रियायोगो भवतां किं विचारितः ।**
**अथवा लौकिकस्तन्मे पृच्छतः साधु भण्यताम् ॥७॥**

*tatra tāvat kriyā-yogo*
*bhavatāṁ kiṁ vicāritaḥ*
*atha vā laukikas tan me*
*pṛcchataḥ sādhu bhaṇyatām*

*tatra tāvat*—that being the case; *kriyā-yogaḥ*—this fruitive endeavor; *bhavatām*—of yours; *kim*—whether; *vicāritaḥ*—learned from the scriptures; *atha vā*—or else; *laukikaḥ*—of ordinary custom; *tat*—that; *me*—to Me; *pṛcchataḥ*—who am inquiring; *sādhu*—clearly; *bhaṇyatām*—it should be explained.

## TRANSLATION

**Such being the case, this ritualistic endeavor of yours should be clearly explained to Me. Is it a ceremony based on scriptural injunction, or simply a custom of ordinary society?**

## TEXT 8

श्रीनन्द उवाच
पर्जन्यो भगवानिन्द्रो मेघास्तस्यात्ममूर्तयः ।
तेऽभिवर्षन्ति भूतानां प्रीणनं जीवनं पयः ॥८॥

*śrī-nanda uvāca*
*parjanyo bhagavān indro*
*meghās tasyātma-mūrtayaḥ*
*te 'bhivarṣanti bhūtānāṁ*
*prīṇanaṁ jīvanaṁ payaḥ*

*śrī-nandaḥ uvāca*—Śrī Nanda Mahārāja said; *parjanyaḥ*—the rain; *bhagavān*—the great lord; *indraḥ*—Indra; *meghāḥ*—the clouds; *tasya*—his; *ātma-mūrtayaḥ*—personal representatives; *te*—they; *abhivarṣanti*—directly give rain; *bhūtānām*—for all living entities; *prīṇanam*—the gratification; *jīvanam*—the life-giving force; *payaḥ*—(like) milk.

## TRANSLATION

**Nanda Mahārāja replied: The great Lord Indra is the controller of the rain. The clouds are his personal representatives, and they directly provide rainwater, which gives happiness and sustenance to all creatures.**

## PURPORT

Without clean rainwater, the earth could not possibly provide food or drink for anyone, nor could there be cleanliness. Thus it would be difficult to overestimate the value of rain.

## TEXT 9

तं तात वयमन्ये च वार्मुचां पतिमीश्वरम् ।
द्रव्यैस्तद्रेतसा सिद्धैर्यजन्ते क्रतुभिर्नराः ॥९॥

*taṁ tāta vayam anye ca*
*vārmucāṁ patim īśvaram*
*dravyais tad-retasā siddhair*
*yajante kratubhir narāḥ*

*tam*—him; *tāta*—my dear son; *vayam*—we; *anye*—others; *ca*—also; *vāḥ-mucām*—of the clouds; *patim*—the master; *īśvaram*—the powerful controller; *dravyaiḥ*—with various items; *tat-retasā*—by his liquid discharge; *siddhaiḥ*—produced; *yajante*—they worship; *kratubhiḥ*—by fire sacrifices; *narāḥ*—men.

## TRANSLATION

**Not only we, my dear son, but also many other men worship him, the lord and master of the rain-giving clouds. We offer him grain and other paraphernalia of worship produced through his own discharge in the form of rain.**

## PURPORT

Nanda Mahārāja patiently tried to explain the "facts of life" to his young son, Śrī Kṛṣṇa, but in fact Nanda and all the residents of Vṛndāvana would learn an astonishing lesson, as explained in this chapter.

## TEXT 10

तच्छेषेणोपजीवन्ति त्रिवर्गफलहेतवे ।
पुंसां पुरुषकाराणां पर्जन्यः फलभावनः ॥१०॥

*tac-cheṣeṇopajīvanti*
*tri-varga-phala-hetave*
*puṁsāṁ puruṣa-kārāṇāṁ*
*parjanyaḥ phala-bhāvanaḥ*

*tat*—of that sacrifice; *śeṣeṇa*—by the remnants; *upajīvanti*—they sustain their lives; *tri-varga*—consisting of the three aims of human life (religiosity, economic development and sense gratification); *phala-hetave*—for the sake of fruit; *puṁsām*—for persons; *puruṣa-kārāṇām*—engaged in human endeavor; *parjanyaḥ*—Lord Indra; *phala-bhāvanaḥ*—the means of effecting the intended goals.

## TRANSLATION

**By accepting the remnants of sacrifices performed to Indra, people sustain their lives and accomplish the threefold aims of religiosity, economic development and sense gratification. Thus Lord Indra is the agent responsible for the fruitive success of industrious people.**

## PURPORT

One might object that people sustain themselves by farming, industry and so on. But as previously mentioned, all human and nonhuman endeavor depends on food and drink, which cannot be produced without ample rain. By the word *tri-varga* Nanda further points out that the prosperity achieved through sacrifice for Indra is meant not merely for sense gratification but also for religiosity and economic development. Unless people are well fed, it is difficult for them to execute their duties, and without performance of duty, it is very difficult to be religious.

## TEXT 11

य एनं विसृजेद्धर्मं परम्पर्यागतं नरः ।
कामाद् द्वेषाद् भयाल्लोभात्स वै नाप्नोति शोभनम् ॥११॥

*ya enaṁ visṛjed dharmaṁ*
*paramparyāgataṁ naraḥ*

*kāmād dveṣād bhayāl lobhāt*
*sa vai nāpnoti śobhanam*

*yaḥ*—anyone who; *enam*—this; *visṛjet*—rejects; *dharmam*—the religious principle; *paramparya*—from traditional authority; *āgatam*—received; *naraḥ*—a person; *kāmāt*—because of lust; *dveṣāt*—because of enmity; *bhayāt*—because of fear; *lobhāt*—or because of greed; *saḥ*—he; *vai*—certainly; *na āpnoti*—cannot achieve; *śobhanam*—auspiciousness.

## TRANSLATION

**This religious principle is based on sound tradition. Anyone who rejects it out of lust, enmity, fear or greed will certainly fail to achieve good fortune.**

## PURPORT

If a person neglects his religious duties because of lust, envy, fear or greed, his life will never be brilliant or perfect.

## TEXT 12

श्रीशुक उवाच
वचो निशम्य नन्दस्य तथान्येषां व्रजौकसाम् ।
इन्द्राय मन्युं जनयन् पितरं प्राह केशवः ॥१२॥

*śrī-śuka uvāca*
*vaco niśamya nandasya*
*tathānyeṣāṁ vrajaukasām*
*indrāya manyuṁ janayan*
*pitaraṁ prāha keśavaḥ*

*śrī-śukaḥ uvāca*—Śrī Śukadeva Gosvāmī said; *vacaḥ*—the words; *niśamya*—hearing; *nandasya*—of Mahārāja Nanda; *tathā*—and also; *anyeṣām*—of the others; *vraja-okasām*—the residents of Vraja; *indrāya*—in Lord Indra; *manyum*—anger; *janayan*—generating; *pitaram*—to His father; *prāha*—spoke; *keśavaḥ*—Lord Keśava.

## TRANSLATION

**Śukadeva Gosvāmī said: When Lord Keśava [Kṛṣṇa] heard the**

**statements of His father, Nanda, and other senior residents of Vraja, He addressed His father as follows, to arouse anger in Lord Indra.**

## PURPORT

Śrīla Śrīdhara Svāmī explains that Lord Kṛṣṇa's intention was not simply to insult a demigod, but rather to knock down the great mountain of false pride that had arisen within the Lord's tiny servant, who was supposed to represent the Lord as Indra. By lifting Govardhana Hill Lord Kṛṣṇa would thus initiate a blissful annual festival called Govardhana-pūjā, and He would further enjoy the pleasant pastime of dwelling for several days beneath the hill with all His loving devotees.

## TEXT 13

श्रीभगवानुवाच
कर्मणा जायते जन्तुः कर्मणैव प्रलीयते ।
सुखं दुःखं भयं क्षेमं कर्मणैवाभिपद्यते ॥१३॥

*śrī-bhagavān uvāca*
*karmaṇā jāyate jantuḥ*
*karmaṇaiva pralīyate*
*sukhaṁ duḥkhaṁ bhayaṁ kṣemaṁ*
*karmaṇaivābhipadyate*

*śrī-bhagavān uvāca*—the Supreme Personality of Godhead said; *karmaṇā*—by the force of *karma; jāyate*—takes birth; *jantuḥ*—the living entity; *karmaṇā*—by *karma; eva*—alone; *pralīyate*—he meets his destruction; *sukham*—happiness; *duḥkham*—unhappiness; *bhayam*—fear; *kṣemam*—security; *karmaṇā eva*—by *karma* alone; *abhipadyate*—are obtained.

## TRANSLATION

**Lord Kṛṣṇa said: It is by the force of *karma* that a living entity takes birth, and it is by *karma* alone that he meets his destruction. His happiness, distress, fear and sense of security all arise as the effects of *karma*.**

## PURPORT

Lord Kṛṣṇa minimized the importance of the demigods by speaking the philosophy known as Karma-vāda or Karma-mīmāṁsā, which, basically, is atheism with a belief in reincarnation. According to this philosophy, there are subtle laws of nature that reward or punish us according to how we act: "As you sow, so shall you reap." In a future life one reaps the fruit of his present work, and this is the sum and substance of reality. Lord Kṛṣṇa, being God Himself, could hardly be a serious proponent of this mediocre philosophy. In the role of a young boy He was simply teasing His pure devotees by preaching it.

Śrīla Jīva Gosvāmī points out that Lord Kṛṣṇa was thinking, "Why are these eternal associates of Mine, appearing as My father and other relatives and friends, so caught up in this worship of Indra?" Thus although the Lord's main purpose was to take away the false pride of Indra, He also wanted to remind His eternal devotees that they need not divert their attention to other so-called gods, since in fact His devotees were already living with the Supreme Absolute Truth, the almighty Lord Himself.

## TEXT 14

अस्ति चेदीश्वरः कश्चित् फलरूप्यन्यकर्मणाम् ।
कर्तारं भजते सोऽपि न ह्यकर्तुः प्रभुर्हि सः ॥१४॥

*asti ced īśvaraḥ kaścit*
*phala-rūpy anya-karmaṇām*
*kartāraṁ bhajate so 'pi*
*na hy akartuḥ prabhur hi saḥ*

*asti*—there is; *cet*—if hypothetically; *īśvaraḥ*—a supreme controller; *kaścit*—someone; *phala-rūpī*—serving to award fruitive results; *anya-karmaṇām*—of the activities of other persons; *kartāram*—the performer of activity; *bhajate*—depends upon; *saḥ*—He; *api*—even; *na*—not; *hi*—after all; *akartuḥ*—of one who performs no activity; *prabhuḥ*—the master; *hi*—certainly; *saḥ*—He.

## TRANSLATION

**Even if there is some supreme controller who awards all others**

**the results of their activities, He must also depend upon a performer's engaging in activity. After all, there is no question of being the bestower of fruitive results unless fruitive activities have actually been performed.**

## PURPORT

Here Lord Kṛṣṇa argues that if there is a supreme controller, He must depend on a performer of activity to reciprocate with and must therefore also be subject to the laws of *karma,* being obliged to award happiness and distress to conditioned souls according to the laws of good and evil.

This superficial argument neglects the obvious point that the laws of nature that prescribe the good and bad results of pious and impious acts are themselves creations of the all-good Supreme Lord. Being the creator and sustainer of these laws, the Lord is not subject to them. Furthermore, the Lord is not dependent on the work of the conditioned souls, since He is satisfied and complete within Himself. Out of His all-merciful nature He awards the results appropriate to our activities. That which we call destiny, fate or *karma* is an elaborate and subtle system of rewards and punishments meant for gradually encouraging conditioned souls to evolve to the stage of perfect consciousness, which is their original, constitutional nature.

The Supreme Personality of Godhead has so dexterously formulated and applied the laws of material nature governing punishment and reward for human behavior that the living being is discouraged from sin and encouraged toward goodness without suffering any significant inteference with his free will as an eternal soul.

In contrast to the material nature, the Lord exhibits His essential nature in the spiritual world, where He reciprocates the eternal love of His pure devotees. Such loving affairs are based completely on the mutual freedom of the Lord and His devotees, not on a mechanical reciprocity of coinciding selfish interests. The Supreme Lord, assisted by His pure devotees, repeatedly offers the conditioned souls of this world the opportunity to give up their bizarre attempt at exploiting the material universe and go back home, back to Godhead, for an eternal life of bliss and knowledge. Considering all these points, the atheistic arguments given here by Lord Kṛṣṇa in a playful mood are not to be taken seriously.

## TEXT 15

किमिन्द्रेणेह भूतानां स्वस्वकर्मानुवर्तिनाम् ।
अनीशेनान्यथा कर्तुं स्वभावविहितं नृणाम् ॥१५॥

*kim indreṇeha bhūtānāṁ*
*sva-sva-karmānuvartinām*
*anīśenānyathā kartuṁ*
*svabhāva-vihitaṁ nṛṇām*

*kim*—what; *indreṇa*—with Indra; *iha*—here; *bhūtānām*—for living entities; *sva-sva*—each their own; *karma*—of fruitive action; *anuvartinām*—who are experiencing the consequences; *anīśena*—(Indra) who is incapable; *anyathā*—otherwise; *kartum*—to make; *svabhāva*—by their conditioned natures; *vihitam*—that which is ordained; *nṛṇām*—for men.

### TRANSLATION

**Living beings in this world are forced to experience the consequences of their own particular previous work. Since Lord Indra cannot in any way change the destiny of human beings, which is born of their own nature, why should people worship him?**

### PURPORT

Lord Kṛṣṇa's argument here is not a negation of free will. If one accepts the existence of *karma* as a system of laws awarding reactions for our present activities, then we ourselves, according to our nature, will decide our future. Our happiness and distress in this life have already been adjudicated and fixed according to our previous activities, and not even the demigods can change that. They must award us the prosperity or poverty, sickness or health, happiness or distress due us by our previous work. However, we still retain the freedom to select a pious or impious mode of activity in this life, and the choice we make will determine our future suffering and enjoyment.

For example, if I was pious in my last life, in this life the demigods may award me great material wealth. But I am free to spend my riches for good or for bad purposes, and my choice will determine my future life. Thus, although no one can change the karmic results due him in this life, everyone still retains his free will, by which he determines what his future situation will be. Lord Kṛṣṇa's argument here is quite interesting; however, it neglects the overriding consideration that we are all eternal servants of God and must satisfy Him by all that we do.

## TEXT 16

स्वभावतन्त्रो हि जनः स्वभावमनुवर्तते ।
स्वभावस्थमिदं सर्वं सदेवासुरमानुषम् ॥१६॥

*svabhāva-tantro hi janaḥ*
*svabhāvam anuvartate*
*svabhāva-stham idaṁ sarvaṁ*
*sa-devāsura-mānuṣam*

*svabhāva*—of his conditioned nature; *tantraḥ*—under the control; *hi*—indeed; *janaḥ*—a person; *svabhāvam*—his nature; *anuvartate*—he follows; *svabhāva-stham*—based on conditioned propensities; *idam*—this world; *sarvam*—entire; *sa*—together with; *deva*—the demigods; *asura*—the demons; *mānuṣam*—and humankind.

## TRANSLATION

**Every individual is under the control of his own conditioned nature, and thus he must follow that nature. This entire universe, with all its demigods, demons and human beings, is based on the conditioned nature of the living entities.**

## PURPORT

Lord Kṛṣṇa here elaborates upon the argument given in the previous verse. Since everything depends on *svabhāva*, or one's conditioned nature, why bother worshiping God or the demigods? This argument would be sublime if *svabhāva*, or conditioned nature, were all-powerful. But unfortunately it is not. There is a supreme controller and we must worship Him, as Lord Kṛṣṇa will emphatically reveal in this chapter of the *Śrīmad-Bhāgavatam*. For now, however, He is content to tease His relatives.

## TEXT 17

देहानुच्चावचाञ्जन्तुः प्राप्योत्सृजति कर्मणा ।
शत्रुर्मित्रमुदासीनः कर्मैव गुरुरीश्वरः ॥१७॥

*dehān uccāvacāñ jantuḥ*
*prāpyotsṛjati karmaṇā*
*śatrur mitram udāsīnaḥ*
*karmaiva gurur īśvaraḥ*

*dehān*—material bodies; *ucca-avacān*—high- and low-class; *jantuḥ*—the conditioned living entity; *prāpya*—obtaining; *utsṛjati*—gives up; *karmaṇā*—by the reactions of his material activities; *śatruḥ*—his enemy; *mitram*—friend; *udāsīnaḥ*—and neutral party; *karma*—material work; *eva*—alone; *guruḥ*—his spiritual master; *īśvaraḥ*—his lord.

## TRANSLATION

**Because it is *karma* that causes the conditioned living entity to accept and then give up different high- and low-grade material bodies, this *karma* is his enemy, friend and neutral witness, his spiritual master and controlling lord.**

## PURPORT

Even the demigods are bound and limited by the laws of *karma*. That Indra himself is subordinate to the laws of *karma* is explicitly stated in the *Brahma-saṁhitā* (5.54): *yas tv indra-gopam atha vendram aho sva-karma-bandhānurūpa-phala-bhājanam ātanoti*. The Supreme Lord, Govinda, awards all creatures the appropriate results of their work. This is as true for mighty Indra, the lord of the material heavens, as it is for the germ called *indra-gopa*. The *Bhagavad-gītā* (7.20) also states, *kāmais tais tair hṛta-jñānāḥ prapadyante 'nya-devatāḥ*. Only those who have lost their intelligence because of various material desires surrender unto demigods rather than worship the Supreme Lord. In fact, the demigods cannot award benefits to anyone independently, as stated by Lord Kṛṣṇa in the *Gītā: mayaiva vihitān hi tān*. All benefits are ultimately issued by the Lord Himself.

Thus it is not altogether incorrect to say that demigod worship is useless, since even the demigods are under the laws of *karma*. In fact, this is the case. But Lord Kṛṣṇa, the Supreme Absolute Truth, is not subordinate to the law of *karma;* rather, He can independently offer or withold His favor. This is confirmed in the verse from the *Brahma-saṁhitā* quoted above, the third line of which is *karmāṇi nirdahati kintu ca bhakti-bhājām:* "The Supreme Lord burns up all the accumulated *karma* of those engaged in His loving service." Not only is Lord Kṛṣṇa above the laws of material action and reaction, but He can immediately dissolve these laws for anyone who satisfies Him through loving service. Thus the Almighty God is supreme in absolute freedom, and by surrendering to Him we can escape the bonds of *karma* and stop accepting their dismal rule as supreme.

## TEXT 18

तस्मात्सम्पूजयेत्कर्म स्वभावस्थः स्वकर्मकृत् ।
अञ्जसा येन वर्तेत तदेवास्य हि दैवतम् ॥१८॥

*tasmāt sampūjayet karma*
*svabhāva-sthaḥ sva-karma-kṛt*
*añjasā yena varteta*
*tad evāsya hi daivatam*

*tasmāt*—therefore; *sampūjayet*—one should fully worship; *karma*—his prescribed activity; *svabhāva*—in the position corresponding to his own conditioned nature; *sthaḥ*—remaining; *sva-karma*—his own prescribed duty; *kṛt*—performing; *añjasā*—without difficulty; *yena*—by which; *varteta*—one lives; *tat*—that; *eva*—certainly; *asya*—his; *hi*—indeed; *daivatam*—worshipable deity.

## TRANSLATION

**Therefore one should seriously worship work itself. A person should remain in the position corresponding to his nature and should perform his own duty. Indeed, that by which we may live nicely is really our worshipable deity.**

## PURPORT

Lord Kṛṣṇa here proposes the modern if absurd philosophy that our work or occupation is really God and that we should therefore simply worship our work. Upon close scrutiny, we observe that our work is nothing more than the interaction of the material body with material nature, as Lord Kṛṣṇa Himself states, in a more serious mood, in the *Bhagavad-gītā* (3.28): *guṇā guṇeṣu vartante.* Karma-mīmāṁsā philosophy accepts that good activity in this life will give us a better next life. If this is true, there must be some type of conscious soul different from the body. And if that is the case, why should a transcendental soul worship the interaction of the temporary body with material nature? If the words *sampūjayet karma* here mean that one should worship the laws of *karma* governing our activities, then one may astutely ask what it means to worship laws and, indeed, what might be the origin of such laws and who is maintaining them. To say that laws have created or are maintaining the world is a meaningless proposition, since there is nothing about the nature of a law that indicates it could generate the existential situation it is supposed to govern. In fact, worship is meant for Kṛṣṇa Himself, and this real conclusion will be clearly revealed in this chapter.

## TEXT 19

आजीव्यैकतरं भावं यस्त्वन्यमुपजीवति ।
न तस्माद् विन्दते क्षेमं जारान्नार्यसती यथा ॥१९॥

*ājīvyaikataraṁ bhāvaṁ*
*yas tv anyam upajīvati*
*na tasmād vindate kṣemaṁ*
*jārān nāry asatī yathā*

*ājīvya*—sustaining his life; *ekataram*—one; *bhāvam*—entity; *yaḥ*—who; *tu*—but; *anyam*—another; *upajīvati*—resorts to; *na*—not; *tasmāt*—from that one; *vindate*—gains; *kṣemam*—real benefit; *jārāt*—from a paramour; *nārī*—a woman; *asatī*—who is unchaste; *yathā*—as.

## TRANSLATION

**If one thing is actually sustaining our life but we take shelter of something else, how can we achieve any real benefit? We would be**

**like an unfaithful woman, who can never achieve any actual benefit by consorting with her paramour.**

## PURPORT

The word *kṣemam* means actual prosperity, not merely the accumulation of money. Here Lord Kṛṣṇa boldly argues that just as a woman can never achieve actual dignity or enlightenment from an illicit lover, the residents of Vṛndāvana will never be happy by neglecting the real source of their prosperity and worshiping Indra instead. According to Śrīla Jīva Gosvāmī, the audacity that child Kṛṣṇa displayed before His father and other elders should be understood as an exhibition of transcendental anger aroused when He saw His eternal devotees worshiping an insignificant demigod.

## TEXT 20

**वर्तेत ब्रह्मणा विप्रो राजन्यो रक्षया भुवः ।**
**वैश्यस्तु वार्तया जीवेच्छूद्रस्तु द्विजसेवया ॥२०॥**

*varteta brahmaṇā vipro*
*rājanyo rakṣayā bhuvaḥ*
*vaiśyas tu vārtayā jīvec*
*chūdras tu dvija-sevayā*

*varteta*—lives; *brahmaṇā*—by the *Vedas; vipraḥ*—the *brāhmaṇa; rājanyaḥ*—the member of the ruling class; *rakṣayā*—by protection; *bhuvaḥ*—of the earth; *vaiśyaḥ*—the *vaiśya; tu*—on the other hand; *vārtayā*—by trade; *jīvet*—lives; *śūdraḥ*—the *śūdra; tu*—and; *dvija-sevayā*—by serving the twice-born *brāhmaṇas, kṣatriya*s and *vaiśyas.*

## TRANSLATION

**The *brāhmaṇa* maintains his life by studying and teaching the *Vedas*, the member of the royal order by protecting the earth, the *vaiśya* by trade, and the *śūdra* by serving the higher, twice-born classes.**

## PURPORT

After glorifying *karma*, or work, Lord Kṛṣṇa now explains what He means by prescribed duties born of one's nature. He was not referring to any whimsical activity, but rather to the religious duties prescribed in the *varṇāśrama*, or Vedic social system.

## TEXT 21

**कृषिवाणिज्यगोरक्षा कुसीदं तूर्यमुच्यते ।**
**वार्ता चतुर्विधा तत्र वयं गोवृत्तयोऽनिशम् ॥२१॥**

*kṛṣi-vāṇijya-go-rakṣā*
*kusīdaṁ tūryam ucyate*
*vārtā catur-vidhā tatra*
*vayaṁ go-vṛttayo 'niśam*

*kṛṣi*—farming; *vāṇijya*—commerce; *go-rakṣā*—and protecting cows; *kusīdam*—banking; *tūryam*—the fourth; *ucyate*—is said; *vārtā*—the occupational duty; *catuḥ-vidhā*—fourfold; *tatra*—among these; *vayam*—we; *go-vṛttayaḥ*—engaged in protecting the cows; *aniśam*—without cessation.

## TRANSLATION

**The occupational duties of the *vaiśya* are conceived in four divisions: farming, commerce, cow protection and moneylending. Out of these, we as a community are always engaged in cow protection.**

## TEXT 22

**सत्त्वं रजस्तम इति स्थित्युत्पत्त्यन्तहेतवः ।**
**रजसोत्पद्यते विश्वमन्योन्यं विविधं जगत् ॥२२॥**

*sattvaṁ rajas tama iti*
*sthity-utpatty-anta-hetavaḥ*
*rajasotpadyate viśvam*
*anyonyaṁ vividhaṁ jagat*

*sattvam*—goodness; *rajaḥ*—passion; *tamaḥ*—and ignorance; *iti*—thus; *sthiti*—of maintenance; *utpatti*—creation; *anta*—and destruction; *hetavaḥ*—the causes; *rajasā*—by the mode of passion; *utpadyate*—is generated; *viśvam*—this universe; *anyonyam*—by combination of male and female; *vividham*—becomes variegated; *jagat*—the world.

## TRANSLATION

**The causes of creation, maintenance and destruction are the three modes of nature—namely goodness, passion and ignorance. In particular, the mode of passion creates this universe and through sexual combination causes it to become full of variety.**

## PURPORT

Anticipating the possible objection that a livelihood based on cows certainly depends on Lord Indra, who supplies rain, Lord Kṛṣṇa here introduces a mechanistic theory of existence known as atheistic Sāṅkhya. The tendency to attribute exclusive causality to the apparently mechanistic functions of nature is an old tendency indeed. Five thousand years ago Lord Kṛṣṇa referred to a doctrine already well known in human society.

## TEXT 23

रजसा चोदिता मेघा वर्षन्त्यम्बूनि सर्वतः ।
प्रजास्तैरेव सिध्यन्ति महेन्द्रः किं करिष्यति ॥२३॥

*rajasā coditā meghā*
*varṣanty ambūni sarvataḥ*
*prajās tair eva sidhyanti*
*mahendraḥ kiṁ kariṣyati*

*rajasā*—by passion; *coditāḥ*—impelled; *meghāḥ*—the clouds; *varṣanti*—pour down; *ambūni*—their water; *sarvataḥ*—everywhere; *prajāḥ*—the population; *taiḥ*—by that water; *eva*—simply; *sidhyanti*—maintain their existence; *mahā-indraḥ*—the great Indra; *kim*—what; *kariṣyati*—can do.

## TRANSLATION

**Impelled by the material mode of passion, the clouds pour down their rain everywhere, and by this rain all creatures gain their sustenance. What has the great Indra to do with this arrangement?**

## PURPORT

Lord Kṛṣṇa continues His mechanistic explanation of existence, concluding *mahendraḥ kiṁ kariṣyati:* "Who needs the great Indra, since the rain, sent by the clouds, which in turn are impelled by the mode of passion, is actually producing everyone's food?" The word *sarvataḥ* indicates that the clouds magnanimously send their rain even on the ocean, rocks and barren land, where there is no apparent necessity for such sweet water.

## TEXT 24

**न नः पुरो जनपदा न ग्रामा न गृहा वयम् ।**
**वनौकसस्तात नित्यं वनशैलनिवासिनः ॥२४॥**

*na naḥ puro janapadā*
*na grāmā na gṛhā vayam*
*vanaukasas tāta nityaṁ*
*vana-śaila-nivāsinaḥ*

*na*—not; *naḥ*—for us; *puraḥ*—the cities; *jana-padāḥ*—developed inhabited area; *na*—not; *grāmāḥ*—villages; *na*—not; *gṛhāḥ*—living in permanent homes; *vayam*—we; *vana-okasaḥ*—dwelling in the forests; *tāta*—My dear father; *nityam*—always; *vana*—in the forests; *śaila*—and on the hills; *nivāsinaḥ*—living.

## TRANSLATION

**My dear father, our home is not in the cities or towns or villages. Being forest dwellers, we always live in the forest and on the hills.**

## PURPORT

Lord Kṛṣṇa here points out that the residents of Vṛndāvana should recognize their relationship with Govardhana Hill and with the forests of

Vṛndāvana, and not worry about a distant demigod like Indra. Having concluded His argument, Lord Kṛṣṇa makes a radical proposal in the following verse.

## TEXT 25

तस्माद् गवां ब्राह्मणानामद्रेश्चारभ्यतां मखः ।
य इन्द्रयागसम्भारास्तैरयं साध्यतां मखः ॥२५॥

*tasmād gavāṁ brāhmaṇānām*
*adreś cārabhyatāṁ makhaḥ*
*ya indra-yāga-sambhārās*
*tair ayaṁ sādhyatāṁ makhaḥ*

*tasmāt*—therefore; *gavām*—of the cows; *brāhmaṇānām*—of the *brāhmaṇas; adreḥ*—and of the hill (Govardhana); *ca*—also; *ārabhyatām*—let it begin; *makhaḥ*—the sacrifice; *ye*—which; *indra-yāga*—for the sacrifice to Indra; *sambhārāḥ*—the ingredients; *taiḥ*—by them; *ayam*—this; *sadhyatām*—may it be carried out; *makhaḥ*—the sacrifice.

## TRANSLATION

**Therefore may a sacrifice for the pleasure of the cows, the *brāhmaṇas* and Govardhana Hill begin! With all the paraphernalia collected for worshiping Indra, let this sacrifice be performed instead.**

## PURPORT

Lord Kṛṣṇa is famous as *go-brāhmaṇa-hita,* the well-wishing friend of the cows and the *brāhmaṇas.* Lord Kṛṣṇa specifically included the local *brāhmaṇas* in His proposal because He is always devoted to those who are devoted to the godly Vedic culture.

## TEXT 26

पच्यन्तां विविधाः पाकाः सूपान्ताः पायसादयः ।
संयावापूपशष्कुल्यः सर्वदोहश्च गृह्यताम् ॥२६॥

*pacyantāṁ vividhāḥ pākāḥ*
*sūpāntāḥ pāyasādayaḥ*
*saṁyāvāpūpa-śaṣkulyaḥ*
*sarva-dohaś ca gṛhyatām*

*pacyantām*—let the people cook; *vividhāḥ*—many varieties; *pākāḥ*—of cooked foods; *sūpa-antāḥ*—ending with liquid vegetable preparations; *pāyasa-ādayaḥ*—beginning with sweet rice; *saṁyāva-āpūpa*—fried and baked cakes; *śaṣkulyaḥ*—large, round cakes made from rice flour; *sarva*—all; *dohaḥ*—what is obtained by milking the cows; *ca*—and; *gṛhyatām*—let it be taken.

## TRANSLATION

**Let many different kinds of food be cooked, from sweet rice to vegetable soups! Many kinds of fancy cakes, both baked and fried, should be prepared. And all the available milk products should be taken for this sacrifice.**

## PURPORT

The word *sūpa* indicates bean broth and also liquid vegetables. Thus to celebrate the Govardhana-pūjā, Lord Kṛṣṇa called for hot preparations such as soup, cold preparations like sweet rice, and all types of milk products.

## TEXT 27

हूयन्तामग्नयः सम्यग् ब्राह्मणैर्ब्रह्मवादिभिः ।
अन्नं बहुगुणं तेभ्यो देयं वो धेनुदक्षिणाः ॥२७॥

*hūyantām agnayaḥ samyag*
*brāhmaṇair brahma-vādibhiḥ*
*annaṁ bahu-guṇaṁ tebhyo*
*deyaṁ vo dhenu-dakṣiṇāḥ*

*hūyantām*—should be invoked; *agnayaḥ*—the sacrificial fires; *samyak*—in the proper manner; *brāhmaṇaiḥ*—by the *brāhmaṇas; brahma-vādibhiḥ*—who are learned in the *Vedas; annam*—food; *bahu-guṇam*—well prepared; *tebhyaḥ*—to them; *deyam*—should be given; *vaḥ*—by you; *dhenu-dakṣiṇāḥ*—cows and other gifts as remuneration.

## TRANSLATION

**The *brāhmaṇas* who are learned in the Vedic *mantras* must properly invoke the sacrificial fires. Then you should feed the priests with nicely prepared food and reward them with cows and other gifts.**

## PURPORT

According to Śrīla Śrīdhara Svāmī, Lord Śrī Kṛṣṇa instructed His father and other residents of Vṛndāvana in the technical details of this Vedic sacrifice to assure the quality of the sacrifice and also to inspire Nanda and the others with faith in the concept of such a sacrifice. Thus the Lord mentioned that there must be orthodox *brāhmaṇas*, regular sacrificial fires and proper distribution of charity. And things were to be done in the order given by the Lord.

## TEXT 28

अन्येभ्यश्चाश्वचाण्डालपतितेभ्यो यथार्हतः ।
यवसं च गवां दत्त्वा गिरये दीयतां बलिः ॥२८॥

*anyebhyaś cāśva-cāṇḍāla-*
*patitebhyo yathārhataḥ*
*yavasaṁ ca gavāṁ dattvā*
*giraye dīyatāṁ baliḥ*

*anyebhyaḥ*—to the others; *ca*—also; *ā-śva-cāṇḍāla*—even down to the dogs and the dog-eaters; *patitebhyaḥ*—to such fallen persons; *yathā*—as; *arhataḥ*—is proper in each case; *yavasam*—grass; *ca*—and; *gavām*—to the cows; *dattvā*—having given; *giraye*—to the mountain called Govardhana; *dīyatām*—should be presented; *baliḥ*—respectful offerings.

## TRANSLATION

**After giving the appropriate food to each of the others, including the dog-eaters, the dogs and other fallen personalities, you should give grass to the cows and then present your respectful offerings to Govardhana Hill.**

## TEXT 29

स्वलंकृता भुक्तवन्तः स्वनुलिप्ताः सुवाससः ।
प्रदक्षिणां च कुरुत गोविप्रानलपर्वतान् ॥२९॥

*sv-alaṅkṛtā bhuktavantaḥ*
*sv-anuliptāḥ su-vāsasaḥ*
*pradakṣiṇāṁ ca kuruta*
*go-viprānala-parvatān*

*su-alaṅkṛtāḥ*—handsomely adorned; *bhuktavantaḥ*—having eaten to your satisfaction; *su-anuliptāḥ*—anointed with auspicious sandalwood pulp; *su-vāsasaḥ*—wearing fine garments; *pradakṣiṇām*—circumambulation; *ca*—and; *kuruta*—you should perform; *go*—of the cows; *vipra*—the *brāhmaṇas; anala*—the sacrificial fires; *parvatān*—and the hill, Govardhana.

## TRANSLATION

**After everyone has eaten to his satisfaction, you should all dress and decorate yourselves handsomely, smear your bodies with sandalwood paste and then circumambulate the cows, the *brāhmaṇas,* the sacrificial fires and Govardhana Hill.**

## PURPORT

Lord Kṛṣṇa wanted all the human beings and even the animals to eat nice *bhagavat-prasādam,* sanctified foods offered to the Lord. To enthuse His relatives with a festive mood, He requested them to dress beautifully with fine clothes and ornaments and to refresh their bodies with luxurious sandalwood paste. The essential activity, however, was the circumambulation of the holy *brāhmaṇas,* cows, sacrificial fires and especially Govardhana Hill.

## TEXT 30

एतन्मम मतं तात क्रियतां यदि रोचते ।
अयं गोब्राह्मणाद्रीणां मह्यं च दयितो मखः ॥३०॥

*etan mama mataṁ tāta*
*kriyatāṁ yadi rocate*
*ayaṁ go-brāhmaṇādrīṇāṁ*
*mahyaṁ ca dayito makhaḥ*

*etat*—this; *mama*—My; *matam*—idea; *tāta*—O father; *kriyatām*—may it be carried out; *yadi*—if; *rocate*—it is pleasing; *ayam*—this; *go-brāhmaṇa-adrīṇām*—for the cows, *brāhmaṇas* and Govardhana Hill; *mahyam*—for Me; *ca*—also; *dayitaḥ*—cherished; *makhaḥ*—sacrifice.

## TRANSLATION

**This is My idea, O father, and you may carry it out if it appeals to you. Such a sacrifice will be very dear to the cows, the *brāhmaṇas* and Govardhana Hill, and also to Me.**

## PURPORT

Whatever is pleasing to the *brāhmaṇas,* the cows and the Supreme Lord Himself is auspicious and beneficial for the entire world. Spiritually blind "modern" people do not understand this and instead adopt a "scientific" approach to life that is rapidly destroying the entire earth.

## TEXT 31

श्रीशुक उवाच
कालात्मना भगवता शक्रदर्पजिघांसया ।
प्रोक्तं निशम्य नन्दाद्याः साध्वगृह्णन्त तद्वचः ॥३१॥

*śrī-śuka uvāca*
*kālātmanā bhagavatā*
*śakra-darpa-jighāṁsayā*
*proktaṁ niśamya nandādyāḥ*
*sādhv agṛhṇanta tad-vacaḥ*

*śrī-śukaḥ uvāca*—Śrī Śukadeva Gosvāmī said; *kāla-ātmanā*—manifesting as the force of time; *bhagavatā*—by the Supreme Personality of Godhead; *śakra*—of Indra; *darpa*—the pride; *jighāṁsayā*—with a desire to destroy; *proktam*—what was spoken; *niśamya*—hearing; *nanda-ādyāḥ*—Nanda and the other elder cowherd men; *sādhu*—as excellent; *agṛhṇanta*—they accepted; *tat-vacaḥ*—His words.

## TRANSLATION

**Śukadeva Gosvāmī said: Lord Kṛṣṇa, who is Himself powerful time, desired to destroy the false pride of Lord Indra. When Nanda and the other senior men of Vṛndāvana heard Śrī Kṛṣṇa's statement, they accepted His words as proper.**

## TEXTS 32–33

तथा च व्यदधुः सर्वं यथाह मधुसूदनः ।
वाचयित्वा स्वस्त्ययनं तद्‌द्रव्येण गिरिद्विजान् ॥३२॥
उपहृत्य बलीन् सम्यगादृता यवसं गवाम् ।
गोधनानि पुरस्कृत्य गिरिं चक्रुः प्रदक्षिणम् ॥३३॥

*tathā ca vyadadhuḥ sarvaṁ*
*yathāha madhusūdanaḥ*
*vācayitvā svasty-ayanaṁ*
*tad-dravyeṇa giri-dvijān*

*upahṛtya balīn samyag*
*ādṛtā yavasaṁ gavām*
*go-dhanāni puraskṛtya*
*giriṁ cakruḥ pradakṣiṇam*

*tathā*—thus; *ca*—and; *vyadadhuḥ*—they executed; *sarvam*—everything; *yathā*—as; *āha*—He spoke; *madhusūdanaḥ*—Lord Kṛṣṇa; *vācayitvā*—making (the *brāhmaṇas*) recite; *svasti-ayanam*—the auspicious chants; *tat-dravyeṇa*—with the paraphernalia intended for Indra's sacrifice; *giri*—to the hill; *dvijān*—and the *brāhmaṇas; upahṛtya*—offering; *balīn*—the presentations of tribute; *samyak*—all together; *ādṛtāḥ*—respectfully; *yavasam*—grass; *gavām*—to the cows; *go-dhanāni*—the bulls, cows and calves; *puraskṛtya*—placing in front; *girim*—of the hill; *cakruḥ*—they performed; *pradakṣiṇam*—circumambulation.

## TRANSLATION

**The cowherd community then did all that Madhusūdana had suggested. They arranged for the *brāhmaṇas* to recite the auspicious Vedic *mantras,* and using the paraphernalia that had been intended for Indra's sacrifice, they presented offerings to Govardhana Hill and the *brāhmaṇas* with reverential respect. They also gave grass to the cows. Then, placing the cows, bulls and calves in front of them, they circumambulated Govardhana.**

## PURPORT

The residents of Vṛndāvana were simply devoted to Lord Kṛṣṇa; that was the sum and substance of their existence. Being the Lord's eternal associates, they were ultimately not concerned with Lord Indra or ritualistic sacrifice, and they were certainly not interested in the mechanistic philosophy that Kṛṣṇa had just spoken to them. They simply loved Kṛṣṇa, and out of intense affection they did exactly what He had requested.

Their simple loving mentality was not small-mindedness or ignorance, since they were devoted to the Supreme Absolute Truth, who contains within Himself all existence. Thus the residents of Vṛndāvana constantly experienced the highest, essential truth underlying all other truths—and that is Śrī Kṛṣṇa Himself, the cause of all causes and that which sustains the existence of all that exists. The residents of Vṛndāvana were overwhelmed in loving service to that Supreme Absolute Truth; therefore they were the most fortunate, most intelligent and most pragmatic of all living beings.

## TEXT 34

अनांस्यनडुद्युक्तानि ते चारुह्य स्वलंकृताः ।
गोप्यश्च कृष्णवीर्याणि गायन्त्यः सद्विजाशिषः ॥३४॥

*anāṁsy anaḍud-yuktāni*
*te cāruhya sv-alaṅkṛtāḥ*
*gopyaś ca kṛṣṇa-vīryāṇi*
*gāyantyaḥ sa-dvijāśiṣaḥ*

*anāṁsi*—wagons; *anaḍut-yuktāni*—yoked with oxen; *te*—they; *ca*—and; *āruhya*—riding; *su-alaṅkṛtāḥ*—nicely ornamented; *gopyaḥ*—the cowherd women; *ca*—and; *kṛṣṇa-vīryāṇi*—the glories of Lord Kṛṣṇa; *gāyantyaḥ*—singing; *sa*—together with; *dvija*—of the *brāhmaṇas; āśiṣaḥ*—the benedictions.

## TRANSLATION

**As the beautifully ornamented cowherd ladies followed along, riding on wagons drawn by oxen, they sang the glories of Lord Kṛṣṇa, and their songs mingled with the *brāhmaṇas'* chanting of benedictions.**

## TEXT 35

कृष्णस्त्वन्यतमं रूपं गोपविश्रम्भणं गतः ।
शैलोऽस्मीति ब्रुवन् भूरि बलिमादद् बृहद्वपुः ॥३५॥

*kṛṣṇas tv anyatamaṁ rūpaṁ*
*gopa-viśrambhaṇaṁ gataḥ*
*śailo 'smīti bruvan bhūri*
*balim ādad bṛhad-vapuḥ*

*kṛṣṇaḥ*—Lord Kṛṣṇa; *tu*—and then; *anyatamam*—another; *rūpam*—transcendental form; *gopa-viśrambhaṇam*—for generating the faith of the cowherds; *gataḥ*—assumed; *śailaḥ*—the mountain; *asmi*—I am; *iti*—these words; *bruvan*—saying; *bhūri*—abundant; *balim*—the offerings; *ādat*—He devoured; *bṛhat-vapuḥ*—in His huge form.

## TRANSLATION

**Kṛṣṇa then assumed an unprecedented, huge form to instill faith in the cowherd men. Declaring "I am Govardhana Mountain!" He ate the abundant offerings.**

## PURPORT

In Chapter Twenty-four of *Kṛṣṇa, the Supreme Personality of Godhead,* Śrīla Prabhupāda writes, "When everything was complete, Kṛṣṇa assumed a great transcendental form and declared to the inhabitants of Vṛndāvana that He was Himself Govardhana Hill in order to convince the devotees that Govardhana Hill and Kṛṣṇa are identical. Then Kṛṣṇa began to eat all the food offered there. The identity of Kṛṣṇa and Govardhana Hill is still honored, and great devotees take rocks from Govardhana Hill and worship them exactly as they worship the Deity of Kṛṣṇa in the temples. Devotees therefore collect small rocks or pebbles from Govardhana Hill and worship them at home, because this worship is as good as Deity worship."

Lord Kṛṣṇa had induced the residents of Vṛndāvana to assume a significant risk on His behalf. He convinced them to neglect a sacrifice to what is, after all, the powerful government of the universe and to worship a hill called Govardhana instead. The cowherd community did all this simply out of love for Kṛṣṇa, and now to convince them that their decision was correct, Lord Kṛṣṇa appeared in an unprecedented, huge transcendental form and demonstrated that He Himself was Govardhana Hill.

## TEXT 36

तस्मै नमो व्रजजनैः सह चक्र आत्मनात्मने ।
अहो पश्यत शैलोऽसौ रूपी नोऽनुग्रहं व्यधात् ॥३६॥

*tasmai namo vraja-janaiḥ*
*saha cakra ātmanātmane*
*aho paśyata śailo 'sau*
*rūpī no 'nugrahaṁ vyadhāt*

*tasmai*—to Him; *namaḥ*—obeisances; *vraja-janaiḥ*—with the people of Vraja; *saha*—together; *cakre*—He made; *ātmanā*—by Himself; *ātmane*—to Himself; *aho*—ah; *paśyata*—just see; *śailaḥ*—hill; *asau*—this; *rūpī*—manifest in person; *naḥ*—upon us; *anugraham*—mercy; *vyadhāt*—has bestowed.

## TRANSLATION

**Together with the people of Vraja, the Lord bowed down to this form of Govardhana Hill, thus in effect offering obeisances to Himself. Then He said, "Just see how this hill has appeared in person and bestowed mercy upon us!**

## PURPORT

It is clear from this verse that Lord Kṛṣṇa had expanded Himself and was appearing in His normal form among the festival-goers of Vṛndāvana while simultaneously manifesting Himself as the great form of Govardhana Hill. Thus, in His form as a child, Kṛṣṇa led the residents of Vṛndāvana in bowing down to His new incarnation as Govardhana Hill, and to all He pointed out the great mercy bestowed by this divine form of Govardhana. Lord Kṛṣṇa's amazing transcendental activities were certainly in keeping with the festive atmosphere.

## TEXT 37

एषोऽवजानतो मर्त्यान् कामरूपी वनौकसः ।
हन्ति ह्यस्मै नमस्यामः शर्मणे आत्मनो गवाम् ॥३७॥

*eṣo 'vajānato martyān*
*kāma-rūpī vanaukasaḥ*
*hanti hy asmai namasyāmaḥ*
*śarmaṇe ātmano gavām*

*eṣaḥ*—this one; *avajānataḥ*—those who are neglectful; *martyān*—mortals; *kāma-rūpī*—assuming any form at will (such as that of the snakes who live upon the hill); *vana-okasaḥ*—residents of the forest; *hanti*—will kill; *hi*—certainly; *asmai*—to him; *namasyāmaḥ*—let us pay our obeisances; *śarmaṇe*—for the protection; *ātmanaḥ*—of ourselves; *gavām*—and of the cows.

## TRANSLATION

**"This Govardhana Hill, assuming any form he wishes, will kill any residents of the forest who neglect him. Therefore let us pay our obeisances to him for the safety of ourselves and our cows."**

## PURPORT

*Kāma-rūpī* indicates that the form of Govardhana can manifest as poisonous snakes, wild animals, falling rocks and so on, all of which are competent to kill a human being.

According to Śrīla Śrīdhara Svāmī, the Lord presented six theoretical points in this chapter: 1) that *karma* alone is sufficient to determine one's destiny; 2) that one's conditioned nature is the supreme controller; 3) that the modes of nature are the supreme controller; 4) that the Supreme Lord is simply a dependent aspect of *karma;* 5) that He is under the control of *karma;* and 6) that one's occupation is the actual worshipable deity.

The Lord presented these arguments not because He believed them but rather because He wanted to stop the impending sacrifice to Indra and divert it to Himself in the form of Govardhana Hill. In this way the Lord desired to agitate that falsely proud demigod.

## TEXT 38

इत्यद्रिगोद्विजमखं वासुदेवप्रचोदिताः ।
यथा विधाय ते गोपा सहकृष्णा व्रजं ययुः ॥३८॥

*ity adri-go-dvija-makhaṁ*
*vāsudeva-pracoditāḥ*
*yathā vidhāya te gopā*
*saha-kṛṣṇā vrajaṁ yayuḥ*

*iti*—in this manner; *adri*—to Govardhana Hill; *go*—the cows; *dvija*—and the *brāhmaṇas; makham*—the great sacrifice; *vāsudeva*—by Lord Kṛṣṇa; *pracoditāḥ*—urged; *yathā*—properly; *vidhāya*—executing; *te*—they; *gopāḥ*—the cowherds; *saha-kṛṣṇāḥ*—together with Lord Kṛṣṇa; *vrajam*—to Vraja; *yayuḥ*—they went.

## TRANSLATION

**The members of the cowherd community, having thus been inspired by Lord Vāsudeva to properly execute the sacrifice to Govardhana Hill, the cows and the *brāhmaṇas,* returned with Lord Kṛṣṇa to their village, Vraja.**

## PURPORT

Although the Govardhana-pūjā was performed in a blissful and successful way, the matter was hardly finished. Lord Indra is, after all, tremendously powerful, and he received the news of the Govardhana sacrifice with burning anger. What ensued will be described in the following chapter.

*Thus end the purports of the humble servant of His Divine Grace A. C. Bhaktivedanta Swami Prabhupāda to the Tenth Canto, Twenty-fourth Chapter, of the* Śrīmad-Bhāgavatam, *entitled "Worshiping Govardhana Hill."*

## CHAPTER TWENTY-FIVE

# Lord Kṛṣṇa Lifts Govardhana Hill

This chapter describes how Lord Indra was overcome by anger when the residents of Vraja canceled his sacrifice, how he tried to punish them by sending forth a devastating rainfall to Vṛndāvana, and how Lord Śrī Kṛṣṇa protected Gokula by lifting Govardhana Hill and for seven days using it as an umbrella to ward off the rain.

Indra, angered at the disruption of the sacrifice meant for him and falsely presuming himself the supreme controller, said, "People often give up the pursuit of transcendental knowledge—the means for self-realization—and imagine that they can cross over the ocean of material existence by mundane fruitive sacrifices. Similarly, these cowherd men have become intoxicated by pride and have offended me by taking shelter of an ignorant, ordinary child—Kṛṣṇa."

To remove this supposed pride of the residents of Vraja, Indra sent the clouds known as Sāṁvartaka, whose function is to facilitate the destruction of the world. He sent them to harass the Vrajavāsīs with downpours of rain and hail. The cowherd community was very disturbed by this and approached Kṛṣṇa for shelter. Understanding that this trouble was the work of Indra, Kṛṣṇa decided to smash to pieces Indra's false prestige, and thus He lifted Govardhana Hill with one hand. He then invited the entire cowherd community to take shelter in the dry space beneath the mountain. For seven successive days He held up the hill, until Indra finally understood Kṛṣṇa's mystic power and ordered the clouds to withdraw.

When the cowherd villagers emerged from beneath the mountain, Kṛṣṇa put Govardhana Hill back in its proper place. The cowherds were in ecstasy, showing loving symptoms such as flowing tears and bodily hairs standing on end. They embraced Kṛṣṇa and offered Him benedictions according to their respective positions, while the demigods in heaven rained down flowers and sang the Lord's praises.

### TEXT 1

श्रीशुक उवाच
इन्द्रस्तदात्मनः पूजां विज्ञाय विहतां नृप ।
गोपेभ्यः कृष्णनाथेभ्यो नन्दादिभ्यश्चुकोप ह ॥१॥

*śrī-śuka uvāca*
*indras tadātmanaḥ pūjāṁ*
*vijñāya vihatāṁ nṛpa*
*gopebhyaḥ kṛṣṇa-nāthebhyo*
*nandādibhyaś cukopa ha*

*śrī-śukaḥ uvāca*—Śrī Śukadeva Gosvāmī said; *indraḥ*—Lord Indra; *tadā*—then; *ātmanaḥ*—his own; *pūjām*—worship; *vijñāya*—understanding; *vihatām*—diverted; *nṛpa*—O King (Parīkṣit); *gopebhyaḥ*—at the cowherds; *kṛṣṇa-nāthebhyaḥ*—who took Kṛṣṇa as their Lord; *nanda-ādibhyaḥ*—headed by Nanda Mahārāja; *cukopa ha*—he became angry.

### TRANSLATION

**Śukadeva Gosvāmī said: My dear King Parīkṣit, when Indra understood that his sacrifice had been put aside, he became furious with Nanda Mahārāja and the other cowherd men, who were accepting Kṛṣṇa as their Lord.**

### PURPORT

At the very beginning of this chapter Śukadeva Gosvāmī reveals the foolishness of Indra and the absurdity of his anger. Indra was frustrated because the residents of Vṛndāvana accepted Śrī Kṛṣṇa as their Lord. But the simple fact is that Śrī Kṛṣṇa *is* the Lord, not only of the residents of Vṛndāvana but of all that exists, including Indra himself. Thus Indra's petulant reaction was ridiculous. As the common saying goes, "Pride goes before a fall."

### TEXT 2

गणं सांवर्तकं नाम मेघानां चान्तकारिणाम् ।
इन्द्रः प्रचोदयत् क्रुद्धो वाक्यं चाहेशमान्युत ॥२॥

*gaṇaṁ sāṁvartakaṁ nāma*
*meghānāṁ cānta-kāriṇām*
*indraḥ pracodayat kruddho*
*vākyaṁ cāheśa-māny uta*

*gaṇam*—the group; *sāṁvartakam nāma*—named Sāṁvartaka; *meghānām*—of clouds; *ca*—and; *anta-kāriṇām*—who effect the end of the universe; *indraḥ*—Indra; *pracodayat*—sent forth; *kruddhaḥ*—angry; *vākyam*—words; *ca*—and; *āha*—spoke; *īśa-mānī*—falsely thinking himself the supreme controller; *uta*—indeed.

### TRANSLATION

**Angry Indra sent forth the clouds of universal destruction, known as Sāṁvartaka. Imagining himself the supreme controller, he spoke as follows.**

### PURPORT

The word *īśa-mānī* here is very significant. Indra arrogantly considered himself to be the Lord, and thus he exhibited the typical attitude of a conditioned soul. Many thinkers in the twentieth century have noted the exaggerated sense of individual prestige characteristic of our culture; indeed, writers have even coined the phrase "the me generation." Everyone in this world is more or less guilty of the syndrome called *īśa-māna*, or proudly considering oneself the Lord.

### TEXT 3

अहो श्रीमदमाहात्म्यं गोपानां काननौकसाम् ।
कृष्णं मर्त्यमुपाश्रित्य ये चक्रुर्देवहेलनम् ॥३॥

*aho śrī-mada-māhātmyaṁ*
*gopānāṁ kānanaukasām*
*kṛṣṇaṁ martyam upāśritya*
*ye cakrur deva-helanam*

*aho*—just see; *śrī*—because of opulence; *mada*—of intoxication; *māhātmyam*—the great extent; *gopānām*—of the cowherds; *kānana*—in the forest; *okasām*—who dwell; *kṛṣṇam*—Kṛṣṇa; *martyam*—an ordinary human; *upāśritya*—taking shelter of; *ye*—who; *cakruḥ*—have committed; *deva*—against the demigods; *helanam*—offense.

## TRANSLATION

**Just see how these cowherd men living in the forest have become so greatly intoxicated by their prosperity! They have surrendered to an ordinary human being, Kṛṣṇa, and thus they have offended the gods.**

## PURPORT

Of course, Indra was really saying that the cowherd men had offended him by taking shelter of Kṛṣṇa, whom Indra considered to be *martya,* a mortal. This was certainly a gross miscalculation on Indra's part.

## TEXT 4

यथादृढैः कर्ममयैः क्रतुभिर्नामनौनिभैः ।
विद्यामान्वीक्षिकीं हित्वा तितीर्षन्ति भवार्णवम् ॥४॥

*yathādṛḍhaiḥ karma-mayaiḥ*
*kratubhir nāma-nau-nibhaiḥ*
*vidyām ānvīkṣikīṁ hitvā*
*titīrṣanti bhavārṇavam*

*yathā*—as; *adṛḍhaiḥ*—which are inadequate; *karma-mayaiḥ*—based on fruitive activity; *kratubhiḥ*—by ritual sacrifices; *nāma*—in name only; *nau-nibhaiḥ*—which serve as boats; *vidyām*—knowledge; *ānvīkṣikīm*—spiritual; *hitvā*—abandoning; *titīrṣanti*—they try to cross beyond; *bhava-arṇavam*—the ocean of material existence.

## TRANSLATION

**Their taking shelter of Kṛṣṇa is just like the foolish attempt of men who abandon transcendental knowledge of the self and instead try to cross over the great ocean of material existence in the false boats of fruitive, ritual sacrifices.**

## TEXT 5

वाचालं बालिशं स्तब्धमज्ञं पण्डितमानिनम् ।
कृष्णं मर्त्यमुपाश्रित्य गोपा मे चक्रुरप्रियम् ॥५॥

*vācālaṁ bāliśaṁ stabdham*
*ajñaṁ paṇḍita-māninam*
*kṛṣṇaṁ martyam upāśritya*
*gopā me cakrur apriyam*

*vācālam*—overtalkative; *bāliśam*—child; *stabdham*—arrogant; *ajñam*—foolish; *paṇḍita-māninam*—thinking Himself wise; *kṛṣṇam*—Kṛṣṇa; *martyam*—a human being; *upāśritya*—taking shelter of; *gopāḥ*—the cowherds; *me*—against me; *cakruḥ*—have acted; *apriyam*—unfavorably.

## TRANSLATION

**These cowherd men have acted inimically toward me by taking shelter of this ordinary human being, Kṛṣṇa, who thinks Himself very wise but who is simply a foolish, arrogant, overtalkative child.**

## PURPORT

According to Śrīla Śrīdhara Svāmī, through the insults of Indra goddess Sarasvatī is actually praising Kṛṣṇa. The *ācārya* explains: '*Bāliśam*' means 'free from pretension, just like a child.' *Stabdham* means that He bows down to no one because there is no one for Him to offer homage to, *ajñam* means that there is nothing more for Him to know because He is omniscient, *paṇḍita-māninam* means that He is highly honored by the knowers of the Absolute Truth, and *kṛṣṇam* means He is the Supreme Absolute Truth, whose transcendental form is full of eternity and ecstasy. *Martyam* means that although He is the Absolute Truth, He nevertheless appears in this world as a human being out of affection for His devotees."

Indra wanted to rebuke Kṛṣṇa as *vācālam* because the Lord had presented many audacious arguments in the line of Karma-mīmāṁsā and Sāṅkhya philosophy even though He did not accept these arguments; thus Indra called the Lord *bāliśa,* or foolish. Indra called Him *stabdha* because He had spoken boldly even in the presence of His own father. Thus although Indra attempted to criticize Śrī Kṛṣṇa, the Lord's transcendental character is in fact impeccable, and this chapter will demonstrate how Indra came to recognize the position of the Lord.

## TEXT 6

**एषां श्रियावलिप्तानां कृष्णेनाध्मापितात्मनाम् ।**
**धुनुत श्रीमदस्तम्भं पशून्नयत सङ्क्षयम् ॥६॥**

*eṣāṁ śriyāvaliptānāṁ*
*kṛṣṇenādhmāpitātmanām*
*dhunuta śrī-mada-stambhaṁ*
*paśūn nayata saṅkṣayam*

*eṣām*—of them; *śriyā*—by their opulences; *avaliptānām*—who are intoxicated; *kṛṣṇena*—by Kṛṣṇa; *ādhmāpita*—fortified; *ātmanām*—whose hearts; *dhunuta*—remove; *śrī*—based on their wealth; *mada*—being maddened; *stambham*—their false pride; *paśūn*—their animals; *nayata*—bring; *saṅkṣayam*—to destruction.

## TRANSLATION

**[To the clouds of destruction King Indra said:] The prosperity of these people has made them mad with pride, and their arrogance is backed up by Kṛṣṇa. Now go and remove their pride and bring their animals to destruction.**

## PURPORT

It is clear from this verse that the residents of Vṛndāvana had become highly prosperous simply by protecting cows, since Indra wanted to destroy their so-called pride based on wealth by killing their animals. Well-tended cows produce large quantities of milk, cheese, butter, yogurt, ghee and so on. These foods are delicious by themselves and also enhance other foods such as fruits, vegetables and grains. Bread and vegetables are rich and delicious with butter, and fruit is especially appetizing when mixed with cream or yogurt. Dairy products are always desirable in civilized society, and the surplus can be traded for many valuable com-

His Divine Grace
A. C. Bhaktivedanta Swami Prabhupāda
*Founder-Ācārya of the International Society for Krishna Consciousness*

PLATE ONE: **The Forest Creatures Enchanted by Kṛṣṇa's Flute**

"The peacocks dance madly when they hear Govinda's flute, and when other creatures see them from the hilltops, they all become stunned. Blessed are all these foolish deer because they have approached Mahārāja Nanda's son, who is gorgeously dressed and is playing on His flute. Indeed, both the doe and the bucks worship the Lord with looks of love and affection.

"Using their upraised ears as vessels, the cows are drinking the nectar of the flute-song flowing out of Kṛṣṇa's mouth. The calves, their mouths full of milk from their mothers' moist nipples, stand still as they take Govinda within themselves through their tear-filled eyes and embrace Him within their hearts.

"In this forest all the birds have risen onto the beautiful branches of the trees to see Kṛṣṇa. With closed eyes they are simply listening in silence to the sweet vibrations of His flute, and they are not attracted by any other sound. Surely these birds are on the same level as great sages.

"When the rivers hear the flute-song of Kṛṣṇa, their minds begin to desire Him, and thus the flow of their currents is broken and their waters are agitated, moving around in whirlpools. Then with the arms of their waves the rivers embrace Murāri's lotus feet and, holding on to them, present offerings of lotus flowers." (*pp. 10–17*)

PLATE THREE: **The *Brāhmaṇas'* Wives Offer Food to Kṛṣṇa and Balarāma**

"When the cowherd boys became very hungry, they asked Śrī Kṛṣṇa about obtaining food, and He sent them to beg some from a group of *brāhmaṇas* who were performing a sacrifice nearby. But these *brāhmaṇas* ignored the boys, thinking Śrī Kṛṣṇa an ordinary human being. The

PLATE TWO: **Kṛṣṇa Returns the Clothing of the Unmarried Cowherd Girls**

"During the month of Mārgaśīrṣa, every day early in the morning the young daughters of the cowherds would take one another's hands and, singing of Kṛṣṇa's transcendental qualities, go to the Yamunā to bathe. Desiring to obtain Kṛṣṇa as their husband, they would then worship the goddess Kātyāyanī with incense, flowers and other items.

"One day, the young *gopīs* left their garments on the shore as usual and began playing in the water while chanting of Lord Kṛṣṇa's activities. Suddenly Kṛṣṇa Himself came there, took away all the garments and climbed a nearby *kadamba* tree. Wanting to tease the *gopīs,* Kṛṣṇa said, 'I understand how fatigued you *gopīs* are from your austerities, so please come onto the shore and take back your clothes.'

"Satisfied, He gave them back their clothing. But the young girls' hearts had become so attracted to Him that they could not leave. Understanding their minds, Kṛṣṇa said that He knew they had worshiped Kātyāyanī to get Him as their husband." (*pp. 25–51*)

PLATE THREE: **The *Brāhmaṇas'* Wives Offer Food to Kṛṣṇa and Balarāma**

"When the cowherd boys became very hungry, they asked Śrī Kṛṣṇa about obtaining food, and He sent them to beg some from a group of *brāhmaṇas* who were performing a sacrifice nearby. But these *brāhmaṇas* ignored the boys, thinking Śrī Kṛṣṇa an ordinary human being. The

boys returned disappointed, but the Lord sent them off again, advising them to ask the *brāhmaṇas'* wives for the food. These ladies had heard of Kṛṣṇa's transcendental qualities and were very much attached to Him. Thus as soon as they learned He was nearby, they went to Him in great haste, bringing all four varieties of food. In this way they offered themselves to Śrī Kṛṣṇa." *(pp. 59–99)*

PLATE FOUR: **Kṛṣṇa Convincing Nanda Mahārāja to Worship Govardhana Hill**

"When Śrī Kṛṣṇa saw the cowherd men busily preparing for a sacrifice to Indra, He inquired about it from their king [and His father], Nanda. Nanda explained that the rain given by Indra enables all living entities to maintain their lives, and therefore this sacrifice would be executed to satisfy him. Kṛṣṇa responded that it is because of *karma* alone that living entities take their birth in a certain body, experience varieties of happiness and suffering in that body, and then give it up as

the *karma* pertaining to it runs out. Thus it is *karma* alone that is our enemy, our friend, our *guru* and our lord, and Indra can do nothing to alter the happiness and distress of anyone, for everyone is tightly bound by his karmic reactions. The material modes of goodness, passion, and ignorance bring about the creation, maintenance and destruction of this world. The clouds give forth rain when they are impelled by the mode of passion, and cowherds prosper by protecting the cows. Furthermore, the cowherds' proper residence is in the forest and on the hills. Therefore they should offer worship to the cows, the *brāhmaṇas* and Govardhana Hill." (*pp. 101–123*)

PLATE FIVE: **Lord Kṛṣṇa Lifting Govardhana Hill**

"Indra, angered at the disruption of the sacrifice meant for him and falsely presuming himself to be the supreme controller, said, 'These cowherd men have become intoxicated by pride and have offended me by taking shelter of an ignorant, ordinary child—Kṛṣṇa.'

"To remove this supposed pride of the residents of Vraja, Indra sent the clouds known as Sāṁvartaka, whose function is to facilitate the destruction of the world. He sent them to harass the Vrajavāsīs with

downpours of rain and hail. The cowherd community was very disturbed by this and approached Kṛṣṇa for shelter. Understanding that this trouble was the work of Indra, Kṛṣṇa decided to smash to pieces Indra's false prestige, and thus He lifted Govardhana Hill with one hand. He then invited the entire cowherd community to take shelter in the dry space beneath the mountain. For seven successive days He held up the hill, until Indra finally understood Kṛṣṇa's mystic power and ordered the clouds to withdraw." (*pp. 135–154*)

PLATE SIX: **Indra Offers Prayers to Lord Kṛṣṇa**

"Fearing that Śrī Kṛṣṇa might be tired from lifting Govardhana Hill, Indra secretly came into His presence, offered obeisances and praised Him. Indra stated that although Śrī Kṛṣṇa is never caught in the current of material illusion, which is born of ignorance, He nevertheless accepts a humanlike body and performs various activities to establish religious principles and chastise the wicked.

"Satisfied with Indra's prayers, Śrī Kṛṣṇa told him that He had stopped the *indra-yajña* (sacrifice to Indra) so that Indra, puffed up as he was with false pride, would remember the Lord. Persons intoxicated by material opulence never see Him standing before them with the rod of punishment in His hand. Therefore if Lord Kṛṣṇa desires the actual good fortune of some person, He brings him down from his position of opulence.

"Lord Kṛṣṇa ordered Indra to return to his proper position in heaven and to serve there without egotism. Indra, along with the cow Surabhi, then performed a bathing ceremony for Kṛṣṇa, using the water of the heavenly Ganges and the milk of mother Surabhi." (*pp. 183–211*)

PLATE SEVEN: **Kṛṣṇa Rescues Nanda Mahārāja from the Abode of Varuṇa**

"The king of the cowherds, Nanda Mahārāja, observed the prescribed fast on the eleventh day of the lunar month and then considered how to break his fast properly on the twelfth day. By circumstance only a few more minutes remained, and so he decided to take his bath at the very end of the night, although astrologically that was an inauspicious time. Thus he entered the water of the Yamunā. A servant of Varuṇa, the demigod of the ocean, noticed Nanda Mahārāja entering the water at a time forbidden by scripture and took him away to the demigod's abode. In the early morning the cowherd men unsuccessfully searched for Nanda, but Lord Kṛṣṇa immediately understood the situation and went to see Varuṇa. Varuṇa worshiped Kṛṣṇa with great and variegated festivity. Afterwards he begged the Lord to forgive his servant for having foolishly arrested the king of the cowherds." (*pp. 213–221*)

modities. Thus, simply by a Vedic dairy enterprise, the residents of Vṛndāvana were wealthy, healthy and happy, even in the material sense, and most of all they were eternal associates of the Supreme Lord Kṛṣṇa.

## TEXT 7

अहं चैरावतं नागमारुह्यानुव्रजे व्रजम् ।
मरुद्गणैर्महावेगैर्नन्दगोष्ठजिघांसया ॥७॥

*ahaṁ cairāvataṁ nāgam*
*āruhyānuvraje vrajam*
*marud-gaṇair mahā-vegair*
*nanda-goṣṭha-jighāṁsayā*

*aham*—I; *ca*—also; *airāvatam*—named Airāvata; *nāgam*—my elephant; *āruhya*—riding; *anuvraje*—will follow along; *vrajam*—to Vraja; *marut-gaṇaiḥ*—accompanied by the wind-gods; *mahā-vegaiḥ*—who move with great power; *nanda-goṣṭha*—the cowherd community of Nanda Mahārāja; *jighāṁsayā*—with the intent of destroying.

## TRANSLATION

**I will follow you to Vraja, riding on my elephant Airāvata and taking with me the swift and powerful wind-gods to decimate the cowherd village of Nanda Mahārāja.**

## PURPORT

The Sāṁvartaka clouds were frightened by Indra's powerful mood and thus carried out his order, as described in the following verse.

## TEXT 8

श्रीशुक उवाच
इत्थं मघवताज्ञप्ता मेघा निर्मुक्तबन्धनाः ।
नन्दगोकुलमासारैः पीडयामासुरोजसा ॥८॥

*śrī-śuka uvāca*
*itthaṁ maghavatājñaptā*
*meghā nirmukta-bandhanāḥ*
*nanda-gokulam āsāraiḥ*
*pīḍayām āsur ojasā*

*śrī-śukaḥ uvāca*—Śrī Śukadeva Gosvāmī said; *ittham*—in this manner; *maghavatā*—by Indra; *ājñaptāḥ*—ordered; *meghāḥ*—the clouds; *nirmukta-bandhanāḥ*—released from their bonds (although they were supposed to be kept in check until the time for the destruction of the world); *nanda-gokulam*—the cowherd pastures of Nanda Mahārāja; *āsāraiḥ*—by great downpours of rain; *pīḍayām āsuḥ*—they tormented; *ojasā*—with all their power.

## TRANSLATION

**Śukadeva Gosvāmī said: On Indra's order the clouds of universal destruction, released untimely from their bonds, went to the cowherd pastures of Nanda Mahārāja. There they began to torment the inhabitants by powerfully pouring down torrents of rain upon them.**

## PURPORT

The Sāṁvartaka clouds could cover the entire earth with a single great ocean. With great strength, these clouds began flooding the simple land of Vraja.

## TEXT 9

विद्योतमाना विद्युद्भिः स्तनन्तः स्तनयित्नुभिः ।
तीव्रैर्मरुद्गणैर्नुन्ना ववृषुर्जलशर्कराः ॥९॥

*vidyotamānā vidyudbhiḥ*
*stanantaḥ stanayitnubhiḥ*
*tīvrair marud-gaṇair nunnā*
*vavṛṣur jala-śarkarāḥ*

*vidyotamānāḥ*—being illuminated; *vidyudbhiḥ*—by bolts of lightning; *stanantaḥ*—roaring; *stanayitnubhiḥ*—with thunder; *tīvraiḥ*—fearsome;

*marut-gaṇaiḥ*—by the wind-gods; *nunnāḥ*—propelled; *vavṛṣuḥ*—they poured down; *jala-śarkarāḥ*—hailstones.

## TRANSLATION

**Propelled by the fearsome wind-gods, the clouds blazed with lightning bolts and roared with thunder as they hurled down hailstones.**

## PURPORT

Śrīla Śrīdhara Svāmī explains that the word *marud-gaṇaiḥ* indicates the seven great winds, such as Āvaha, who presides over the region of Bhuvarloka, and Pravaha, who holds the planets in their places.

## TEXT 10

स्थूणास्थूला वर्षधारा मुञ्चत्स्वभ्रेष्वभीक्ष्णशः ।
जलौघैः प्लाव्यमाना भूर्नादृश्यत नतोन्नतम् ॥१०॥

*sthūṇā-sthūlā varṣa-dhārā*
*muñcatsv abhreṣv abhīkṣṇaśaḥ*
*jalaughaiḥ plāvyamānā bhūr*
*nādṛśyata natonnatam*

*sthūṇā*—like columns; *sthūlāḥ*—massive; *varṣa-dhārāḥ*—downpours of rain; *muñcatsu*—releasing; *abhreṣu*—the clouds; *abhīkṣṇaśaḥ*—incessantly; *jala-oghaiḥ*—by the flood of water; *plāvyamānā*—being submerged; *bhūḥ*—the earth; *na adṛśyata*—could not be seen; *nata-unnatam*—low or high.

## TRANSLATION

**As the clouds released torrents of rain as thick as massive columns, the earth was submerged in the flood, and high ground could no longer be distinguished from low.**

## TEXT 11

**अत्यासारातिवातेन पशवो जातवेपनाः ।**
**गोपा गोप्यश्च शीतार्ता गोविन्दं शरणं ययुः ॥११॥**

*aty-āsārāti-vātena*
*paśavo jāta-vepanāḥ*
*gopā gopyaś ca śītārtā*
*govindaṁ śaraṇaṁ yayuḥ*

*ati-āsāra*—by the excessive rainfall; *ati-vātena*—and the excessive wind; *paśavaḥ*—the cows and other animals; *jāta-vepanāḥ*—trembling; *gopāḥ*—the cowherd men; *gopyaḥ*—the cowherd ladies; *ca*—also; *śīta*—by the cold; *ārtāḥ*—distressed; *govindam*—to Lord Govinda; *śaraṇam*—for shelter; *yayuḥ*—they went.

## TRANSLATION

**The cows and other animals, shivering from the excessive rain and wind, and the cowherd men and ladies, pained by the cold, all approached Lord Govinda for shelter.**

## TEXT 12

**शिरः सुतांश्च कायेन प्रच्छाद्यासारपीडिताः ।**
**वेपमाना भगवतः पादमूलमुपाययुः ॥१२॥**

*śiraḥ sutāṁś ca kāyena*
*pracchādyāsāra-pīḍitāḥ*
*vepamānā bhagavataḥ*
*pāda-mūlam upāyayuḥ*

*śiraḥ*—their heads; *sutān*—their children; *ca*—and; *kāyena*—by their bodies; *pracchādya*—covering; *āsāra-pīḍitāḥ*—distressed by the rainfall; *vepamānāḥ*—trembling; *bhagavataḥ*—of the Supreme Personality of Godhead; *pāda-mūlam*—the base of the lotus feet; *upāyayuḥ*—they approached.

## TRANSLATION

**Trembling from the distress brought about by the severe rainfall, and trying to cover their heads and calves with their own bodies, the cows approached the lotus feet of the Supreme Personality of Godhead.**

## TEXT 13

कृष्ण कृष्ण महाभाग त्वन्नाथं गोकुलं प्रभो ।
त्रातुमर्हसि देवान्नः कुपिताद् भक्तवत्सल ॥१३॥

*kṛṣṇa kṛṣṇa mahā-bhāga*
*tvan-nāthaṁ gokulaṁ prabho*
*trātum arhasi devān naḥ*
*kupitād bhakta-vatsala*

*kṛṣṇa kṛṣṇa*—O Kṛṣṇa, Kṛṣṇa; *mahā-bhāga*—O all-fortunate one; *tvat-nātham*—whose master is Yourself; *go-kulam*—the community of cows; *prabho*—O Lord; *trātum arhasi*—kindly protect; *devāt*—from the demigod Indra; *naḥ*—us; *kupitāt*—who is angry; *bhakta-vatsala*—O You who are very affectionate to Your devotees.

## TRANSLATION

**[The cowherd men and women addressed the Lord:] Kṛṣṇa, Kṛṣṇa, O most fortunate one, please deliver the cows from the wrath of Indra! O Lord, You are so affectionate to Your devotees. Please save us also.**

## PURPORT

At the time of Lord Kṛṣṇa's birth, Garga Muni had predicted, *anena sarva-durgāṇi yūyam añjas tariṣyatha* (*Bhāg.* 10.8.16): "By His grace you will easily cross beyond all difficulties." The residents of Vṛndāvana were confident that in such a great emergency Lord Śrī Nārāyaṇa would empower Kṛṣṇa to protect them. They accepted Kṛṣṇa as everything, and Kṛṣṇa reciprocated their love.

## TEXT 14

शिलावर्षातिवातेन हन्यमानमचेतनम् ।
निरीक्ष्य भगवान्मेने कुपितेन्द्रकृतं हरिः ॥१४॥

*śilā-varṣāti-vātena*
*hanyamānam acetanam*
*nirīkṣya bhagavān mene*
*kupitendra-kṛtaṁ hariḥ*

*śilā*—of (hail)stones; *varṣa*—by the rain; *ati-vātena*—and by the extreme wind; *hanyamānam*—being attacked; *acetanam*—unconscious; *nirīkṣya*—seeing; *bhagavān*—the Supreme Personality of Godhead; *mene*—considered; *kupita*—angry; *indra*—by Indra; *kṛtam*—done; *hariḥ*—Lord Hari.

## TRANSLATION

**Seeing the inhabitants of His Gokula rendered practically unconscious by the onslaught of hail and blasting wind, the Supreme Lord Hari understood that this was the work of angry Indra.**

## PURPORT

Śrīla Viśvanātha Cakravartī Ṭhākura explains that the severe distress Indra apparently inflicted upon the residents of Vṛndāvana was an arrangement made by Śrī Kṛṣṇa's pastime potency to enhance the loving dealings between the residents and the Lord. The *ācārya* gives the analogy that for a hungry person, the pain of hunger increases the happiness he feels when he finally eats excellent food, and thus hunger can be said to enhance the pleasure of eating. Similarly, the residents of Vṛndāvana, although not experiencing ordinary, material anxiety, felt a type of distress at the activities of Indra and thus intensified their meditation on Kṛṣṇa. When the Lord finally acted, the result was wonderful.

## TEXT 15

अपर्त्वत्युल्बणं वर्षमतिवातं शिलामयम् ।
स्वयागे विहतेऽस्माभिरिन्द्रो नाशाय वर्षति ॥१५॥

*apartv aty-ulbaṇaṁ varṣam*
*ati-vātaṁ śilā-mayam*
*sva-yāge vihate 'smābhir*
*indro nāśāya varṣati*

*apa-ṛtu*—out of season; *ati-ulbaṇam*—unusually fierce; *varṣam*—rain; *ati-vātam*—accompanied by great wind; *śilā-mayam*—full of hailstones; *sva-yāge*—his sacrifice; *vihate*—having been stopped; *asmābhiḥ*—by Ourselves; *indraḥ*—King Indra; *nāśāya*—for destruction; *varṣati*—is raining.

## TRANSLATION

**[Śrī Kṛṣṇa thought:] Because We have stopped his sacrifice, Indra has caused this unusually fierce, unseasonable rain, together with terrible winds and hail.**

## TEXT 16

तत्र प्रतिविधिं सम्यगात्मयोगेन साधये ।
लोकेशमानिनां मौढ्याद्धनिष्ये श्रीमदं तमः ॥१६॥

*tatra pratividhiṁ samyag*
*ātma-yogena sādhaye*
*lokeśa-māninām mauḍhyād*
*dhaniṣye śrī-madaṁ tamaḥ*

*tatra*—in that regard; *prati-vidhim*—counteracting measures; *samyak*—properly; *ātma-yogena*—by My mystic power; *sādhaye*—I shall arrange; *loka-īśa*—lords of the world; *māninām*—of those who falsely consider themselves; *mauḍhyāt*—out of foolishness; *haniṣye*—I shall defeat; *śrī-madam*—their pride in opulence; *tamaḥ*—the ignorance.

## TRANSLATION

**By My mystic power I will completely counteract this disturbance caused by Indra. Demigods like Indra are proud of their opulence, and out of foolishness they falsely consider themselves the Lord of the universe. I will now destroy such ignorance.**

## TEXT 17

न हि सद्भावयुक्तानां सुराणामीशविस्मयः ।
मत्तोऽसतां मानभंगः प्रशमायोपकल्पते ॥१७॥

*na hi sad-bhāva-yuktānāṁ*
*surāṇām īśa-vismayaḥ*
*matto 'satāṁ māna-bhaṅgaḥ*
*praśamāyopakalpate*

*na*—not; *hi*—certainly; *sat-bhāva*—with the mode of goodness; *yuktānām*—who are endowed; *surāṇām*—of the demigods; *īśa*—as controlling lords; *vismayaḥ*—false identification; *mattaḥ*—by Me; *asatām*—of the impure; *māna*—of the false prestige; *bhaṅgaḥ*—the eradication; *praśamāya*—for relieving them; *upakalpate*—is intended.

## TRANSLATION

**Since the demigods are endowed with the mode of goodness, the false pride of considering oneself the Lord should certainly not affect them. When I break the false prestige of those bereft of goodness, My purpose is to bring them relief.**

## PURPORT

The demigods are supposed to be *sad-bhāva-yukta,* endowed with spiritual existence, since they are deputed servants of the Supreme Lord. In the *Bhagavad-gītā* (4.24) it is stated:

*brahmārpaṇaṁ brahma havir*
*brahmāgnau brahmaṇā hutam*
*brahmaiva tena gantavyaṁ*
*brahma-karma-samādhinā*

"That which is duly offered to the Lord becomes spiritualized." The demigods engage in the devotional service of the Lord by managing various departments of cosmic administration. Therefore as demigods, or as servants of the Lord, their existence is pure (*sad-bhāva*). When the demigods fail to live up to the high position given them by the Lord and deviate from proper behavior, they are not acting as demigods but rather as conditioned souls.

*Māna,* or false prestige, is certainly an anxiety-ridden burden for the conditioned soul. A falsely proud person is not truly peaceful or satisfied, because his understanding of himself is false and inflated. When a servant of the Lord becomes *asat,* or irreligious, the Lord saves him from impiety by breaking the false prestige that has led him to be offensive or sinful. As stated by the Lord Himself, *yasyāhaṁ anugṛhṇāmi hariṣye tad-dhanaṁ śanaiḥ:* "I give My blessings to a person by taking away his so-called opulence."

Of course, the advanced stage of devotional service to the Lord, as described by Rūpa Gosvāmī, is *yukta-vairāgya,* utilizing the opulence of this world to execute the Lord's mission. Obviously the things of this world can be used wonderfully to spread the glories of God and to create a godly society, and a more advanced devotee will not be seduced by material paraphernalia but will dutifully and honestly engage it solely for the pleasure of the Lord. In this particular case, Lord Indra forgot that he was a humble servant of God, and Lord Kṛṣṇa therefore arranged to bring this bewildered demigod to his senses.

## TEXT 18

तस्मान्मच्छरणं गोष्ठं मन्नाथं मत्परिग्रहम् ।
गोपाये स्वात्मयोगेन सोऽयं मे व्रत आहितः ॥१८॥

*tasmān mac-charaṇaṁ goṣṭhaṁ*
*man-nāthaṁ mat-parigraham*
*gopāye svātma-yogena*
*so 'yaṁ me vrata āhitaḥ*

*tasmāt*—therefore; *mat-śaraṇam*—having taken shelter of Me; *goṣṭham*—the cowherd community; *mat-nātham*—who have Me as their master; *mat-parigraham*—My own family; *gopāye*—I shall protect; *sva-ātma-yogena*—by My personal mystic power; *saḥ ayam*—this; *me*—by Me; *vrataḥ*—vow; *āhitaḥ*—has been taken.

## TRANSLATION

**I must therefore protect the cowherd community by My transcendental potency, for I am their shelter, I am their master, and**

**indeed they are My own family. After all, I have taken a vow to protect My devotees.**

### PURPORT

The word *mac-charaṇam* indicates not only that Lord Kṛṣṇa was the sole shelter for the *vraja-jana*, the people of Vṛndāvana, but also that Lord Kṛṣṇa had established His home among them. Śrīla Viśvanātha Cakravartī Ṭhākura quotes from the *Anekārtha-varga* dictionary, *śaraṇaṁ gṛha-rakṣitroḥ:* "The word *śaraṇam* can represent either home or protector." The residents of Vṛndāvana adopted Kṛṣṇa as their beloved child, friend, lover and life itself, and the Lord reciprocated their feelings. Thus Śrī Kṛṣṇa lived among these fortunate people, moving in their houses and fields; naturally He would protect such intimate devotees from all types of danger.

### TEXT 19

इत्युक्त्वैकेन हस्तेन कृत्वा गोवर्धनाचलम् ।
दधार लीलया विष्णुश्छत्राकमिव बालकः ॥१९॥

*ity uktvaikena hastena*
*kṛtvā govardhanācalam*
*dadhāra līlayā viṣṇuś*
*chatrākam iva bālakaḥ*

*iti*—thus; *uktvā*—having spoken; *ekena*—with one; *hastena*—hand; *kṛtvā*—taking; *govardhana-acalam*—Govardhana Hill; *dadhāra*—He held it; *līlayā*—very easily; *viṣṇuḥ*—Lord Viṣṇu; *chatrākam*—a mushroom; *iva*—just as; *bālakaḥ*—a child.

### TRANSLATION

**Having said this, Lord Kṛṣṇa, who is Viṣṇu Himself, picked up Govardhana Hill with one hand and held it aloft just as easily as a child holds up a mushroom.**

## PURPORT

It is confirmed in the *Hari-vaṁśa* that Śrī Kṛṣṇa picked up the Govardhana Mountain with His left hand: *sa dhṛtaḥ saṅgato meghair giriḥ savyena pāṇinā.* "With His left hand He picked up that mountain, which was touching the clouds." According to Śrīla Viśvanātha Cakravartī Ṭhākura, when Lord Kṛṣṇa was preparing to lift Govardhana Hill, a partial expansion of His Yogamāyā potency named Saṁhārikī temporarily removed all the rain from the sky so that as He ran very swiftly from the porch of His house to the mountain, neither His turban nor other garments became wet.

## TEXT 20

अथाह भगवान् गोपान् हेऽम्ब तात व्रजौकसः ।
यथोपजोषं विशत गिरिगर्तं सगोधनाः ॥२०॥

*athāha bhagavān gopān*
*he 'mba tāta vrajaukasaḥ*
*yathopajoṣaṁ viśata*
*giri-gartaṁ sa-go-dhanāḥ*

*atha*—then; *āha*—addressed; *bhagavān*—the Supreme Lord; *gopān*—the cowherds; *he*—O; *amba*—mother; *tāta*—O father; *vraja-okasaḥ*—O residents of Vraja; *yathā-upajoṣam*—as suits your pleasure; *viśata*—please enter; *giri*—this hill; *gartam*—the empty space below; *sa-go-dhanāḥ*—together with your cows.

## TRANSLATION

**The Lord then addressed the cowherd community: O Mother, O Father, O residents of Vraja, if you wish you may now come under this hill with your cows.**

## PURPORT

Śrīla Viśvanātha Cakravartī Ṭhākura provides the following insight in this regard: Ordinarily a large cowherd community, which included many thousands of cows, calves, bulls and so on, could not fit under the base of a medium-sized hill like Śrī Govardhana. However, because the hill was in ecstasy, being touched by the hand of the Supreme Personality of Godhead, it acquired inconceivable power and even felt the hundreds of deadly thunderbolts thrown upon its back by angry Indra to be offerings of soft, fragrant flowers. At times Śrī Govardhana was not even aware that the thunderbolts were striking. From the *Hari-vaṁśa* the *ācārya* has also quoted Śrī Kṛṣṇa Himself as saying, *trai-lokyam apy utsahate rakṣituṁ kiṁ punar vrajam:* "Śrī Govardhana can give shelter to all the three worlds, what to speak of the simple land of Vraja."

When Indra's attack began and Kṛṣṇa lifted the hill, the deer, wild hogs, and other animals and birds standing on the hill's flanks climbed up to its peaks, and even they did not experience the slightest distress.

## TEXT 21

न त्रास इह वः कार्यो मद्धस्ताद्रिनिपातनात् ।
वातवर्षभयेनालं तत्त्राणं विहितं हि वः ॥२१॥

*na trāsa iha vaḥ kāryo*
*mad-dhastādri-nipātanāt*
*vāta-varṣa-bhayenālaṁ*
*tat-trāṇaṁ vihitaṁ hi vaḥ*

*na*—not; *trāsaḥ*—fear; *iha*—in this matter; *vaḥ*—by you; *kāryaḥ*—should be felt; *mat-hasta*—from My hand; *adri*—of the mountain; *nipātanāt*—of the falling; *vāta*—of the wind; *varṣa*—and the rain; *bhayena*—with fear; *alam*—enough; *tat-trāṇam*—the deliverance from that; *vihitam*—has been provided; *hi*—certainly; *vaḥ*—for you.

## TRANSLATION

**You should have no fear that this mountain will fall from My hand. And don't be afraid of the wind and rain, for your deliverance from these afflictions has already been arranged.**

## TEXT 22

तथा निर्विविशुर्गर्तं कृष्णाश्वासितमानसः ।
यथावकाशं सधनाः सव्रजाः सोपजीविनः ॥२२॥

*tathā nirviviśur gartaṁ*
*kṛṣṇāśvāsita-mānasaḥ*
*yathāvakāśaṁ sa-dhanāḥ*
*sa-vrajāḥ sopajīvinaḥ*

*tathā*—thus; *nirviviśuḥ*—they entered; *gartam*—the hollow; *kṛṣṇa*—by Lord Kṛṣṇa; *āśvāsita*—pacified; *mānasaḥ*—their minds; *yathā-avakāśam*—comfortably; *sa-dhanāḥ*—with their cows; *sa-vrajāḥ*—and with their wagons; *sa-upajīvinaḥ*—together with their dependents (such as their servants and *brāhmaṇa* priests).

## TRANSLATION

**Their minds thus pacified by Lord Kṛṣṇa, they all entered beneath the hill, where they found ample room for themselves and all their cows, wagons, servants and priests, and for all other members of the community as well.**

## PURPORT

All the domestic animals of Vṛndāvana were brought beneath Govardhana Hill for shelter.

## TEXT 23

क्षुत्तृड्व्यथां सुखापेक्षां हित्वा तैर्व्रजवासिभिः ।
वीक्ष्यमाणो दधाराद्रिं सप्ताहं नाचलत्पदात् ॥२३॥

*kṣut-tṛḍ-vyathāṁ sukhāpekṣāṁ*
*hitvā tair vraja-vāsibhiḥ*
*vīkṣyamāṇo dadhārādriṁ*
*saptāhaṁ nācalat padāt*

*kṣut*—of hunger; *tṛṭ*—and thirst; *vyathām*—the pain; *sukha*—of personal happiness; *apekṣām*—all consideration; *hitvā*—putting aside; *taiḥ*—by them; *vraja-vāsibhiḥ*—the residents of Vraja; *vīkṣyamāṇaḥ*—being glanced upon; *dadhāra*—He held; *adrim*—the mountain; *sapta-aham*—for seven days; *na acalat*—He did not move; *padāt*—from that place.

## TRANSLATION

**Forgetting hunger and thirst, and putting aside all considerations of personal pleasure, Lord Kṛṣṇa stood there holding up the hill for seven days as the people of Vraja gazed upon Him.**

## PURPORT

According to the *Viṣṇu Purāṇa*,

*vrajaika-vāsibhir harṣa-*
*vismitākṣair nirīkṣitaḥ*
*gopa-gopī-janair hṛṣṭaiḥ*
*prīti-visphāritekṣaṇaiḥ*
*saṁstūyamāna-caritaḥ*
*kṛṣṇaḥ śailam adhārayat*

"Lord Kṛṣṇa held up the mountain while His praises were chanted by the residents of Vraja, all of whom now had the opportunity to dwell together with Him, and who glanced at Him with joyful and amazed eyes. Thus the cowherd men and women were all elated, and out of loving affection they opened their eyes wide."

By continuously drinking the nectar of the beauty and sweetness of Śrī Kṛṣṇa, the residents of Vṛndāvana felt no hunger, thirst or fatigue, and Lord Kṛṣṇa, by seeing their beautiful forms, also forgot about eating, drinking and sleeping. Śrīla Viśvanātha Cakravartī Ṭhākura points out that seven days of continuous rain from the Sāṁvartaka clouds failed to flood the district of Mathurā because the Supreme Lord, simply by His potency, immediately dried up the water as it fell to the ground. Thus Kṛṣṇa's lifting of Govardhana Hill is full of fascinating details and has remained for thousands of years one of His most famous pastimes.

## TEXT 24

कृष्णयोगानुभावं तं निशम्येन्द्रोऽतिविस्मितः ।
निस्तम्भो भ्रष्टसंकल्पः स्वान्मेघान् संन्यवारयत् ॥२४॥

*kṛṣṇa-yogānubhāvaṁ taṁ*
*niśamyendro 'ti-vismitaḥ*
*nistambho bhraṣṭa-saṅkalpaḥ*
*svān meghān sannyavārayat*

*kṛṣṇa*—of Lord Kṛṣṇa; *yoga*—of the mystic power; *anubhāvam*—the influence; *tam*—that; *niśamya*—seeing; *indraḥ*—Lord Indra; *ati-vismitaḥ*—most amazed; *nistambhaḥ*—whose false pride was brought down; *bhraṣṭa*—ruined; *saṅkalpaḥ*—whose determination; *svān*—his own; *meghān*—clouds; *sannyavārayat*—stopped.

## TRANSLATION

**When Indra observed this exhibition of Lord Kṛṣṇa's mystic power, he became most astonished. Pulled down from his platform of false pride, and his intentions thwarted, he ordered his clouds to desist.**

## TEXT 25

खं व्यभ्रमुदितादित्यं वातवर्षं च दारुणम् ।
निशम्योपरतं गोपान् गोवर्धनधरोऽब्रवीत् ॥२५॥

*khaṁ vyabhram uditādityaṁ*
*vāta-varṣaṁ ca dāruṇam*
*niśamyoparataṁ gopān*
*govardhana-dharo 'bravīt*

*kham*—the sky; *vi-abhram*—empty of clouds; *udita*—arisen; *ādityam*—with the sun; *vāta-varṣam*—the wind and rain; *ca*—and; *dāruṇam*—fierce; *niśamya*—seeing; *uparatam*—ceased; *gopān*—to the cowherds; *govardhana-dharaḥ*—the lifter of Govardhana Hill; *abravīt*—spoke.

## TRANSLATION

**Seeing that the fierce wind and rain had now ceased, the sky had become clear of rainclouds, and the sun had risen, Lord Kṛṣṇa, the lifter of Govardhana Hill, spoke to the cowherd community as follows.**

## TEXT 26

निर्यात त्यजत त्रासं गोपाः सस्त्रीधनार्भकाः ।
उपारतं वातवर्षं व्युदप्रायाश्च निम्नगाः ॥२६॥

*niryāta tyajata trāsaṁ*
*gopāḥ sa-strī-dhanārbhakāḥ*
*upāratam vāta-varṣaṁ*
*vyuda-prāyāś ca nimnagāḥ*

*niryāta*—please go out; *tyajata*—give up; *trāsam*—your fear; *gopāḥ*—O cowherd men; *sa*—together with; *strī*—your women; *dhana*—property; *arbhakāḥ*—and children; *upāratam*—finished; *vāta-varṣam*—the wind and rain; *vi-uda*—without water; *prāyāḥ*—practically; *ca*—and; *nimna-gāḥ*—the rivers.

## TRANSLATION

**My dear cowherd men, please go out with your wives, children and possessions. Give up your fear. The wind and rain have stopped, and the rivers' high waters have subsided.**

## TEXT 27

ततस्ते निर्ययुर्गोपाः स्वं स्वमादाय गोधनम् ।
शकटोढोपकरणं स्त्रीबालस्थविराः शनैः ॥२७॥

*tatas te niryayur gopāḥ*
*svaṁ svam ādāya go-dhanam*
*śakaṭoḍhopakaraṇaṁ*
*strī-bāla-sthavirāḥ śanaiḥ*

*tataḥ*—then; *te*—they; *niryayuḥ*—went out; *gopāḥ*—the cowherd men; *svam svam*—each his own; *ādāya*—taking; *go-dhanam*—their cows; *śakaṭa*—upon their wagons; *ūḍha*—loaded; *upakaraṇam*—their paraphernalia; *strī*—the women; *bāla*—children; *sthavirāḥ*—and old people; *śanaiḥ*—slowly.

### TRANSLATION

**After collecting their respective cows and loading their paraphernalia into their wagons, the cowherd men went out. The women, children and elderly persons gradually followed them.**

### TEXT 28

भगवानपि तं शैलं स्वस्थाने पूर्ववत्प्रभुः ।
पश्यतां सर्वभूतानां स्थापयामास लीलया ॥२८॥

*bhagavān api taṁ śailaṁ*
*sva-sthāne pūrva-vat prabhuḥ*
*paśyatāṁ sarva-bhūtānāṁ*
*sthāpayām āsa līlayā*

*bhagavān*—the Supreme Personality of Godhead; *api*—and; *tam*—that; *śailam*—hill; *sva-sthāne*—upon its place; *pūrva-vat*—as originally; *prabhuḥ*—the almighty Lord; *paśyatām*—while they were looking on; *sarva-bhūtānām*—all the living creatures; *sthāpayām āsa*—He put; *līlayā*—with ease.

### TRANSLATION

**While all living creatures looked on, the Supreme Personality of Godhead put down the hill in its original place, just as it had stood before.**

### TEXT 29

तं प्रेमवेगान्निर्भृता व्रजौकसो
यथा समीयुः परिरम्भणादिभिः ।

गोप्यश्च सस्नेहमपूजयन्मुदा
दध्यक्षताद्भिर्युयुजुः सदाशिषः ॥२९॥

*taṁ prema-vegān nirbhṛtā vrajaukaso*
*yathā samīyuḥ parirambhaṇādibhiḥ*
*gopyaś ca sa-sneham apūjayan mudā*
*dadhy-akṣatādbhir yuyujuḥ sad-āśiṣaḥ*

*tam*—to Him; *prema*—of their pure love; *vegāt*—by the force; *nirbhṛtāḥ*—fulfilled; *vraja-okasaḥ*—the residents of Vraja; *yathā*—each according to his position; *samīyuḥ*—came forward; *parirambhaṇa-ādibhiḥ*—with embracing and so forth; *gopyaḥ*—the cowherd ladies; *ca*—and; *sa-sneham*—with great affection; *apūjayan*—showed their respect; *mudā*—joyfully; *dadhi*—with yogurt; *akṣata*—unbroken grains; *adbhiḥ*—and water; *yuyujuḥ*—they presented; *sat*—excellent; *āśiṣaḥ*—benedictions.

## TRANSLATION

**All the residents of Vṛndāvana were overwhelmed with ecstatic love, and they came forward and greeted Śrī Kṛṣṇa according to their individual relationships with Him—some embracing Him, others bowing down to Him, and so forth. The cowherd women presented water mixed with yogurt and unbroken barleycorns as a token of honor, and they showered auspicious benedictions upon Him.**

## PURPORT

Śrīla Viśvanātha Cakravartī Ṭhākura explains that each of the residents of Vṛndāvana regarded Kṛṣṇa in his own way—as an inferior, younger member of the community; as an equal; or as a superior—and they dealt with Him accordingly. Kṛṣṇa's superiors offered auspicious benedictions, lovingly smelled His head, kissed Him, rubbed His arms and fingers, and inquired with parental affection as to whether He was tired or pained. Kṛṣṇa's equals laughed or joked with Him, and those who were younger fell at His feet, massaged His feet, and so on.

The word *ca* in this verse indicates that the wives of the *brāhmaṇas* joined with the cowherd ladies to offer auspicious items like yogurt and unbroken grains. Lord Kṛṣṇa received benedictions such as this: "May You subdue the wicked, protect the decent people, give pleasure to Your parents and be enriched with all wealth and opulence."

## TEXT 30

यशोदा रोहिणी नन्दो रामश्च बलिनां वरः ।
कृष्णमालिंग्य युयुजुराशिषः स्नेहकातराः ॥३०॥

*yaśodā rohiṇī nando*
*rāmaś ca balināṁ varaḥ*
*kṛṣṇam āliṅgya yuyujur*
*āśiṣaḥ sneha-kātarāḥ*

*yaśodā*—mother Yaśodā; *rohiṇī*—Rohiṇī; *nandaḥ*—Nanda Mahārāja; *rāmaḥ*—Balarāma; *ca*—also; *balinām*—of the strong; *varaḥ*—the greatest; *kṛṣṇam*—Kṛṣṇa; *āliṅgya*—embracing; *yuyujuḥ*—they all offered; *āśiṣaḥ*—benedictions; *sneha*—by their affection for Him; *kātarāḥ*—beside themselves.

## TRANSLATION

**Mother Yaśodā, mother Rohiṇī, Nanda Mahārāja and Balarāma, the greatest of the strong, all embraced Kṛṣṇa. Overwhelmed with affection, they offered Him their blessings.**

## TEXT 31

दिवि देवगणाः सिद्धाः साध्या गन्धर्वचारणाः ।
तुष्टुवुर्मुमुचुस्तुष्टाः पुष्पवर्षाणि पार्थिव ॥३१॥

*divi deva-gaṇāḥ siddhāḥ*
*sādhyā gandharva-cāraṇāḥ*
*tuṣṭuvur mumucus tuṣṭāḥ*
*puṣpa-varṣāṇi pārthiva*

*divi*—in the heavens; *deva-gaṇāḥ*—the demigods; *siddhāḥ*—the Siddhas; *sādhyāḥ*—the Sādhyas; *gandharva-cāraṇāḥ*—the Gandharvas and

Cāraṇas; *tuṣṭuvuḥ*—they recited the Lord's praises; *mumucuḥ*—they released; *tuṣṭāḥ*—being satisfied; *puṣpa-varṣāṇi*—downpours of flowers; *pārthiva*—O King (Parīkṣit).

## TRANSLATION

**In the heavens, O King, all the demigods, including the Siddhas, Sādhyas, Gandharvas and Cāraṇas, sang the praises of Lord Kṛṣṇa and showered down flowers in great satisfaction.**

## PURPORT

The demigods in heaven were just as jubilant as the residents of Vṛndāvana, and thus a great universal festival took place.

## TEXT 32

**शंखदुन्दुभयो नेदुर्दिवि देवप्रचोदिताः ।**
**जगुर्गन्धर्वपतयस्तुम्बुरुप्रमुखा नृप ॥३२॥**

*śaṅkha-dundubhayo nedur*
*divi deva-pracoditāḥ*
*jagur gandharva-patayas*
*tumburu-pramukhā nṛpa*

*śaṅkha*—conchshells; *dundubhayaḥ*—and kettledrums; *neduḥ*—resounded; *divi*—in the heavenly planets; *deva-pracoditāḥ*—played by the demigods; *jaguḥ*—sang; *gandharva-patayaḥ*—the chiefs of the Gandharvas; *tumburu-pramukhāḥ*—led by Tumburu; *nṛpa*—my dear King.

## TRANSLATION

**My dear Parīkṣit, the demigods in heaven resoundingly played their conchshells and kettledrums, and the best of the Gandharvas, led by Tumburu, began to sing.**

## TEXT 33

ततोऽनुरक्तैः पशुपैः परिश्रितो
राजन् स्वगोष्ठं सबलोऽव्रजद्धरिः ।
तथाविधान्यस्य कृतानि गोपिका
गायन्त्य ईयुर्मुदिता हृदिस्पृशः ॥३३॥

*tato 'nuraktaiḥ paśupaiḥ pariśrito*
*rājan sva-goṣṭhaṁ sa-balo 'vrajad dhariḥ*
*tathā-vidhāny asya kṛtāni gopikā*
*gāyantya īyur muditā hṛdi-spṛśaḥ*

*tataḥ*—then; *anuraktaiḥ*—loving; *paśu-paiḥ*—by the cowherd boys; *pariśritaḥ*—surrounded; *rājan*—O King; *sva-goṣṭham*—to the place where He was tending His own cows; *sa-balaḥ*—together with Lord Balarāma; *avrajat*—went off; *hariḥ*—Kṛṣṇa; *tathā-vidhāni*—such as this (lifting of Govardhana); *asya*—of Him; *kṛtāni*—the activities; *gopikāḥ*—the cowherd girls; *gāyantyaḥ*—singing; *īyuḥ*—they went; *muditāḥ*—happily; *hṛdi-spṛśaḥ*—of Him who touched them within their hearts.

## TRANSLATION

**Surrounded by His loving cowherd boyfriends and Lord Balarāma, Kṛṣṇa then went off to the place where He had been tending His cows. The cowherd girls returned to their homes, singing joyfully about the lifting of Govardhana Hill and other glorious activities of Lord Kṛṣṇa, who had so deeply touched their hearts.**

## PURPORT

Before returning to their homes, the *gopīs* shared intimate association with their lover, Śrī Kṛṣṇa, by exchanging secret glances. Ordinarily they could not publicly talk about Kṛṣṇa, since they were chaste young girls in a religious village, but now they took advantage of this wonderful exhibition by the Lord and freely sang of His beautiful qualities. It is natural that a young man wants to do something wonderful in the presence of a beautiful young girl. The *gopīs* were the most beautiful and pure-hearted young girls, and Śrī Kṛṣṇa performed the most wonderful activities in their presence. Thus He entered deep within their tender hearts, enlivening their eternal devotion to Him.

*Thus end the purports of the humble servant of His Divine Grace A. C. Bhaktivedanta Swami Prabhupāda to the Tenth Canto, Twenty-fifth Chapter, of the* Śrīmad-Bhāgavatam, *entitled "Lord Kṛṣṇa Lifts Govardhana Hill."*

CHAPTER TWENTY-SIX

# Wonderful Kṛṣṇa

In this chapter Nanda Mahārāja describes Kṛṣṇa's opulences to the cowherd men, as Nanda had heard of them from Garga Muni.

The cowherd men, unaware of Lord Kṛṣṇa's power, were amazed to see His various extraordinary activities. The men approached Nanda Mahārāja and told him that after seeing how Kṛṣṇa, a boy only seven years old, had lifted a mountain, and how He had previously killed the demoness Pūtanā and generated extreme attraction in the hearts of everyone in Vṛndāvana, the men had become doubtful and bewildered about how Śrī Kṛṣṇa could possibly have taken birth in the unsuitable environment of a cowherd community. Nanda replied by relating to them what Garga Muni had told him about Śrī Kṛṣṇa.

Garga Muni had said that in the previous three ages Nanda's boy had manifested Himself in white, red and yellow forms, whereas now, in the Dvāpara age, He had assumed His darkish-blue form, *kṛṣṇa-rūpa.* Because He descended as the son of Vasudeva, one of His many names is Vāsudeva, and He has innumerable other names indicating His many qualities and activities.

Garga Muni had predicted that Kṛṣṇa would prevent all sorts of catastrophes in Gokula, spread unlimited auspiciousness, and increase the ecstasy of the cowherd men and women. In a previous age He had provided protection for the saintly *brāhmaṇas* when they were harassed by low-class dacoits and there was no proper ruler in society. As the demons in the higher planets can never defeat the demigods who have Lord Viṣṇu on their side, no enemy can ever defeat those who love Kṛṣṇa. In His affinity for His devotees and in His opulence and power, Kṛṣṇa is just like Lord Nārāyaṇa Himself.

Overjoyed and awestruck by Garga Muni's statements, the cowherd men concluded that Kṛṣṇa must be an empowered representative of the Supreme Lord, Nārāyaṇa. Thus they worshiped Him and Nanda Mahārāja.

## TEXT 1

श्रीशुक उवाच
एवंविधानि कर्माणि गोपाः कृष्णस्य वीक्ष्य ते ।
अतद्वीर्यविदः प्रोचुः समभ्येत्य सुविस्मिताः ॥१॥

*śrī-śuka uvāca*
*evaṁ-vidhāni karmāṇi*
*gopāḥ kṛṣṇasya vīkṣya te*
*atad-vīrya-vidaḥ procuḥ*
*samabhyetya su-vismitāḥ*

*śrī-śukaḥ uvāca*—Śrī Śukadeva Gosvāmī said; *evam-vidhāni*—like this; *karmāṇi*—activities; *gopāḥ*—the cowherd men; *kṛṣṇasya*—of Lord Kṛṣṇa; *vīkṣya*—seeing; *te*—they; *atat-vīrya-vidaḥ*—unable to understand His power; *procuḥ*—they spoke; *samabhyetya*—approaching (Nanda Mahārāja); *su-vismitāḥ*—very astonished.

### TRANSLATION

**Śukadeva Gosvāmī said: The cowherd men were astonished when they saw Kṛṣṇa's activities, such as lifting Govardhana Hill. Unable to understand His transcendental potency, they approached Nanda Mahārāja and spoke as follows.**

### PURPORT

Śrīla Viśvanātha Cakravartī Ṭhākura explains this verse as follows: "During Lord Kṛṣṇa's pastime of lifting Śrī Govardhana Hill, the cowherd men simply enjoyed the spiritual bliss of the Lord's activities without analyzing them. But afterwards, when they had returned to their homes, perplexity arose within their hearts. Thus they thought, 'Now we have directly seen child Kṛṣṇa lift Govardhana Hill, and we remember how He killed Pūtanā and other demons, extinguished the forest fire, and so on. At the time, we thought that these extraordinary acts occurred because of a benediction from the *brāhmaṇas* or because of Nanda Mahārāja's great fortune, or that perhaps this boy had achieved the mercy of Lord Nārāyaṇa and was thus empowered by Him.

"'But all these presumptions are false, because an ordinary seven-year-old boy could never hold up the king of mountains for seven whole days. Kṛṣṇa is not a human. He must be the Supreme Lord Himself.

"'But on the other hand, child Kṛṣṇa loves it when we coddle Him, and He becomes morose when we—His uncles and well-wishers, simply worldly cowherd men—do not give Him attention. He appears to become hungry and thirsty, steals yogurt and milk, sometimes plays tricks, tells lies, chatters childishly and tends the calves. If He is actually the Supreme Lord, why would He do these things? Don't these things indicate that He is an ordinary human child?

"'We are totally unable to establish the truth of His identity. Therefore let us go and inquire from the highly intelligent king of Vraja, Nanda Mahārāja, and he shall free us from our doubts.'"

According to Śrīla Viśvanātha Cakravartī Ṭhākura, the cowherd men thus made up their minds, and then they entered Nanda Mahārāja's great assembly hall and questioned him as described in the following verse.

## TEXT 2

बालकस्य यदेतानि कर्माण्यत्यद्भुतानि वै ।
कथमर्हत्यसौ जन्म ग्राम्येष्वात्मजुगुप्सितम् ॥२॥

*bālakasya yad etāni*
*karmāṇy aty-adbhutāni vai*
*katham arhaty asau janma*
*grāmyeṣv ātma-jugupsitam*

*bālakasya*—of the boy; *yat*—because; *etāni*—these; *karmāṇi*—activities; *ati-adbhutāni*—most amazing; *vai*—certainly; *katham*—how; *arhati*—should deserve; *asau*—He; *janma*—birth; *grāmyeṣu*—among worldly men; *ātma*—for Himself; *jugupsitam*—contemptible.

## TRANSLATION

**Since this boy performs such extraordinary activities, how could He warrant a birth among worldly men like ourselves—a birth that for Him would seem to be contemptible?**

## PURPORT

An ordinary living being cannot avoid unpleasant circumstances, but the supreme controller can always make perfect arrangements for His pleasure.

## TEXT 3

**यः सप्तहायनो बालः करेणैकेन लीलया ।**
**कथं बिभ्रद् गिरिवरं पुष्करं गजराडिव ॥३॥**

*yaḥ sapta-hāyano bālaḥ*
*kareṇaikena līlayā*
*kathaṁ bibhrad giri-varaṁ*
*puṣkaraṁ gaja-rāḍ iva*

*yaḥ*—who; *sapta-hāyanaḥ*—seven years of age; *bālaḥ*—a boy; *kareṇa*—with a hand; *ekena*—one; *līlayā*—playfully; *katham*—how; *bibhrat*—He held up; *giri-varam*—the best of mountains, Govardhana; *puṣkaram*—a lotus flower; *gaja-rāṭ*—a mighty elephant; *iva*—as.

## TRANSLATION

**How could this seven-year-old boy playfully hold up the great hill Govardhana with one hand, just as a mighty elephant holds up a lotus flower?**

## TEXT 4

**तोकेनामीलिताक्षेण पूतनाया महौजसः ।**
**पीतः स्तनः सह प्राणैः कालेनेव वयस्तनोः ॥४॥**

*tokenāmīlitākṣeṇa*
*pūtanāyā mahaujasaḥ*
*pītaḥ stanaḥ saha prāṇaiḥ*
*kāleneva vayas tanoḥ*

*tokena*—by the young child; *ā-mīlita*—almost closed; *akṣeṇa*—whose eyes; *pūtanāyāḥ*—of the witch Pūtanā; *mahā-ojasaḥ*—whose power was very great; *pītaḥ*—drunk; *stanaḥ*—the breast; *saha*—along with;

*prāṇaiḥ*—her life air; *kālena*—by the force of time; *iva*—as; *vayaḥ*—the life span; *tanoḥ*—of a material body.

## TRANSLATION

**As a mere infant who had hardly yet opened His eyes, He drank the breast milk of the powerful demoness Pūtanā and then sucked out her very life air as well, just as the force of time sucks out the youth of one's body.**

## PURPORT

The word *vayaḥ* in this verse indicates youth or life span in general. With irresistible power, time takes away our life, and that time is actually Lord Kṛṣṇa Himself. Thus in the case of the powerful witch Pūtanā, Lord Kṛṣṇa accelerated the time process and within an instant withdrew the duration of her life. Here the cowherd men mean to say, "How could a mere infant who could barely open His eyes so easily kill a very powerful demoness?"

## TEXT 5

हिन्वतोऽधः शयानस्य मास्यस्य चरणावुदक् ।
अनोऽपतद् विपर्यस्तं रुदतः प्रपदाहतम् ॥५॥

*hinvato 'dhaḥ śayānasya*
*māsyasya caraṇāv udak*
*ano 'patad viparyastaṁ*
*rudataḥ prapadāhatam*

*hinvataḥ*—moving; *adhaḥ*—beneath; *śayānasya*—of Him who was lying; *māsyasya*—the child only a few months old; *caraṇau*—His two feet; *udak*—upwards; *anaḥ*—the cart; *apatat*—fell; *viparyastam*—turned upside-down; *rudataḥ*—of Him who was crying; *prapada*—by the tip of the foot; *āhatam*—struck.

## TRANSLATION

**Once, when only three months old, little Kṛṣṇa was crying and kicking up His feet as He lay beneath a huge cart. Then the cart fell and turned upside-down simply because it was struck by the tip of His toe.**

## TEXT 6

एकहायन आसीनो ह्रियमाणो विहायसा ।
दैत्येन यस्तृणावर्तमहन् कण्ठग्रहातुरम् ॥६॥

*eka-hāyana āsīno*
*hriyamāṇo vihāyasā*
*daityena yas tṛṇāvartam*
*ahan kaṇṭha-grahāturam*

*eka-hāyanaḥ*—one year old; *āsīnaḥ*—sitting; *hriyamāṇaḥ*—being taken away; *vihāyasā*—in the sky; *daityena*—by the demon; *yaḥ*—who; *tṛṇāvartam*—named Tṛṇāvarta; *ahan*—killed; *kaṇṭha*—his neck; *graha*—by being seized; *āturam*—tormented.

## TRANSLATION

**At the age of one, while sitting peacefully He was taken up into the sky by the demon Tṛṇāvarta. But baby Kṛṣṇa grabbed the demon's neck, causing him great pain, and thus killed him.**

## PURPORT

The cowherd men, who loved Kṛṣṇa as an ordinary child, were astonished by all these activities. A newborn infant cannot ordinarily kill a powerful witch, and one would hardly think that a one-year-old baby could kill a demon who has kidnapped him and carried him up into the sky. But Kṛṣṇa did all of these wonderful things, and the cowherd men were enhancing their love for Him by remembering and discussing His activities.

## TEXT 7

क्वचिद्धैयंगवस्तैन्ये मात्रा बद्ध उदूखले ।
गच्छन्नर्जुनयोर्मध्ये बाहुभ्यां तावपातयत् ॥७॥

*kvacid dhaiyaṅgava-stainye*
*mātrā baddha udūkhale*

*gacchann arjunayor madhye*
*bāhubhyāṁ tāv apātayat*

*kvacit*—once; *haiyaṅgava*—butter; *stainye*—engaged in stealing; *mātrā*—by His mother; *baddhaḥ*—bound up; *udūkhale*—to a large mortar; *gacchan*—moving; *arjunayoḥ*—the twin *arjuna* trees; *madhye*—between; *bāhubhyām*—by His hands; *tau apātayat*—He made them fall.

### TRANSLATION

**Once, His mother tied Him with ropes to a mortar because she had caught Him stealing butter. Then, crawling on His hands, He dragged the mortar between a pair of *arjuna* trees and pulled them down.**

### PURPORT

The two *arjuna* trees were old and thick, and they towered above little Kṛṣṇa's courtyard. Nevertheless, they were pulled down quite easily by the naughty child.

### TEXT 8

वने सञ्चारयन् वत्सान् सरामो बालकैर्वृतः ।
हन्तुकामं बकं दोर्भ्यां मुखतोऽरिमपाटयत् ॥८॥

*vane sañcārayan vatsān*
*sa-rāmo bālakair vṛtaḥ*
*hantu-kāmaṁ bakaṁ dorbhyāṁ*
*mukhato 'rim apāṭayat*

*vane*—in the forest; *sañcārayan*—grazing; *vatsān*—the calves; *sa-rāmaḥ*—together with Lord Balarāma; *bālakaiḥ*—by the cowherd boys; *vṛtaḥ*—surrounded; *hantu-kāmam*—desiring to kill; *bakam*—the demon Baka; *dorbhyām*—with His arms; *mukhataḥ*—from the mouth; *arim*—the enemy; *apāṭayat*—tore apart.

### TRANSLATION

**Another time, when Kṛṣṇa was tending the calves in the forest**

**together with Balarāma and the cowherd boys, the demon Bakāsura came with the intention of killing Kṛṣṇa. But Kṛṣṇa seized this inimical demon by the mouth and tore him apart.**

### TEXT 9

वत्सेषु वत्सरूपेण प्रविशन्तं जिघांसया ।
हत्वा न्यपातयत्तेन कपित्थानि च लीलया ॥९॥

*vatseṣu vatsa-rūpeṇa*
*praviśantaṁ jighāṁsayā*
*hatvā nyapātayat tena*
*kapitthāni ca līlayā*

*vatseṣu*—among the calves; *vatsa-rūpeṇa*—appearing as if another calf; *praviśantam*—who had entered; *jighāṁsayā*—wanting to kill; *hatvā*—killing him; *nyapātayat*—He made to fall; *tena*—by him; *kapitthāni*—the *kapittha* fruits; *ca*—and; *līlayā*—as a sport.

### TRANSLATION

**Desiring to kill Kṛṣṇa, the demon Vatsa disguised himself as a calf and entered among Kṛṣṇa's calves. But Kṛṣṇa killed the demon and, using his body, enjoyed the sport of knocking *kapittha* fruits down from the trees.**

### TEXT 10

हत्वा रासभदैतेयं तद्बन्धूंश्च बलान्वितः ।
चक्रे तालवनं क्षेमं परिपक्वफलान्वितम् ॥१०॥

*hatvā rāsabha-daiteyaṁ*
*tad-bandhūṁś ca balānvitaḥ*
*cakre tāla-vanaṁ kṣemaṁ*
*paripakva-phalānvitam*

*hatvā*—killing; *rāsabha*—who appeared as a jackass; *daiteyam*—the descendant of Diti; *tat-bandhūn*—the demon's companions; *ca*—and;

*bala-anvitaḥ*—accompanied by Balarāma; *cakre*—He made; *tāla-vanam*—the Tālavana forest; *kṣemam*—auspicious; *paripakva*—fully ripened; *phala*—with fruits; *anvitam*—filled.

## TRANSLATION

**Together with Lord Balarāma, Kṛṣṇa killed the jackass demon and all his friends, thereby securing the safety of the Tālavana forest, which abounded with fully ripened palm fruits.**

## PURPORT

Long, long ago, the powerful demons Hiraṇyakaśipu and Hiraṇyākṣa were born of the goddess Diti. Therefore demons are commonly called *daiteyas* or *daityas,* meaning "descendants of Diti." Dhenukāsura, the ass demon, terrorized the Tāla forest with his friends, but Śrī Kṛṣṇa and Śrī Balarāma killed them just as modern governments kill terrorists who harass innocent people.

## TEXT 11

प्रलम्बं घातयित्वोग्रं बलेन बलशालिना ।
अमोचयद् व्रजपशून् गोपांश्चारण्यवह्नितः ॥११॥

*pralambaṁ ghātayitvograṁ*
*balena bala-śālinā*
*amocayad vraja-paśūn*
*gopāṁś cāraṇya-vahnitaḥ*

*pralambam*—the demon named Pralamba; *ghātayitvā*—arranging to be killed; *ugram*—terrible; *balena*—by Lord Balarāma; *bala-śālinā*—who is very powerful; *amocayat*—He liberated; *vraja-paśūn*—the animals of Vraja; *gopān*—the cowherd boys; *ca*—and; *āraṇya*—of the forest; *vahnitaḥ*—from the fire.

## TRANSLATION

**After arranging for the mighty Lord Balarāma to kill the terrible demon Pralamba, Kṛṣṇa freed Vraja's cowherd boys and their animals from a forest fire.**

## TEXT 12

आशीविषतमाहीन्द्रं दमित्वा विमदं ह्रदात् ।
प्रसह्योद्वास्य यमुनां चक्रेऽसौ निर्विषोदकाम् ॥१२॥

*āśī-viṣatamāhīndraṁ*
*damitvā vimadaṁ hradāt*
*prasahyodvāsya yamunāṁ*
*cakre 'sau nirviṣodakām*

*āśī*—of his fangs; *viṣa-tama*—having the most powerful poison; *ahi*—of the snakes; *indram*—the chief; *damitvā*—subduing; *vimadam*—whose pride was removed; *hradāt*—from the lake; *prasahya*—by force; *ud-vāsya*—sending him away; *yamunām*—the river Yamunā; *cakre*—made; *asau*—He; *nirviṣa*—free from poison; *udakām*—its water.

## TRANSLATION

**Kṛṣṇa chastised the most poisonous serpent, Kāliya, and after humbling him He drove him forcibly from the lake of the Yamunā. In this way the Lord made the water of that river free of the snake's powerful poison.**

## TEXT 13

दुस्त्यजश्चानुरागोऽस्मिन् सर्वेषां नो व्रजौकसाम् ।
नन्द ते तनयेऽस्मासु तस्याप्यौत्पत्तिकः कथम् ॥१३॥

*dustyajaś cānurāgo 'smin*
*sarveṣāṁ no vrajaukasām*
*nanda te tanaye 'smāsu*
*tasyāpy autpattikaḥ katham*

*dustyajaḥ*—impossible to give up; *ca*—and; *anurāgaḥ*—loving affection; *asmin*—for Him; *sarveṣām*—on the part of all; *naḥ*—us; *vraja-okasām*—the residents of Vraja; *nanda*—dear Nanda Mahārāja; *te*—your; *tanaye*—for the son; *asmāsu*—toward us; *tasya*—on His part; *api*—also; *autpattikaḥ*—natural; *katham*—how.

## TRANSLATION

**[The cowherd men continued:] Dear Nanda, how is it that we and all the other residents of Vraja cannot give up our constant affection for your son? And how is it that He is so spontaneously attracted to us?**

## PURPORT

The very word *kṛṣṇa* means "the all-attractive one." The residents of Vṛndāvana could not give up their constant love (*anurāga*) for Lord Kṛṣṇa. Their attitude toward Him was not particularly theistic, because they were unsure whether He was God or not. But He attracted all their love precisely because as God He is the all-attractive person, the supreme object of our love.

The cowherd men also asked, "How is it that young Kṛṣṇa feels such constant love for us?" In fact the Supreme Lord loves all living beings, who are eternally His children. At the end of the *Bhagavad-gītā*, Lord Kṛṣṇa dramatically declares His affection for Arjuna and urges Arjuna to reciprocate that love by surrendering to Him. Śrī Caitanya Mahāprabhu, in His prayers to Lord Kṛṣṇa, states, *etādṛśī tava kṛpā bhagavan mamāpi durdaivam īdṛśam ihājani nānurāgaḥ:* "My Lord, You are so merciful toward Me, but I am so unfortunate that love for You has not awakened within Me." (*Śikṣāṣṭaka* 2) In this statement Śrī Caitanya Mahāprabhu also uses the word *anurāga*. Our misfortune is that we cannot reciprocate the *anurāga*, or loving affection, that the Lord feels for us. Although we are infinitesimal and insignificant and the Lord is infinitely attractive, somehow we do not give Him our love. We must accept responsibility for this foolish decision, since to surrender to God or not is the essential expression of our free will.

The Kṛṣṇa consciousness movement provides an efficient, systematic program to help conditioned souls revive their original, blissful consciousness, which is love of God, Kṛṣṇa consciousness. The intricacies of Kṛṣṇa consciousness are so wonderful that even Kṛṣṇa's eternal associates, the residents of Vṛndāvana, are astonished by them, as shown by these verses.

## TEXT 14

क्व सप्तहायनो बालः क्व महाद्रिविधारणम् ।
ततो नो जायते शंका व्रजनाथ तवात्मजे ॥१४॥

*kva sapta-hāyano bālaḥ*
*kva mahādri-vidhāraṇam*
*tato no jāyate śaṅkā*
*vraja-nātha tavātmaje*

*kva*—where, in comparison; *sapta-hāyanaḥ*—seven years old; *bālaḥ*—this boy; *kva*—where; *mahā-adri*—of the great mountain; *vidhāraṇam*—the lifting; *tataḥ*—thus; *naḥ*—for us; *jāyate*—arises; *śaṅkā*—doubt; *vraja-nātha*—O master of Vraja; *tava*—your; *ātmaje*—concerning the son.

## TRANSLATION

**On the one hand this boy is only seven years old, and on the other we see that He has lifted the great hill Govardhana. Therefore, O King of Vraja, a doubt about your son arises within us.**

## TEXT 15

श्रीनन्द उवाच
श्रूयतां मे वचो गोपा व्येतु शंका च वोऽर्भके ।
एनं कुमारमुद्दिश्य गर्गो मे यदुवाच ह ॥१५॥

*śrī-nanda uvāca*
*śrūyatāṁ me vaco gopā*
*vyetu śaṅkā ca vo 'rbhake*
*enaṁ kumāram uddiśya*
*gargo me yad uvāca ha*

*śrī-nandaḥ uvāca*—Śrī Nanda Mahārāja said; *śrūyatām*—please hear; *me*—my; *vacaḥ*—words; *gopāḥ*—my dear cowherd men; *vyetu*—let it go away; *śaṅkā*—the doubt; *ca*—and; *vaḥ*—your; *arbhake*—concerning the boy; *enam*—this; *kumāram*—to the child; *uddiśya*—referring; *gargaḥ*—the sage Garga; *me*—to me; *yat*—which; *uvāca*—spoke; *ha*—in the past.

## TRANSLATION

**Nanda Mahārāja replied: O cowherd men, just hear my words and let all your doubts concerning my son be gone. Some time ago Garga Muni spoke to me as follows about this boy.**

## PURPORT

Śrīla Śrīdhara Svāmī comments, "The words previously heard from Gargācārya awakened Nanda Mahārāja to the truth about Kṛṣṇa, and thus, by Nanda's constantly remembering His activities, all thoughts about their being impossible ceased in him. Now he is instructing the cowherd men with these same words."

## TEXT 16

वर्णास्त्रयः किलास्यासन् गृह्णतोऽनुयुगं तनूः ।
शुक्लो रक्तस्तथा पीत इदानीं कृष्णतां गतः ॥१६॥

*varṇās trayaḥ kilāsyāsan*
*gṛhṇato 'nu-yugaṁ tanūḥ*
*śuklo raktas tathā pīta*
*idānīṁ kṛṣṇatāṁ gataḥ*

*varṇāḥ trayaḥ*—three colors; *kila*—indeed; *asya*—by your son Kṛṣṇa; *āsan*—were assumed; *gṛhṇataḥ*—accepting; *anu-yugam tanūḥ*—transcendental bodies according to the different *yugas; śuklaḥ*—sometimes white; *raktaḥ*—sometimes red; *tathā*—as well as; *pītaḥ*—sometimes yellow; *idānīm kṛṣṇatām gataḥ*—at the present moment He has assumed a blackish color.

## TRANSLATION

**Your son Kṛṣṇa appears as an incarnation in every millennium. In the past He assumed three different colors—white, red and yellow—and now He has appeared in a blackish color.**

## PURPORT

This and the next six verses (16 through 22) are taken from the eighth chapter of this canto, in which Garga Muni instructs Nanda Mahārāja about Nanda's son Kṛṣṇa. The translations found herein for these verses are based on those of His Divine Grace A. C. Bhaktivedanta Swami Prabhupāda. In Chapter Eight, where the verses originally appear, the reader will find extensive purports by Śrīla Prabhupāda.

## TEXT 17

प्रागयं वसुदेवस्य क्वचिज्जातस्तवात्मजः ।
वासुदेव इति श्रीमानभिज्ञाः सम्प्रचक्षते ॥१७॥

*prāg ayaṁ vasudevasya*
*kvacij jātas tavātmajaḥ*
*vāsudeva iti śrīmān*
*abhijñāḥ sampracakṣate*

*prāk*—before; *ayam*—this child; *vasudevasya*—of Vasudeva; *kvacit*—sometimes; *jātaḥ*—was born; *tava*—your; *ātmajaḥ*—Kṛṣṇa, who has taken birth as your child; *vāsudevaḥ*—therefore He may be given the name Vāsudeva; *iti*—thus; *śrīmān*—very beautiful; *abhijñāḥ*—those who are learned; *sampracakṣate*—also say that Kṛṣṇa is Vāsudeva.

## TRANSLATION

**For many reasons, this beautiful son of yours sometimes appeared previously as the son of Vasudeva. Therefore, those who are learned sometimes call this child Vāsudeva.**

## TEXT 18

बहूनि सन्ति नामानि रूपाणि च सुतस्य ते ।
गुणकर्मानुरूपाणि तान्यहं वेद नो जनाः ॥१८॥

*bahūni santi nāmāni*
*rūpāṇi ca sutasya te*
*guṇa-karmānurūpāṇi*
*tāny ahaṁ veda no janāḥ*

*bahūni*—various; *santi*—there are; *nāmāni*—names; *rūpāṇi*—forms; *ca*—also; *sutasya*—of the son; *te*—your; *guṇa-karma-anurūpāṇi*—according to His attributes and activities; *tāni*—them; *aham*—I; *veda*—know; *na u janāḥ*—not ordinary persons.

### TRANSLATION

**For this son of yours there are many forms and names according to His transcendental qualities and activities. These are known to me, but people in general do not understand them.**

### TEXT 19

एष वः श्रेय आधास्यद् गोपगोकुलनन्दनः ।
अनेन सर्वदुर्गाणि यूयमञ्जस्तरिष्यथ ॥१९॥

*eṣa vaḥ śreya ādhāsyad*
*gopa-gokula-nandanaḥ*
*anena sarva-durgāṇi*
*yūyam añjas tariṣyatha*

*eṣaḥ*—this child; *vaḥ*—for all of you people; *śreyaḥ ādhāsyat*—will act all-auspiciously; *gopa-gokula-nandanaḥ*—just like a cowherd boy born in a family of cowherd men as the son of the estate of Gokula; *anena*—by Him; *sarva-durgāṇi*—all kinds of miserable conditions; *yūyam*—all of you; *añjaḥ*—easily; *tariṣyatha*—will overcome.

### TRANSLATION

**To increase the transcendental bliss of the cowherd men of Gokula, this child will always act auspiciously for you. And by His grace only, you will surpass all difficulties.**

### TEXT 20

पुरानेन व्रजपते साधवो दस्युपीडिताः ।
अराजके रक्ष्यमाणा जिग्युर्दस्यून् समेधिताः ॥२०॥

*purānena vraja-pate*
*sādhavo dasyu-pīḍitāḥ*
*arājake rakṣyamāṇā*
*jigyur dasyūn samedhitāḥ*

*purā*—formerly; *anena*—by Kṛṣṇa; *vraja-pate*—O King of Vraja; *sādhavaḥ*—those who were honest; *dasyu-pīḍitāḥ*—being disturbed by rogues and thieves; *arājake*—when there was an irregular government; *rakṣyamāṇāḥ*—were protected; *jigyuḥ*—conquered; *dasyūn*—the rogues and thieves; *samedhitāḥ*—flourished.

## TRANSLATION

**O Nanda Mahārāja, as recorded in history, when there was an irregular, incapable government, Indra having been dethroned, and when honest people were being harassed and disturbed by thieves, this child appeared in order to curb the rogues and to protect the people and enable them to flourish.**

## TEXT 21

य एतस्मिन्महाभागे प्रीतिं कुर्वन्ति मानवाः ।
नारयोऽभिभवन्त्येतान् विष्णुपक्षानिवासुराः ॥२१॥

*ya etasmin mahā-bhāge*
*prītiṁ kurvanti mānavāḥ*
*nārayo 'bhibhavanty etān*
*viṣṇu-pakṣān ivāsurāḥ*

*ye*—those persons who; *etasmin*—unto this child; *mahā-bhāge*—most auspicious; *prītim*—affection; *kurvanti*—execute; *mānavāḥ*—such persons; *na*—not; *arayaḥ*—their enemies; *abhibhavanti*—do overcome; *etān*—those who are attached to Kṛṣṇa; *viṣṇu-pakṣān*—the demigods, who always have Lord Viṣṇu on their side; *iva*—like; *asurāḥ*—the demons.

## TRANSLATION

**Demons cannot harm the demigods, who always have Lord Viṣṇu on their side. Similarly, any person or group attached to all-auspicious Kṛṣṇa cannot be defeated by enemies.**

## PURPORT

Śrīla Prabhupāda has especially indicated in this connection that just as Lord Kṛṣṇa's associates could not be defeated by Kaṁsa, so His modern-day devotees will not be defeated by their demoniac opponents, nor will the Lord's devotees be defeated by the internal enemies—the lusty, materialistic senses.

## TEXT 22

तस्मान्नन्द कुमारोऽयं नारायणसमो गुणैः ।
श्रिया कीर्त्यानुभावेन तत्कर्मसु न विस्मयः ॥२२॥

*tasmān nanda kumāro 'yaṁ*
*nārāyaṇa-samo guṇaiḥ*
*śriyā kīrtyānubhāvena*
*tat-karmasu na vismayaḥ*

*tasmāt*—therefore; *nanda*—O Nanda Mahārāja; *kumāraḥ*—child; *ayam*—this; *nārāyaṇa-samaḥ*—is as good as Nārāyaṇa; *guṇaiḥ*—by His qualities; *śriyā*—by His opulence; *kīrtyā*—especially by His name and fame; *anubhāvena*—and by His influence; *tat*—His; *karmasu*—concerning the activities; *na*—there is no; *vismayaḥ*—surprise.

## TRANSLATION

**Therefore, O Nanda Mahārāja, this child of yours is as good as Nārāyaṇa. In His transcendental qualities, opulence, name, fame and influence, He is exactly like Nārāyaṇa. Thus you should not be astonished by His activities.**

## PURPORT

Nanda here reports to the cowherd men the concluding remarks of Garga Muni, who spoke at the secret birth ceremony of Lord Kṛṣṇa.

## TEXT 23

इत्यद्धा मां समादिश्य गर्गे च स्वगृहं गते ।
मन्ये नारायणस्यांशं कृष्णमक्लिष्टकारिणम् ॥२३॥

*ity addhā māṁ samādiśya*
*garge ca sva-gṛhaṁ gate*

*manye nārāyaṇasyāṁśaṁ*
*kṛṣṇam akliṣṭa-kāriṇam*

*iti*—thus speaking; *addhā*—directly; *mām*—me; *samādiśya*—advising; *garge*—Gargācārya; *ca*—and; *sva-gṛham*—to his home; *gate*—going; *manye*—I consider; *nārāyaṇasya*—of the Supreme Personality of Godhead, Nārāyaṇa; *aṁśam*—an empowered expansion; *kṛṣṇam*—Kṛṣṇa; *akliṣṭa-kāriṇam*—who keeps us free from misery.

## TRANSLATION

**[Nanda Mahārāja continued:] After Garga Ṛṣi spoke these words to me and returned home, I began to consider that Kṛṣṇa, who keeps us free from trouble, is actually an expansion of Lord Nārāyaṇa.**

## TEXT 24

इति नन्दवचः श्रुत्वा गर्गगीतं व्रजौकसः ।
मुदिता नन्दमानर्चुः कृष्णं च गतविस्मयाः ॥२४॥

*iti nanda-vacaḥ śrutvā*
*garga-gītaṁ vrajaukasaḥ*
*muditā nandam ānarcuḥ*
*kṛṣṇaṁ ca gata-vismayāḥ*

*iti*—thus; *nanda-vacaḥ*—the words of Nanda Mahārāja; *śrutvā*—hearing; *garga-gītam*—the statements of Garga Ṛṣi; *vraja-okasaḥ*—the residents of Vraja; *muditāḥ*—enlivened; *nandam*—Nanda Mahārāja; *ānarcuḥ*—they honored; *kṛṣṇam*—Lord Kṛṣṇa; *ca*—and; *gata*—gone; *vismayāḥ*—their perplexity.

## TRANSLATION

**[Śukadeva Gosvāmī continued:] Having heard Nanda Mahārāja relate the statements of Garga Muni, the residents of Vṛndāvana became enlivened. Their perplexity was gone, and they worshiped Nanda and Lord Kṛṣṇa with great respect.**

## PURPORT

Śrīla Jīva Gosvāmī explains that in this verse the word *ānarcuḥ* indicates that the residents of Vṛndāvana honored Nanda and Kṛṣṇa with such offerings as fragrances, garlands and garments brought from their homes. Śrīla Viśvanātha Cakravartī Ṭhākura adds that the residents of Vṛndāvana honored Nanda and Kṛṣṇa with loving offerings of jewels and gold coins. Apparently, Lord Kṛṣṇa was playing in the forest when this conversation took place, so when He returned home the residents of Vṛndāvana encouraged Him by decorating Him with beautiful yellow garments, necklaces, armlets, earrings and crowns, and by shouting, "All glories, all glories to the jewel of Vṛndāvana!"

## TEXT 25

**देवे वर्षति यज्ञविप्लवरुषा वज्राश्मवर्षानिलैः**
**सीदत्पालपशुस्त्रियात्मशरणं दृष्ट्वानुकम्प्युत्स्मयन् ।**
**उत्पाट्यैककरेण शैलमबलो लीलोच्छिलीन्ध्रं यथा**
**बिभ्रद् गोष्ठमपान्महेन्द्रमदभित् प्रीयान्न इन्द्रो गवाम् ॥२५॥**

*deve varṣati yajña-viplava-ruṣā vajrāśma-varṣānilaiḥ*
*sīdat-pāla-paśu-striy ātma-śaraṇaṁ dṛṣṭvānukampy utsmayan*
*utpāṭyaika-kareṇa śailam abalo līlocchilīndhraṁ yathā*
*bibhrad goṣṭham apān mahendra-mada-bhit prīyān na indro gavām*

*deve*—when the demigod Indra; *varṣati*—caused rain; *yajña*—of his sacrifice; *viplava*—due to the disturbances; *ruṣā*—out of anger; *vajra*—with lightning bolts; *aśma-varṣa*—hail; *anilaiḥ*—and winds; *sīdat*—suffering; *pāla*—the cowherds; *paśu*—animals; *stri*—and women; *ātma*—Himself; *śaraṇam*—being their only shelter; *dṛṣṭvā*—seeing; *anukampī*—very compassionate by nature; *utsmayan*—smiling broadly; *utpāṭya*—picking up; *eka-kareṇa*—in one hand; *śailam*—the hill, Govardhana; *abalaḥ*—a small child; *līlā*—in play; *ucchilīndhram*—a mushroom; *yathā*—just as; *bibhrat*—He held; *goṣṭham*—the cowherd community; *apāt*—He protected; *mahā-indra*—of King Indra; *mada*—of the false pride; *bhit*—the destroyer; *prīyāt*—may He be satisfied; *naḥ*—with us; *indraḥ*—the Lord; *gavām*—of the cows.

## TRANSLATION

**Indra became angry when his sacrifice was disrupted, and thus he caused rain and hail to fall on Gokula, accompanied by lightning and powerful winds, all of which brought great suffering to the cowherds, animals and women there. When Lord Kṛṣṇa, who is by nature always compassionate, saw the condition of those who had only Him as their shelter, He smiled broadly and lifted Govardhana Hill with one hand, just as a small child picks up a mushroom to play with it. In this way He protected the cowherd community. May He, Govinda, the Lord of the cows and the destroyer of Indra's false pride, be pleased with us.**

## PURPORT

The word *indra* means "lord" or "king." Thus in this verse Kṛṣṇa is pointedly called *indro gavām,* "the Lord of the cows." In fact, He is the real Indra, the real ruler, of everyone, and the demigods are merely His servants, representing His supreme will.

It is apparent from this and the previous verses in this chapter that Lord Kṛṣṇa's lifting of Govardhana Hill made quite an impression on the simple cowherd men of Vṛndāvana, and they repeatedly remembered this feat. Certainly anyone who soberly and objectively considers the activities of young Kṛṣṇa will surrender to Him and become His eternal devotee in loving devotional service. That is the rational conclusion one should come to after reading this chapter.

*Thus end the purports of the humble servant of His Divine Grace A. C. Bhaktivedanta Swami Prabhupāda to the Tenth Canto, Twenty-sixth Chapter, of the* Śrīmad-Bhāgavatam, *entitled "Wonderful Kṛṣṇa."*

CHAPTER TWENTY-SEVEN

# Lord Indra and Mother Surabhi Offer Prayers

This chapter describes how the Surabhi cow and Indra, having seen the amazing power of Lord Kṛṣṇa, performed a bathing ceremony for Him.

Fearing that Śrī Kṛṣṇa might be tired from lifting Govardhana Hill, Indra secretly came into His presence, offered obeisances and praised Him. Indra stated that although Śrī Kṛṣṇa is never caught in the current of material illusion, which is born of ignorance, He nevertheless accepts a humanlike body and performs various activities to establish religious principles and chastise the wicked. By this means He crushes the false prestige of those who presume themselves great controllers. Indra went on to declare that Kṛṣṇa is the father, *guru* and Lord of all living entities, and that in the form of time He is the agent of their punishment.

Satisfied with Indra's prayers, Śrī Kṛṣṇa told him that He had stopped the *indra-yajña* so that Indra, puffed up as he was with false pride, would remember the Lord. Persons intoxicated by material opulence never see Him standing before them with the rod of punishment in His hand. Therefore if Lord Kṛṣṇa desires the actual good fortune of some person, He brings him down from his position of opulence.

Lord Kṛṣṇa ordered Indra to return to his proper position in heaven and to serve there without egotism. Indra, along with the cow Surabhi, then performed a bathing ceremony for Kṛṣṇa, using the water of the heavenly Ganges and the milk of mother Surabhi. Indra and the cow took this opportunity to bestow upon the Lord the name Govinda, and the demigods showered flowers and recited various prayers.

## TEXT 1

श्रीशुक उवाच

**गोवर्धने धृते शैले आसाराद् रक्षिते व्रजे ।**
**गोलोकादाव्रजत् कृष्णं सुरभिः शक्र एव च ॥१॥**

*śrī-śuka uvāca*
*govardhane dhṛte śaile*
*āsārād rakṣite vraje*
*go-lokād āvrajat kṛṣṇaṁ*
*surabhiḥ śakra eva ca*

*śrī-śukaḥ uvāca*—Śrī Śukadeva Gosvāmī said; *govardhane*—Govardhana; *dhṛte*—having been held; *śaile*—the hill; *āsārāt*—from the rainfall; *rakṣite*—having been protected; *vraje*—Vraja; *go-lokāt*—from the planet of the cows; *āvrajat*—came; *kṛṣṇam*—to Kṛṣṇa; *surabhiḥ*—mother Surabhi; *śakraḥ*—Indra; *eva*—also; *ca*—and.

## TRANSLATION

**Śukadeva Gosvāmī said: After Kṛṣṇa had lifted Govardhana Hill and thus protected the inhabitants of Vraja from the terrible rainfall, Surabhi, the mother of the cows, came from her planet to see Kṛṣṇa. She was accompanied by Indra.**

## PURPORT

The word *go-lokāt* here indicates the material planet called Goloka, which is filled with exceptional cows. Surabhi went joyfully to see Lord Kṛṣṇa, but Indra went fearfully. As indicated by this verse, Lord Kṛṣṇa had to adopt extraordinary measures to protect His Vṛndāvana associates from Indra's obnoxious and offensive attack. Certainly Indra was ashamed, and also nervous about his future. Having acted improperly, he had fearfully gone to seek the shelter of Lord Brahmā, who then ordered him to take along Surabhi from the material Goloka planet and go to see Kṛṣṇa.

## TEXT 2

विविक्त उपसंगम्य व्रीडितः कृतहेलनः ।
पस्पर्श पादयोरेनं किरीटेनार्कवर्चसा ॥२॥

*vivikta upasaṅgamya*
*vrīḍitaḥ kṛta-helanaḥ*
*pasparśa pādayor enaṁ*
*kirīṭenārka-varcasā*

*vivikte*—in a solitary place; *upasaṅgamya*—approaching; *vrīḍitaḥ*—ashamed; *kṛta-helanaḥ*—having committed offense; *pasparśa*—he touched; *pādayoḥ*—upon His feet; *enam*—Him; *kirīṭena*—with his helmet; *arka*—like the sun; *varcasā*—the effulgence of which.

## TRANSLATION

**Indra was very ashamed of having offended the Lord. Approaching Him in a solitary place, Indra fell down and lay his helmet, whose effulgence was as brilliant as the sun, upon the Lord's lotus feet.**

## PURPORT

The specific "solitary place" where Indra approached Śrī Kṛṣṇa is mentioned by the sage Śrī Vaiśampāyana in the *Hari-vaṁśa* (*Viṣṇu-parva* 19.3): *sa dadarśopaviṣṭaṁ vai govardhana-śilā-tale.* "He saw Him [Kṛṣṇa] sitting at the base of Govardhana Hill."

From the commentaries of the *ācāryas* we understand that Lord Kṛṣṇa wanted to provide a solitary meeting for Indra so that he would not be further humiliated. Indra came to surrender and beg forgiveness, and the Lord allowed him to do so privately.

## TEXT 3

दृष्टश्रुतानुभावोऽस्य कृष्णस्यामिततेजसः ।
नष्टत्रिलोकेशमद इदमाह कृताञ्जलिः ॥३॥

*dṛṣṭa-śrutānubhāvo 'sya*
*kṛṣṇasyāmita-tejasaḥ*
*naṣṭa-tri-lokeśa-mada*
*idam āha kṛtāñjaliḥ*

*dṛṣṭa*—seen; *śruta*—heard; *anubhāvaḥ*—the power; *asya*—of this; *kṛṣṇasya*—Lord Kṛṣṇa; *amita*—immeasurable; *tejasaḥ*—whose potencies; *naṣṭa*—destroyed; *tri-loka*—of the three worlds; *īśa*—of being the lord; *madaḥ*—his intoxication; *idam*—these words; *āha*—spoke; *kṛta-añjaliḥ*—folding his hands in supplication.

## TRANSLATION

**Indra had now heard of and seen the transcendental power of omnipotent Kṛṣṇa, and his false pride in being the lord of the three worlds was thus defeated. Holding his hands together in supplication, he addressed the Lord as follows.**

## TEXT 4

इन्द्र उवाच
विशुद्धसत्त्वं तव धाम शान्तं
तपोमयं ध्वस्तरजस्तमस्कम् ।
मायामयोऽयं गुणसम्प्रवाहो
न विद्यते तेऽग्रहणानुबन्धः ॥४॥

*indra uvāca*
*viśuddha-sattvaṁ tava dhāma śāntaṁ*
*tapo-mayaṁ dhvasta-rajas-tamaskam*
*māyā-mayo 'yaṁ guṇa-sampravāho*
*na vidyate te 'grahaṇānubandhaḥ*

*indraḥ uvāca*—Indra said; *viśuddha-sattvam*—manifesting transcendental goodness; *tava*—Your; *dhāma*—form; *śāntam*—changeless; *tapaḥ-mayam*—full of knowledge; *dhvasta*—destroyed; *rajaḥ*—the mode of passion; *tamaskam*—and the mode of ignorance; *māyā-mayaḥ*—based on illusion; *ayam*—this; *guṇa*—of the modes of material nature; *sampravāhaḥ*—the great flux; *na vidyate*—is not present; *te*—within You; *agrahaṇa*—ignorance; *anubandhaḥ*—which is due to.

## TRANSLATION

**King Indra said: Your transcendental form, a manifestation of pure goodness, is undisturbed by change, shining with knowledge and devoid of passion and ignorance. In You does not exist the mighty flow of the modes of material nature, which is based on illusion and ignorance.**

## PURPORT

The great *Bhāgavatam* commentator Śrīla Śrīdhara Svāmī has masterfully explained the Sanskrit elements of this profound verse.

The Sanskrit word *dhāma* has several meanings: a) dwelling place, house, abode and so on; b) a favorite thing or person; delight; or pleasure; c) form or appearance; d) power, strength, majesty, glory, splendor or light.

Concerning the first set of meanings, the *Vedānta-sūtra* states that the Absolute Truth is the source and resting place of all existence, and in the first verse of the *Bhāgavatam* that Absolute Truth is said to be Kṛṣṇa. Although Lord Kṛṣṇa exists in His own *dhāma,* or abode, called Kṛṣṇaloka, He Himself is the abode of all existence, as Arjuna confirms in the *Bhagavad-gītā,* where he addresses Kṛṣṇa as *paraṁ dhāma,* "the supreme abode."

The very name Kṛṣṇa indicates the all-attractive person, and thus Lord Kṛṣṇa, the source of all beauty and pleasure, is certainly "the favorite thing or person; delight; and pleasure." Ultimately these terms can refer only to Kṛṣṇa.

*Dhāma* also refers to form or appearance, and as Indra offered these prayers he was in fact directly seeing the form of Kṛṣṇa before him.

As clearly explained in the Vedic literature, Lord Kṛṣṇa's power, strength, majesty, splendor and effulgence are all contained within His transcendental body and thus attest to the infinite glories of the Lord.

Śrīla Śrīdhara Svāmī has brilliantly summarized all these meanings of the word *dhāma* by giving the Sanskrit term *svarūpa* as a synonym. The word *svarūpa* means "one's own form or shape" and also "one's own condition, character or nature." Since Lord Kṛṣṇa, being pure, absolute spirit, is nondifferent from His body, there is absolutely no difference between the Lord and His visible form. By contrast, in this material world we conditioned souls are all distinctly different from our bodies, whether those bodies be male, female, black, white or whatever. All of us are eternal souls, different from our temporary, flimsy bodies.

When the word *svarūpa* is applied to us, it especially indicates our spiritual form, because our "own form" is in fact our "own condition, character or nature" eternally. Thus the liberated condition in which one's outward form is one's deepest spiritual nature is called *svarūpa.* Primarily, however, this term refers to the Supreme Personality of Godhead, Śrī Kṛṣṇa. This is all indicated in this verse by the words *tava dhāma,* as explained by Śrīdhara Svāmī.

Śrīdhara Svāmī has explained that here the word *śāntam* means "always in the same form." *Śāntam* can also mean "undisturbed, free from passion, or purified." According to Vedic philosophy, all change in this world is caused by the influence of passion and ignorance. The passionate mode is creative, and the ignorant mode is destructive, whereas the mode of goodness, *sattva,* is serene and sustaining. In many ways this verse emphasizes that Lord Kṛṣṇa is free from the modes of nature. The words *viśuddha-sattvam, śāntam, dhvasta-rajas-tamaskam* and *guṇa-sampravāho na vidyate te* all indicate this. Unlike Kṛṣṇa, we change from one body to another because of our involvement with the modes of nature; the various transformations of material forms are impelled by the modes of nature, which are themselves set in motion by the influence of time. Therefore one who is free from the material modes of nature is changeless and eternally satisfied in blissful spiritual existence. Thus the word *śāntam* indicates that the Lord is undisturbed by change, since He is free from the material modes of nature.

According to this verse, the powerful flow of the material modes of nature—namely passion, stupidity and mundane piety—are based on *agrahaṇa,* which Śrīla Śrīdhara Svāmī has translated as "ignorance." Since the Sanskrit root *grah* means "to take, accept, grasp or comprehend," *grahaṇa* means "grasp" exactly in the sense of "to grasp an idea or fact." Therefore *agrahaṇa* here means one's failure to understand one's spiritual position, and this failure causes one to fall into the violent currents of material existence.

An additional meaning of the word *agrahaṇa* is derived when it is divided into the compound *agra-haṇa. Agra* means "the first, top or best," and *hana* means "killing." The best part of our existence is the pure soul, which is eternal, in contradistinction to the temporary, material body and mind. Thus one who chooses material existence over Kṛṣṇa consciousness is in fact killing the best part of himself, the soul, which in its pure state can enjoy Kṛṣṇa consciousness unlimitedly.

Śrīla Śrīdhara Svāmī has translated *tapo-mayam* as "full of knowledge." The word *tapas,* generally indicating "austerity," is derived from the Sanskrit verb *tap,* whose meaning can be summarized as indicating the various functions of the sun. *Tap* means "to burn, to shine, to heat and so on." The Supreme Lord is eternally perfect, and therefore here *tapo-mayam* does not indicate that His transcendental body is meant for austerities, since austerities are performed by conditioned souls to purify themselves or to acquire a particular power. An omnipotent, perfect being neither purifies Himself nor acquires power: He is eternally pure and all-powerful. Therefore Śrīdhara Svāmī has intelligently understood that in this case the word *tapas* refers to the illuminating function of the sun and thus indicates that the Lord's self-effulgent body is omniscient. Light is a common symbol of knowledge. The Lord's spiritual effulgence does not merely illuminate physically, as in the case of a candle or light bulb; more importantly, the Lord's body illuminates our consciousness with perfect knowledge because the Lord's effulgence is itself perfect knowledge.

We offer our respectful obeisances at the lotus feet of Śrīla Śrīdhara Svāmī and thank him for his enlightening comments on this verse.

## TEXT 5

कुतो नु तद्धेतव ईश तत्कृता
लोभादयो येऽबुधलिंगभावाः ।
तथापि दण्डं भगवान् बिभर्ति
धर्मस्य गुप्त्यै खलनिग्रहाय ॥५॥

*kuto nu tad-dhetava īśa tat-kṛtā*
*lobhādayo ye 'budha-liṅga-bhāvāḥ*
*tathāpi daṇḍaṁ bhagavān bibharti*
*dharmasya guptyai khala-nigrahāya*

*kutaḥ*—how; *nu*—certainly; *tat*—of that (existence of the material body); *hetavaḥ*—the causes; *īśa*—O Lord; *tat-kṛtāḥ*—produced by one's connection with the material body; *lobha-ādayaḥ*—greed and so forth; *ye*—which; *abudha*—of an ignorant person; *liṅga-bhāvāḥ*—symptoms; *tathā api*—nevertheless; *daṇḍam*—punishment; *bhagavān*—the Supreme Personality of Godhead; *bibharti*—wields; *dharmasya*—of the principles of religion; *guptyai*—for the protection; *khala*—of wicked persons; *nigrahāya*—for the chastisement.

## TRANSLATION

**How, then, could there exist in You the symptoms of an ignorant**

**person—such as greed, lust, anger and envy—which are produced by one's previous involvement in material existence and which cause one to become further entangled in material existence? And yet as the Supreme Lord You impose punishment to protect religious principles and curb down the wicked.**

## PURPORT

This complex philosophical statement by Indra may be analyzed as follows: In the first line of this verse, Indra refers to the main idea expressed at the end of the previous verse—namely, that the great currents of material existence, which are based on ignorance, cannot possibly exist within the Supreme Lord. The words *tad-dhetavaḥ* and *tat-kṛtāḥ* indicate that something causes the modes of nature to manifest, and that they in turn become the cause of that which caused them. In the second line of this verse, we find that it is material feelings such as greed, lust, envy and anger that cause the modes of nature to manifest and that are themselves caused by the modes of nature.

The explanation of this seeming paradox is as follows: When the conditioned soul decides to associate with the material qualities, he becomes contaminated by those qualities. As stated in the *Gītā* (13.22), *kāraṇaṁ guṇa-saṅgo 'sya sad-asad-yoni-janmasu.* For example, in the presence of a seductive woman, a man may give in to his lower instincts and try to enjoy sex with her. By his deciding to associate with the lower qualities of nature, those qualities manifest in him very powerfully. He is overwhelmed with lust and driven to try again and again to satisfy his burning desire. Because his mind has been infected by lust, all that he does, thinks and speaks will be influenced by his strong attachment to sex. In other words, by choosing to associate with the lusty qualities of nature, he has caused them to powerfully manifest within himself, and eventually those lusty qualities themselves will cause him to accept another material body suitable for affairs governed by those qualities.

The lower qualities, such as lust, greed, anger and envy, are *abudha-liṅga-bhāvāḥ,* symptoms of ignorance. Indeed, as indicated by Śrīla Śrīdhara Svāmī in his commentary, the manifestation of the modes of nature is synonymous with the manifestation of a particular material body. It is clearly explained throughout Vedic literature that the conditioned soul receives a particular body, gives it up and then accepts another all because of his involvement with the modes of nature (*kāraṇaṁ guṇa-saṅgo 'sya*). Thus to say that one is participating in the modes of nature is to say that one is accepting particular types of bodies suitable for the particular material qualities one is involved with.

An ignorant bystander might have simplistically interpreted Kṛṣṇa's pastime of lifting Govardhana Hill as follows: The residents of Vṛndāvana were obliged by Vedic principles to make certain offerings to the god of heaven, Indra. Child Kṛṣṇa, ignoring the position of Indra, usurped these offerings and took them for His own pleasure. When Indra tried to punish Kṛṣṇa and His associates, the Lord frustrated Indra's attempt, humiliated him, and exhausted his pride and resources.

But this superficial interpretation is refuted in this verse. Here Lord Indra addresses Śrī Kṛṣṇa as *bhagavān,* indicating that He is not an ordinary child but in fact God. Therefore Kṛṣṇa's punishing Indra was part of His mission of protecting religious principles and curbing down the envious; it was not a display of material anger or of greed for the offerings meant for Indra. Śrī Kṛṣṇa is pure spiritual existence, and His simple, sublime desire is to engage all living beings in the perfect, blissful life of Kṛṣṇa consciousness. Kṛṣṇa's desire to make us Kṛṣṇa conscious is not egotistical, since ultimately Kṛṣṇa is everything and Kṛṣṇa consciousness is objectively the best consciousness. Lord Indra is really the humble servant of Kṛṣṇa, a fact he is now beginning to remember.

## TEXT 6

पिता गुरुस्त्वं जगतामधीशो
दुरत्ययः काल उपात्तदण्डः ।
हिताय चेच्छातनुभिः समीहसे
मानं विधुन्वन् जगदीशमानिनाम् ॥६॥

*pitā gurus tvaṁ jagatām adhīśo*
*duratyayaḥ kāla upātta-daṇḍaḥ*
*hitāya cecchā-tanubhiḥ samīhase*
*mānaṁ vidhunvan jagad-īśa-māninām*

*pitā*—the father; *guruḥ*—the spiritual master; *tvam*—You; *jagatām*—of the entire universe; *adhīśaḥ*—the supreme controller; *duratyayaḥ*—insurmountable; *kālaḥ*—time; *upātta*—wielding; *daṇḍaḥ*—punishment;

*hitāya*—for the benefit; *ca*—and; *icchā*—assumed by Your own free will; *tanubhiḥ*—by Your transcendental forms; *samīhase*—You endeavor; *mānam*—the false pride; *vidhunvan*—eradicating; *jagat-īśa*—lords of the universe; *māninām*—of those who presume themselves to be.

## TRANSLATION

**You are the father and spiritual master of this entire universe, and also its supreme controller. You are insurmountable time, imposing punishment upon the sinful for their own benefit. Indeed, in Your various incarnations, selected by Your own free will, You act decisively to remove the false pride of those who presume themselves masters of this world.**

## PURPORT

The word *hitāya* is significant here. Lord Kṛṣṇa protects religion and chastises the wicked for the benefit of the entire universe. Foolish and faithless pseudopriests criticize God for punishing the living entities through the actions of nature. But whether Lord Kṛṣṇa punishes them indirectly through nature or directly in His incarnations, as mentioned here, He has a perfect right to do so because He is the father, spiritual master and supreme ruler of the entire universe. Another way He curbs down the false attempts of the conditioned souls to establish the kingdom of God without God is through His feature as insurmountable time. It is said, "Spare the rod and spoil the child." That is a fact, and it is actually the Lord's mercy that He takes the trouble to rectify our misbehavior, although faithless persons criticize the Lord's fatherly vigilance.

## TEXT 7

ये मद्विधाज्ञा जगदीशमानिनस्
त्वां वीक्ष्य कालेऽभयमाशु तन्मदम् ।
हित्वार्यमार्गं प्रभजन्त्यपस्मया
ईहा खलानामपि तेऽनुशासनम् ॥७॥

*ye mad-vidhājñā jagad-īśa-māninas*
*tvāṁ vīkṣya kāle 'bhayam āśu tan-madam*

*hitvārya-mārgaṁ prabhajanty apasmayā*
*īhā khalānām api te 'nuśāsanam*

*ye*—those who; *mat-vidha*—like me; *ajñāḥ*—foolish persons; *jagat-īśa*—as lords of the universe; *māninaḥ*—falsely identifying themselves; *tvām*—You; *vīkṣya*—seeing; *kāle*—at time (of fear); *abhayam*—fearless; *āśu*—quickly; *tat*—their; *madam*—false pride; *hitvā*—abandoning; *ārya*—of devotees progressing in spiritual life; *mārgam*—the path; *prabhajanti*—they take to fully; *apa-smayāḥ*—free of pride; *īhā*—the activity; *khalānām*—of the wicked; *api*—indeed; *te*—by You; *anuśāsanam*—the instruction.

## TRANSLATION

**Even fools like me, who proudly think themselves universal lords, quickly give up their conceit and directly take to the path of the spiritually progressive when they see You are fearless even in the face of time. Thus You punish the mischievous only to instruct them.**

## PURPORT

History is filled with examples of the supreme authority breaking the conceit of foolish men. Modern world leaders proudly fight one another, placing the common people in unprecedented jeopardy. Similarly Indra, proud of his apparently illustrious position, dared to threaten the lives of the innocent residents of Vṛndāvana with terrible weapons, until his arrogance was curbed by the dynamic response of the Supreme Lord.

Nowadays, governments in the Western countries tend to be elected democratically, and thus the mass of people become identified with the destiny of their leaders. When the proud leaders engage in violence, the people who elected them bear the brunt of such belligerent decisions. Thus the people in the democratic nations of the world should elect Kṛṣṇa conscious leaders, who will establish an administration consonant with the laws of God. If they fail to do so, their materialistic leaders, oblivious of the will of the Supreme Lord, will undoubtedly be chastised by cataclysmic events, and the people who elected such leaders, being responsible for their leaders' acts, will share in the suffering.

It is ironic that in modern democracies not only do the leaders consider themselves universal controllers, but the mass of people, considering the leaders merely *their* representatives rather than the representatives of God, also consider themselves, as a people, to be the controllers of their nation. Thus the chastisement mentioned in this verse has become unprecedentedly applicable to people in general in the modern world.

Modern man should not simply make himself a lesson of nature by falling down from his proud position; rather he should submissively execute the will of the all-attractive Personality of Godhead, the Absolute Truth, Śrī Kṛṣṇa, and usher in a new era of sanity, tranquillity and widespread enlightenment.

## TEXT 8

स त्वं ममैश्वर्यमदप्लुतस्य
कृतागसस्तेऽविदुषः प्रभावम् ।
क्षन्तुं प्रभोऽथार्हसि मूढचेतसो
मैवं पुनर्भून्मतिरीश मेऽसती ॥८॥

*sa tvaṁ mamaiśvarya-mada-plutasya*
*kṛtāgasas te 'viduṣaḥ prabhāvam*
*kṣantuṁ prabho 'thārhasi mūḍha-cetaso*
*maivaṁ punar bhūn matir īśa me 'satī*

*saḥ*—He; *tvam*—Yourself; *mama*—of me; *aiśvarya*—of rulership; *mada*—in the intoxication; *plutasya*—who is submerged; *kṛta*—having committed; *āgasaḥ*—sinful offense; *te*—Your; *aviduṣaḥ*—not knowing; *prabhāvam*—the transcendental influence; *kṣantum*—to forgive; *prabho*—O master; *atha*—therefore; *arhasi*—You should; *mūḍha*—foolish; *cetasaḥ*—whose intelligence; *mā*—never; *evam*—thus; *punaḥ*—again; *bhūt*—may it be; *matiḥ*—consciousness; *īśa*—O Lord; *me*—my; *asatī*—impure.

## TRANSLATION

**Engrossed in pride over my ruling power, ignorant of Your majesty, I offended You. O Lord, may You forgive me. My intelligence was bewildered, but let my consciousness never again be so impure.**

## PURPORT

Although Lord Kṛṣṇa protected the residents of Vraja by lifting Govardhana Hill, He had not yet punished Indra himself, and Indra feared that at any moment Śrī Kṛṣṇa might call the son of Vivasvān, Yamarāja, who punishes impudent persons who defy the laws of God.

Indra was quite fearful and thus begged the Lord's forgiveness on the plea that he could be purified only by Kṛṣṇa's mercy—that he was too stubborn to learn a good lesson through mere punishment.

In fact, despite Indra's humility in this case, his heart was not completely purified. Later on in this canto we find that when Lord Kṛṣṇa once took a *pārijāta* flower from Indra's kingdom, poor Indra again reacted violently against the Supreme Personality of Godhead. Thus, we should aspire to go back to our eternal home in the kingdom of Kṛṣṇa, and should not become entangled in the imperfect life of the material gods.

## TEXT 9

तवावतारोऽयमधोक्षजेह
भुवो भराणामुरुभारजन्मनाम् ।
चमूपतीनामभवाय देव
भवाय युष्मच्चरणानुवर्तिनाम् ॥९॥

*tavāvatāro 'yam adhokṣajeha*
*bhuvo bharāṇām uru-bhāra-janmanām*
*camū-patīnām abhavāya deva*
*bhavāya yuṣmac-caraṇānuvartinām*

*tava*—Your; *avatāraḥ*—descent; *ayam*—this; *adhokṣaja*—O transcendental Lord; *iha*—into this world; *bhuvaḥ*—of the earth; *bharāṇām*—who constitute a great burden; *uru-bhāra*—to many disturbances; *janmanām*—who have given rise; *camū-patīnām*—of military leaders; *abhavāya*—for the destruction; *deva*—O Supreme Personality of Godhead; *bhavāya*—for the auspicious benefit; *yuṣmat*—Your; *caraṇa*—lotus feet; *anuvartinām*—of those who serve.

## TRANSLATION

**You descend into this world, O transcendent Lord, to destroy**

**the warlords who burden the earth and create many terrible disturbances. O Lord, you simultaneously act for the welfare of those who faithfully serve Your lotus feet.**

## PURPORT

This verse utilizes an attractive poetic device. Lord Kṛṣṇa's descent into the world is said to be for the *abhava,* literally "nonexistence" or "destruction," of the demoniac warlords, and simultaneously for the *bhava,* or "existence, prosperity," of those who faithfully serve the Lord's lotus feet.

True existence, indicated here by the word *bhava,* is *sac-cid-ānanda,* eternal and full of bliss and knowledge. To an uninformed observer, it may appear that Śrī Kṛṣṇa is simply rewarding His followers and punishing His enemies the way any ordinary person might do. This specific doubt about the Lord is raised extensively in the Sixth Canto in connection with Kṛṣṇa's taking the side of the faithful demigods against the faithless demons in a particular cosmic war. In that canto the Vaiṣṇava authorities clearly explain that in fact Lord Kṛṣṇa is the father and Lord of all living beings and that all His activities are therefore meant for the benefit of all existence. Lord Kṛṣṇa does not really cause the nonexistence of anyone; rather He curbs the foolish, destructive, material ways of those who defy the laws of God. These laws are created to ensure the prosperity, harmony and happiness of the entire creation, and their violation is an unjustifiable disturbance.

Certainly Indra hoped that Lord Kṛṣṇa would count him among the devotees and not the demons, although considering Indra's actions one might doubt where his loyalties actually lay. Indra was aware of this possible doubt and thus, as we find in the next verse, he tried his best to surrender to the Supreme Lord.

## TEXT 10

नमस्तुभ्यं भगवते पुरुषाय महात्मने ।
वासुदेवाय कृष्णाय सात्वतां पतये नमः ॥१०॥

*namas tubhyaṁ bhagavate*
*puruṣāya mahātmane*

*vāsudevāya kṛṣṇāya*
*sātvatāṁ pataye namaḥ*

*namaḥ*—obeisances; *tubhyam*—unto You; *bhagavate*—the Supreme Personality of Godhead; *puruṣāya*—the Lord dwelling within the hearts of all; *mahā-ātmane*—the great Soul; *vāsudevāya*—to Him who dwells everywhere; *kṛṣṇāya*—Śrī Kṛṣṇa; *sātvatām*—of the Yadu dynasty; *pataye*—to the master; *namaḥ*—obeisances.

## TRANSLATION

**Obeisances unto You, the Supreme Personality of Godhead, the great Soul, who are all-pervading and who reside in the hearts of all. My obeisances unto You, Kṛṣṇa, the chief of the Yadu dynasty.**

## TEXT 11

स्वच्छन्दोपात्तदेहाय विशुद्धज्ञानमूर्तये ।
सर्वस्मै सर्वबीजाय सर्वभूतात्मने नमः ॥११॥

*svacchandopātta-dehāya*
*viśuddha-jñāna-mūrtaye*
*sarvasmai sarva-bījāya*
*sarva-bhūtātmane namaḥ*

*sva*—of His own (devotees); *chanda*—according to the desire; *upātta*—who assumes; *dehāya*—His transcendental bodies; *viśuddha*—perfectly pure; *jñāna*—knowledge; *mūrtaye*—whose form; *sarvasmai*—to Him who is everything; *sarva-bījāya*—who is the seed of all; *sarva-bhūta*—of all created beings; *ātmane*—who is the indwelling Soul; *namaḥ*—obeisances.

## TRANSLATION

**Unto Him who assumes transcendental bodies according to the desires of His devotees, unto Him whose form is itself pure consciousness, unto Him who is everything, who is the seed of everything and who is the Soul of all creatures, I offer my obeisances.**

## PURPORT

We could hardly construe from the first line of this verse that God is somehow impersonal but assumes a personal material body. It is clearly said here that the Lord assumes different forms according to *sva-cchanda*—according to His own desire or according to the desires of His devotees. An impersonal God could hardly reciprocate with the personal desires of Its devotees, nor could an impersonal God Itself have desires, since desire is characteristic of personality. Therefore, the Lord's manifesting different forms in a personal way, responding to personal desires, indicates that He is eternally a person and manifests His different transcendental bodies as an expression of His own eternal nature.

The word *viśuddha-jñāna-mūrtaye* is most significant. *Mūrti* means the form of the Deity, and it is specifically stated here that the Lord's form is itself completely pure consciousness. Consciousness is the primary spiritual element, distinct from any of the material elements, and even distinct from the subtle or psychological material elements—mundane mind, intelligence and false ego—which are simply a psychic covering over pure consciousness. Since the Lord's form is made of pure consciousness, it can hardly be understood as a material body like the mortal bags of flesh and bones we carry around in this world.

In the last two lines of this verse, there is poetic emphasis on the word *sarva*, "everything." The Lord is everything: He is the seed of everything and He is the Soul of every creature. Therefore, let us join with Indra in offering our obeisances to the Lord.

## TEXT 12

**मयेदं भगवन् गोष्ठनाशायासारवायुभिः ।**
**चेष्टितं विहते यज्ञे मानिना तीव्रमन्युना ॥१२॥**

*mayedaṁ bhagavan goṣṭha-*
*nāśāyāsāra-vāyubhiḥ*
*ceṣṭitaṁ vihate yajñe*
*māninā tīvra-manyunā*

*mayā*—by me; *idam*—this; *bhagavan*—O Lord; *goṣṭha*—of Your cowherd community; *nāśāya*—for the destruction; *āsāra*—by hard rain;

*vāyubhiḥ*—and wind; *ceṣṭitam*—enacted; *vihate*—when it was disrupted; *yajñe*—my sacrifice; *māninā*—(by me) who was falsely proud; *tīvra*—fierce; *manyunā*—whose anger.

### TRANSLATION

**My dear Lord, when my sacrifice was disrupted I became fiercely angry because of false pride. Thus I tried to destroy Your cowherd community with severe rain and wind.**

### TEXT 13

त्वयेशानुगृहीतोऽस्मि ध्वस्तस्तम्भो वृथोद्यमः ।
ईश्वरं गुरुमात्मानं त्वामहं शरणं गतः ॥१३॥

*tvayeśānugṛhīto 'smi*
*dhvasta-stambho vṛthodyamaḥ*
*īśvaraṁ gurum ātmānaṁ*
*tvām ahaṁ śaraṇaṁ gataḥ*

*tvayā*—by You; *īśa*—O Lord; *anugṛhītaḥ*—shown mercy; *asmi*—I am; *dhvasta*—shattered; *stambhaḥ*—my false pride; *vṛthā*—fruitless; *udyamaḥ*—my attempt; *īśvaram*—the Supreme Lord; *gurum*—the spiritual master; *ātmānam*—the true Self; *tvām*—to You; *aham*—I; *śaraṇam*—for shelter; *gataḥ*—have come.

### TRANSLATION

**O Lord, You have shown mercy to me by shattering my false pride and defeating my attempt [to punish Vṛndāvana]. To You, the Supreme Lord, spiritual master and Supreme Soul, I have now come for shelter.**

### TEXT 14

श्रीशुक उवाच
एवं संकीर्तितः कृष्णो मघोना भगवानमुम् ।
मेघगम्भीरया वाचा प्रहसन्निदमब्रवीत् ॥१४॥

*śrī-śuka uvāca*
*evaṁ saṅkīrtitaḥ kṛṣṇo*
*maghonā bhagavān amum*
*megha-gambhīrayā vācā*
*prahasann idam abravīt*

*śrī-śukaḥ uvāca*—Śrī Śukadeva Gosvāmī said; *evam*—in this manner; *saṅkīrtitaḥ*—glorified; *kṛṣṇaḥ*—Lord Kṛṣṇa; *maghonā*—by Indra; *bhagavān*—the Supreme Personality of Godhead; *amum*—to him; *megha*—like the clouds; *gambhīrayā*—grave; *vācā*—with words; *prahasan*—smiling; *idam*—the following; *abravīt*—spoke.

## TRANSLATION

**Śukadeva Gosvāmī said: Thus glorified by Indra, Lord Kṛṣṇa, the Supreme Personality of Godhead, smiled and then spoke to him as follows in a voice resonant like the clouds.**

## PURPORT

Although in this pastime Lord Kṛṣṇa appeared to be a small boy, the words *megha-gambhīrayā vācā* indicate that He spoke to Indra with the deep, resonant voice of the Supreme Lord.

## TEXT 15

श्रीभगवानुवाच
मया तेऽकारि मघवन्मखभंगोऽनुगृह्णता ।
मदनुस्मृतये नित्यं मत्तस्येन्द्रश्रिया भृशम् ॥१५॥

*śrī-bhagavān uvāca*
*mayā te 'kāri maghavan*
*makha-bhaṅgo 'nugṛhṇatā*
*mad-anusmṛtaye nityaṁ*
*mattasyendra-śriyā bhṛśam*

*śrī-bhagavān uvāca*—the Supreme Personality of Godhead said; *mayā*—by Me; *te*—unto you; *akāri*—has been done; *maghavan*—My dear Indra; *makha*—of your sacrifice; *bhaṅgaḥ*—the stopping; *anugṛhṇatā*—acting to show mercy to you; *mat-anusmṛtaye*—for the sake of remembrance of Me; *nityam*—constant; *mattasya*—of one intoxicated; *indra-śriyā*—with the opulence of Indra; *bhṛśam*—greatly.

### TRANSLATION

**The Supreme Personality of Godhead said: My dear Indra, it was out of mercy that I stopped the sacrifice meant for you. You were greatly intoxicated by your opulence as King of heaven, and I wanted you to always remember Me.**

### PURPORT

According to Śrīdhara Svāmī, Indra and Lord Kṛṣṇa here exchange a heart-to-heart talk. Indra revealed his mind to the Lord, and now Lord Kṛṣṇa similarly reveals His own intention.

In Text 11 of this chapter, Indra emphatically declared that Lord Kṛṣṇa is in fact everything, and thus, according to Indra's own criteria, forgetting Lord Kṛṣṇa is clearly a state of insanity. When the Supreme Lord reminds us of His supreme existence, He is not proudly advertising Himself like a mundane politician or entertainer. The Lord is self-satisfied in His own infinite existence and is trying, lovingly, to bring us back to our own perfect existence as His eternal associates.

From God's point of view even the mighty King of heaven, Indra, is a mere child—and a naughty child at that—and thus the Lord, being a caring father, punished His child and brought him back to the sanity of Kṛṣṇa consciousness.

### TEXT 16

**मामैश्वर्यश्रीमदान्धो दण्डपाणिं न पश्यति ।**
**तं भ्रंशयामि सम्पद्भ्यो यस्य चेच्छाम्यनुग्रहम् ॥१६॥**

*mām aiśvarya-śrī-madāndho*
*daṇḍa-pāṇiṁ na paśyati*
*taṁ bhraṁśayāmi sampadbhyo*
*yasya cecchāmy anugraham*

*mām*—Me; *aiśvarya*—of his power; *śrī*—and opulence; *mada*—by the intoxication; *andhaḥ*—rendered blind; *daṇḍa*—with the rod of punishment; *pāṇim*—in My hand; *na paśyati*—one does not see; *tam*—him;

*bhraṁśayāmi*—I make fall; *sampadbhyaḥ*—from his material assets; *yasya*—for whom; *ca*—and; *icchāmi*—I desire; *anugraham*—benefit.

## TRANSLATION

**A man blinded by intoxication with his power and opulence cannot see Me nearby with the rod of punishment in My hand. If I desire his real welfare, I drag him down from his materially fortunate position.**

## PURPORT

One may argue, "God should desire everyone's real welfare; therefore why should Lord Kṛṣṇa state in this verse that He removes the intoxicating opulence of one who is about to receive His mercy, rather than simply stating that He will remove everyone's opulence and bless everyone?" On the other hand, we may point out that irrevocable death occurs for everyone, and thus Lord Kṛṣṇa *does* take away everyone's opulence and everyone's false pride. However, if we apply the Lord's statement to events within one's immediate life, before death, we may refer to Kṛṣṇa's statement in the *Bhagavad-gītā* (4.11): *ye yathā māṁ prapadyante tāṁs tathaiva bhajāmy aham.* "As people surrender to Me, I reward them accordingly." Lord Kṛṣṇa desires everyone's welfare, but when He says here *yasya cecchāmy anugraham,* "for one whose welfare I desire," it is understood that the Lord refers to those who by their own activities and thoughts have manifested a desire to achieve spiritual benefit. Lord Kṛṣṇa wants everyone to be happy in Kṛṣṇa consciousness, but when He sees that a specific person also desires spiritual happiness, the Lord especially desires it for that person. This is a natural act of reciprocation consistent with the Lord's statement *samo 'haṁ sarva-bhūteṣu:* "I am equal in My attitude to all living beings." (Bg. 9.29)

## TEXT 17

गम्यतां शक्र भद्रं वः क्रियतां मेऽनुशासनम् ।
स्थीयतां स्वाधिकारेषु युक्तैर्वः स्तम्भवर्जितैः ॥१७॥

*gamyatāṁ śakra bhadraṁ vaḥ*
*kriyatāṁ me 'nuśāsanam*

*sthīyatāṁ svādhikāreṣu*
*yuktair vaḥ stambha-varjitaiḥ*

*gamyatām*—you may go; *śakra*—O Indra; *bhadram*—good fortune; *vaḥ*—unto you; *kriyatām*—you should execute; *me*—My; *anuśāsanam*—order; *sthīyatām*—you may remain; *sva*—in your own; *adhikāreṣu*—responsibilities; *yuktaiḥ*—soberly engaged; *vaḥ*—you; *stambha*—false pride; *varjitaiḥ*—devoid of.

## TRANSLATION

**Indra, you may now go. Execute My order and remain in your appointed position as King of heaven. But be sober, without false pride.**

## PURPORT

Lord Kṛṣṇa here addresses Indra in the plural form (*vaḥ*) because this grave instruction was meant to be a lesson for all the demigods.

## TEXT 18

**अथाह सुरभिः कृष्णमभिवन्द्य मनस्विनी ।**
**स्वसन्तानैरुपामन्त्र्य गोपरूपिणमीश्वरम् ॥१८॥**

*athāha surabhiḥ kṛṣṇam*
*abhivandya manasvinī*
*sva-santānair upāmantrya*
*gopa-rūpiṇam īśvaram*

*atha*—then; *āha*—spoke; *surabhiḥ*—the mother of the cows, Surabhi; *kṛṣṇam*—to Kṛṣṇa; *abhivandya*—offering respects; *manasvinī*—peaceful in mind; *sva-santānaiḥ*—together with her progeny, the cows; *upāmantrya*—begging for His attention; *gopa-rūpiṇam*—appearing as a cowherd boy; *īśvaram*—the Supreme Lord.

## TRANSLATION

**Mother Surabhi, along with her progeny, the cows, then offered**

**her obeisances to Lord Kṛṣṇa. Respectfully requesting His attention, the gentle lady addressed the Supreme Personality of Godhead, who was present before her as a cowherd boy.**

## PURPORT

The statement here that the heavenly cow Surabhi approached Lord Kṛṣṇa along with her progeny (*sva-santānaiḥ*) is a reference to the transcendental cows who play with Lord Kṛṣṇa in Vṛndāvana. Although Lord Kṛṣṇa's cows are transcendental, the heavenly cow Surabhi affectionately saw them, as indeed Lord Kṛṣṇa Himself did, as related to her. Since Lord Kṛṣṇa was appearing in the form of a cowherd boy, the whole situation was quite congenial, and Surabhi took the opportunity to offer the following prayers.

## TEXT 19

सुरभिरुवाच
कृष्ण कृष्ण महायोगिन् विश्वात्मन् विश्वसम्भव ।
भवता लोकनाथेन सनाथा वयमच्युत ॥१९॥

*surabhir uvāca*
*kṛṣṇa kṛṣṇa mahā-yogin*
*viśvātman viśva-sambhava*
*bhavatā loka-nāthena*
*sa-nāthā vayam acyuta*

*surabhiḥ uvāca*—Surabhi said; *kṛṣṇa kṛṣṇa*—O Kṛṣṇa, Kṛṣṇa; *mahā-yogin*—O greatest of mystics; *viśva-ātman*—O Soul of the universe; *viśva-sambhava*—O origin of the universe; *bhavatā*—by You; *loka-nāthena*—the master of the world; *sa-nāthāḥ*—having a master; *vayam*—we; *acyuta*—O infallible one.

## TRANSLATION

**Mother Surabhi said: O Kṛṣṇa, Kṛṣṇa, greatest of mystics! O Soul and origin of the universe! You are the master of the world, and by Your grace, O infallible Lord, we have You as our master.**

### PURPORT

Śrīla Viśvanātha Cakravartī Ṭhākura points out here that mother Surabhi is feeling great ecstasy as she repeats the words "Kṛṣṇa, Kṛṣṇa." Kṛṣṇa lifted Govardhana Hill by His mystic power and thus protected the cows of Vṛndāvana, whereas her so-called master, Indra, had tried to kill them. Thus Surabhi now clearly understands that it is not the demigods but rather the Supreme God, Kṛṣṇa Himself, who is her real master forever.

### TEXT 20

त्वं नः परमकं दैवं त्वं न इन्द्रो जगत्पते ।
भवाय भव गोविप्रदेवानां ये च साधवः ॥२०॥

*tvaṁ naḥ paramakaṁ daivaṁ*
*tvaṁ na indro jagat-pate*
*bhavāya bhava go-vipra-*
*devānāṁ ye ca sādhavaḥ*

*tvam*—You; *naḥ*—our; *paramakam*—supreme; *daivam*—worshipable Deity; *tvam*—You; *naḥ*—our; *indraḥ*—Lord Indra; *jagat-pate*—O master of the universe; *bhavāya*—for the welfare; *bhava*—please be; *go*—of the cows; *vipra*—the *brāhmaṇas; devānām*—and the demigods; *ye*—who; *ca*—and; *sādhavaḥ*—saintly persons.

### TRANSLATION

**You are our worshipable Deity. Therefore, O Lord of the universe, for the benefit of the cows, the *brāhmaṇas*, the demigods and all other saintly persons, please become our Indra.**

### PURPORT

The Supreme Lord is self-sufficient: He can do everything Himself. The Lord appointed one of His innumerable children to the position of Indra, the lord of the cosmic heaven. But Indra abused his authority, and now Surabhi requests Lord Kṛṣṇa, the Absolute Truth, to directly become her Lord, her Indra. We should carefully perform our duties without false pride; thus we will not become obsolete and embarrassed, as in the present case of King Indra, who actually attacked Lord Kṛṣṇa and His Vṛndāvana devotees.

## TEXT 21

इन्द्रं नस्त्वाभिषेक्ष्यामो ब्रह्मणा चोदिता वयम् ।
अवतीर्णोऽसि विश्वात्मन् भूमेर्भारापनुत्तये ॥२१॥

*indraṁ nas tvābhiṣekṣyāmo*
*brahmaṇā coditā vayam*
*avatīrṇo 'si viśvātman*
*bhūmer bhārāpanuttaye*

*indram*—as Indra; *naḥ*—our; *tvā*—to You; *abhiṣekṣyāmaḥ*—we shall perform the bathing ceremony of coronation; *brahmaṇā*—by Lord Brahmā; *coditāḥ*—ordered; *vayam*—we; *avatīrṇaḥ asi*—You have descended; *viśva-ātman*—O Soul of the universe; *bhūmeḥ*—of the earth; *bhāra*—the burden; *apanuttaye*—in order to alleviate.

## TRANSLATION

**As ordered by Lord Brahmā, we shall perform Your bathing ceremony to coronate You as Indra. O Soul of the universe, You descend to this world to relieve the burden of the earth.**

## PURPORT

Surabhi makes it quite clear in this verse that she has had enough of the leadership of imperfect demigods like Purandara (Indra), and now she is determined to directly serve the Supreme Lord. Since Brahmā has ordered her, her attempt to coronate Lord Kṛṣṇa as her personal Lord is authorized by higher authority. Moreover, Lord Kṛṣṇa Himself comes down to the earth to relieve the burden of self-destructive, mundane administration, and thus it is perfectly consistent with the Lord's own purpose that He become the Lord of Surabhi. Since the Lord rules millions of universes, He can certainly take care of mother Surabhi.

In fact, Surabhi wanted to bathe the Lord for her own purification, and she earnestly makes her proposal to Viśvātmā, the Soul of the universe, Śrī Kṛṣṇa.

## TEXTS 22–23

श्रीशुक उवाच
एवं कृष्णमुपामन्त्र्य सुरभिः पयसात्मनः ।
जलैराकाशगंगाया ऐरावतकरोद्धृतैः ॥२२॥
इन्द्रः सुरर्षिभिः साकं चोदितो देवमातृभिः ।
अभ्यसिञ्चत दाशार्हं गोविन्द इति चाभ्यधात् ॥२३॥

*śrī-śuka uvāca*
*evaṁ kṛṣṇam upāmantrya*
*surabhiḥ payasātmanaḥ*
*jalair ākāśa-gaṅgāyā*
*airāvata-karoddhṛtaiḥ*

*indraḥ surarṣibhiḥ sākaṁ*
*codito deva-mātṛbhiḥ*
*abhyasiñcata dāśārhaṁ*
*govinda iti cābhyadhāt*

*śrī-śukaḥ uvāca*—Śrī Śukadeva Gosvāmī said; *evam*—thus; *kṛṣṇam*—Lord Kṛṣṇa; *upāmantrya*—requesting; *surabhiḥ*—mother Surabhi; *payasā*—with milk; *ātmanaḥ*—her own; *jalaiḥ*—with the water; *ākāśa-gaṅgāyāḥ*—of the Ganges flowing through the heavenly region (known as the Mandākinī); *airāvata*—of Indra's carrier, the elephant Airāvata; *kara*—by the trunk; *uddhṛtaiḥ*—carried; *indraḥ*—Lord Indra; *sura*—by the demigods; *ṛṣibhiḥ*—and the great sages; *sākam*—accompanied; *coditaḥ*—inspired; *deva*—of the demigods; *mātṛbhiḥ*—by the mothers (headed by Aditi); *abhyasiñcata*—he bathed; *dāśārham*—Lord Kṛṣṇa, the descendant of King Daśārha; *govindaḥ iti*—as Govinda; *ca*—and; *abhyadhāt*—he named the Lord.

## TRANSLATION

**Śukadeva Gosvāmī said: Having thus appealed to Lord Kṛṣṇa, mother Surabhi performed His bathing ceremony with her own milk, and Indra, ordered by Aditi and other mothers of the demigods, anointed the Lord with heavenly Gaṅgā water from the trunk of Indra's elephant carrier, Airāvata. Thus, in the company**

**of the demigods and great sages, Indra coronated Lord Kṛṣṇa, the descendant of Daśārha, and gave Him the name Govinda.**

## PURPORT

According to the *ācāryas,* because Indra was embarrassed by his blunder of attacking Vṛndāvana, he was reluctant to worship the Lord. Therefore the heavenly mothers, such as Aditi, encouraged him to go ahead and worship the Lord. Feeling authorized by the encouragement of demigods less offensive than him, he then bathed the Lord. Indra discovered that the beautiful cowherd boy named Kṛṣṇa is indeed the Supreme Personality of Godhead.

## TEXT 24

तत्रागतास्तुम्बुरुनारदादयो
गन्धर्वविद्याधरसिद्धचारणाः ।
जगुर्यशो लोकमलापहं हरेः
सुरांगनाः सन्ननृतुर्मुदान्विताः ॥२४॥

*tatrāgatās tumburu-nāradādayo*
*gandharva-vidyādhara-siddha-cāraṇāḥ*
*jagur yaśo loka-malāpahaṁ hareḥ*
*surāṅganāḥ sannanṛtur mudānvitāḥ*

*tatra*—to that place; *āgatāḥ*—coming; *tumburu*—the Gandharva named Tumburu; *nārada*—Nārada Muni; *ādayaḥ*—and other demigods; *gandharva-vidyādhara-siddha-cāraṇāḥ*—the Gandharvas, Vidyādharas, Siddhas and Cāraṇas; *jaguḥ*—sang; *yaśaḥ*—the glories; *loka*—of the entire world; *mala*—the contamination; *apaham*—which eradicate; *hareḥ*—of Lord Hari; *sura*—of the demigods; *aṅganāḥ*—the wives; *sannanṛtuḥ*—danced together; *mudā anvitāḥ*—filled with joy.

## TRANSLATION

**Tumburu, Nārada and other Gandharvas, along with the Vidyādharas, Siddhas and Cāraṇas, came there to sing the glories of Lord Hari, which purify the entire world. And the wives of the demigods, filled with joy, danced together in the Lord's honor.**

## TEXT 25

तं तुष्टुवुर्देवनिकायकेतवो
ह्यवाकिरंश्चाद्भुतपुष्पवृष्टिभिः ।
लोकाः परां निर्वृतिमाप्नुवंस्त्रयो
गावस्तदा गामनयन् पयोद्रुताम् ॥२५॥

*taṁ tuṣṭuvur deva-nikāya-ketavo*
*hy avākiraṁś cādbhuta-puṣpa-vṛṣṭibhiḥ*
*lokāḥ paraṁ nirvṛtim āpnuvaṁs trayo*
*gāvas tadā gām anayan payo-drutām*

*tam*—Him; *tuṣṭuvuḥ*—praised; *deva-nikāya*—of all the demigods; *ketavaḥ*—the most eminent; *hi*—indeed; *avākiran*—they covered Him; *ca*—and; *adbhuta*—amazing; *puṣpa*—of flowers; *vṛṣṭibhiḥ*—with showers; *lokāḥ*—the worlds; *parām*—supreme; *nirvṛtim*—satisfaction; *āpnuvan*—experienced; *trayaḥ*—three; *gāvaḥ*—the cows; *tadā*—then; *gām*—the earth; *anayan*—brought; *payaḥ*—with their milk; *drutām*—to saturation.

## TRANSLATION

**The most eminent demigods chanted the praises of the Lord and scattered wonderful showers of flowers all around Him. All three worlds felt supreme satisfaction, and the cows drenched the surface of the earth with their milk.**

## PURPORT

The word *ketavaḥ* means, literally, "banners." The leading demigods are the emblems, or banners, of the demigod race, and they took the lead in glorifying the Lord and covering Him with an amazing shower of multicolored, fragrant flowers.

## TEXT 26

नानारसौघाः सरितो वृक्षा आसन्मधुस्रवाः ।
अकृष्टपच्यौषधयो गिरयोऽबिभ्रनुन्मणीन् ॥२६॥

*nānā-rasaughāḥ sarito*
*vṛkṣā āsan madhu-sravāḥ*
*akṛṣṭa-pacyauṣadhayo*
*girayo 'bibhran un maṇīn*

*nānā*—various; *rasa*—liquids; *oghāḥ*—flooding; *saritaḥ*—the rivers; *vṛkṣāḥ*—the trees; *āsan*—became; *madhu*—with sweet sap; *sravāḥ*—flowing; *akṛṣṭa*—even without cultivation; *pacya*—ripened; *oṣadhayaḥ*—the plants; *girayaḥ*—the mountains; *abibhran*—carried; *ut*—above the ground; *maṇīn*—jewels.

## TRANSLATION

**Rivers flowed with various kinds of tasty liquids, trees exuded honey, edible plants came to maturity without cultivation, and hills gave forth jewels formerly hidden in their interiors.**

## TEXT 27

कृष्णेऽभिषिक्त एतानि सर्वाणि कुरुनन्दन ।
निर्वैराण्यभवंस्तात क्रूराण्यपि निसर्गतः ॥२७॥

*kṛṣṇe 'bhiṣikta etāni*
*sarvāṇi kuru-nandana*
*nirvairāṇy abhavaṁs tāta*
*krūrāṇy api nisargataḥ*

*kṛṣṇe*—Lord Kṛṣṇa; *abhiṣikte*—having been bathed; *etāni*—these; *sarvāṇi*—all; *kuru-nandana*—O beloved of the Kuru dynasty; *nirvairāṇi*—free from enmity; *abhavan*—became; *tāta*—my dear Parīkṣit; *krūrāṇi*—vicious; *api*—although; *nisargataḥ*—by nature.

## TRANSLATION

**O Parīkṣit, beloved of the Kuru dynasty, upon the ceremonial bathing of Lord Kṛṣṇa, all living creatures, even those cruel by nature, became entirely free of enmity.**

## PURPORT

Those corrupted by a type of sophisticated cynicism may mock these descriptions of a paradisiacal world situation effected simply by worshiping the Supreme Lord. Unfortunately, modern man has created a hell on earth in his cynical rejection of heaven on earth, which is actually possible through Kṛṣṇa consciousness. The situation described here, created simply by the auspicious bathing ceremony of the Lord, is an authentic historical incident. Since history repeats itself, there is hope that the Kṛṣṇa consciousness movement may again bring the world community to the brilliant reality of self-realized existence.

## TEXT 28

इति गोगोकुलपतिं गोविन्दमभिषिच्य सः ।
अनुज्ञातो ययौ शक्रो वृतो देवादिभिर्दिवम् ॥२८॥

*iti go-gokula-patiṁ*
*govindam abhiṣicya saḥ*
*anujñāto yayau śakro*
*vṛto devādibhir divam*

*iti*—thus; *go*—of the cows; *go-kula*—and of the community of cowherds; *patim*—the master; *govindam*—Lord Kṛṣṇa; *abhiṣicya*—bathing; *saḥ*—he, Indra; *anujñātaḥ*—given permission; *yayau*—went; *śakraḥ*—King Indra; *vṛtaḥ*—surrounded; *deva-ādibhiḥ*—by the demigods and others; *divam*—to heaven.

## TRANSLATION

**After he had ceremonially bathed Lord Govinda, who is the master of the cows and the cowherd community, King Indra took the Lord's permission and, surrounded by the demigods and other higher beings, returned to his heavenly abode.**

*Thus end the purports of the humble servant of His Divine Grace A. C. Bhaktivedanta Swami Prahbupāda to the Tenth Canto, Twenty-seventh Chapter, of the* Śrīmad-Bhāgavatam, *entitled "Lord Indra and Mother Surabhi Offer Prayers."*

CHAPTER TWENTY-EIGHT

# Kṛṣṇa Rescues Nanda Mahārāja from the Abode of Varuṇa

This chapter describes how Lord Kṛṣṇa brought Nanda Mahārāja back from the abode of Varuṇa and how the cowherd men saw Vaikuṇṭha.

The king of the cowherds, Nanda Mahārāja, observed the prescribed fast on the eleventh day of the lunar month and then considered how to break his fast properly on the twelfth day. By circumstance only a few more minutes remained, and so he decided to take his bath at the very end of the night, although astrologically that was an inauspicious time. Thus he entered the water of the Yamunā. A servant of Varuṇa, the demigod of the ocean, noticed Nanda Mahārāja entering the water at a time forbidden by scripture and took him away to the demigod's abode. In the early morning the cowherd men unsuccessfully searched for Nanda, but Lord Kṛṣṇa immediately understood the situation and went to see Varuṇa. Varuṇa worshiped Kṛṣṇa with great and variegated festivity. Afterwards he begged the Lord to forgive his servant for having foolishly arrested the king of the cowherds.

Nanda was amazed to see the influence Śrī Kṛṣṇa exerted in the court of Varuṇadeva, and after returning home he described his experiences to his friends and relatives. They all thought Kṛṣṇa must be the Supreme Personality of Godhead Himself and wanted to see His supreme abode. Thereupon the omniscient Personality of Godhead arranged for them to bathe in the same lake where Akrūra would have his vision of the Absolute Truth. There the Lord revealed to them Brahmaloka, which is realized by great sages in their mystic trance.

## TEXT 1

श्रीबादरायणिरुवाच

**एकादश्यां निराहारः समभ्यर्च्य जनार्दनम् ।**
**स्नातुं नन्दस्तु कालिन्द्यां द्वादश्यां जलमाविशत् ॥१॥**

*śrī-bādarāyaṇir uvāca*
*ekādaśyāṁ nirāhāraḥ*
*samabhyarcya janārdanam*
*snātuṁ nandas tu kālindyāṁ*
*dvādaśyāṁ jalam āviśat*

*śrī-bādarāyaṇiḥ uvāca*—Śrī Bādarāyaṇi (Śukadeva Gosvāmī) said; *ekādaśyām*—on Ekādaśī (the eleventh day of the lunar month); *nirāhāraḥ*—fasting; *samabhyarcya*—having worshiped; *janārdanam*—Lord Janārdana, the Supreme Personality of Godhead; *snātum*—in order to bathe (before breaking the fast at its prescribed completion); *nandaḥ*—Nanda Mahārāja; *tu*—but; *kālindyām*—in the river Yamunā; *dvādaśyām*—on the twelfth day; *jalam*—the water; *āviśat*—entered.

## TRANSLATION

**Śrī Bādarāyaṇi said: Having worshiped Lord Janārdana and fasted on the Ekādaśī day, Nanda Mahārāja entered the water of the Kālindī on the Dvādaśī to take his bath.**

## TEXT 2

तं गृहीत्वानयद् भृत्यो वरुणस्यासुरोऽन्तिकम् ।
अवज्ञायासुरीं वेलां प्रविष्टमुदकं निशि ॥२॥

*taṁ gṛhītvānayad bhṛtyo*
*varuṇasyāsuro 'ntikam*
*avajñāyāsurīṁ velāṁ*
*praviṣṭam udakaṁ niśi*

*tam*—him; *gṛhītvā*—seizing; *anayat*—brought; *bhṛtyaḥ*—a servant; *varuṇasya*—of Varuṇa, the lord of the sea; *asuraḥ*—demon; *antikam*—to the presence (of his master); *avajñāya*—who had disregarded; *āsurīm*—the inauspicious; *velām*—time; *praviṣṭam*—having entered; *udakam*—the water; *niśi*—during the night.

## TRANSLATION

**Because Nanda Mahārāja entered the water in the dark of night, disregarding that the time was inauspicious, a demoniac servant of Varuṇa seized him and brought him to his master.**

## PURPORT

Nanda Mahārāja was intent on breaking his fast during the Dvādaśī day, of which there remained only a few minutes. Thus he entered the water to bathe at an inauspicious time, before the first dawn light.

The servant of Varuṇa who arrested Nanda Mahārāja is stated here to be an *asura,* or demon, for obvious reasons. First, the servant was foolishly ignorant of Nanda Mahārāja's position as the pastime father of the Supreme Absolute Truth. Also, Nanda Mahārāja's intention was to carry out the injunctions of scripture; therefore Varuṇa's servant should not have arrested Nanda on the technical grounds that he bathed in the Yamunā at an inauspicious time. Later in this chapter Varuṇa himself will say, *ajānatā māmakena mūḍhena:* "This was done by my ignorant servant, who is a fool." This foolish servant did not understand the position of Kṛṣṇa or Nanda Mahārāja or devotional service to the Lord.

In conclusion, it is clear that Lord Kṛṣṇa wanted to give His personal audience to Varuṇa and simultaneously accomplish other didactic purposes. Thus this wonderful pastime will now unfold.

## TEXT 3

चुक्रुशुस्तमपश्यन्तः कृष्ण रामेति गोपकाः ।
भगवांस्तदुपश्रुत्य पितरं वरुणाहृतम् ।
तदन्तिकं गतो राजन् स्वानामभयदो विभुः ॥३॥

*cukruśus tam apaśyantaḥ*
*kṛṣṇa rāmeti gopakāḥ*
*bhagavāṁs tad upaśrutya*
*pitaraṁ varuṇāhṛtam*
*tad-antikaṁ gato rājan*
*svānām abhaya-do vibhuḥ*

*cukruśuḥ*—they called out loudly; *tam*—him, Nanda; *apaśyantaḥ*—not seeing; *kṛṣṇa*—O Kṛṣṇa; *rāma*—O Rāma; *iti*—thus; *gopakāḥ*—the cowherd men; *bhagavān*—the Supreme Lord, Kṛṣṇa; *tat*—that; *upaśrutya*—hearing; *pitaram*—His father; *varuṇa*—by Varuṇa; *āhṛtam*—taken away; *tat*—of Varuṇa; *antikam*—to the presence; *gataḥ*—went; *rājan*—my dear King Parīkṣit; *svānām*—of His own devotees; *abhaya*—of fearlessness; *daḥ*—the giver; *vibhuḥ*—the almighty Lord.

## TRANSLATION

**O King, not seeing Nanda Mahārāja, the cowherd men loudly cried out, "O Kṛṣṇa! O Rāma!" Lord Kṛṣṇa heard their cries and understood that His father had been captured by Varuṇa. Therefore the almighty Lord, who makes His devotees fearless, went to the court of Varuṇadeva.**

## PURPORT

Viśvanātha Cakravartī Ṭhākura explains that when Nanda Mahārāja went to bathe in the river, he was accompanied by several cowherd men. When Nanda did not come out of the water, they began to cry out, and Lord Kṛṣṇa immediately came there. Understanding the situation, Śrī Kṛṣṇa entered the water and went to the court of the demigod Varuṇa, determined to free His father and the other cowherd men from fear of a mere demigod.

## TEXT 4

प्राप्तं वीक्ष्य हृषीकेशं लोकपालः सपर्यया ।
महत्या पूजयित्वाह तद्दर्शनमहोत्सवः ॥४॥

*prāptaṁ vīkṣya hṛṣīkeśaṁ*
*loka-pālaḥ saparyayā*
*mahatyā pūjayitvāha*
*tad-darśana-mahotsavaḥ*

*prāptam*—arrived; *vīkṣya*—seeing; *hṛṣīkeśam*—Lord Kṛṣṇa, the controller of the senses; *loka*—of that planet (the watery regions); *pālaḥ*—the presiding deity (Varuṇa); *saparyayā*—with respectful offerings;

*mahatyā*—elaborate; *pūjayitvā*—worshiping; *āha*—spoke; *tat*—of Lord Kṛṣṇa; *darśana*—from the sight; *mahā*—great; *utsavaḥ*—jubilant pleasure.

### TRANSLATION

**Seeing that the Lord, Hṛṣīkeśa, had arrived, the demigod Varuṇa worshiped Him with elaborate offerings. Varuṇa was in a state of great jubilation upon seeing the Lord, and he spoke as follows.**

### TEXT 5

श्रीवरुण उवाच
अद्य मे निभृतो देहोऽद्यैवार्थोऽधिगतः प्रभो ।
त्वत्पादभाजो भगवन्नवापुः पारमध्वनः ॥५॥

*śrī-varuṇa uvāca*
*adya me nibhṛto deho*
*'dyaivārtho 'dhigataḥ prabho*
*tvat-pāda-bhājo bhagavann*
*avāpuḥ pāram adhvanaḥ*

*śrī-varuṇaḥ uvāca*—Śrī Varuṇa said; *adya*—today; *me*—by me; *nibhṛtaḥ*—is carried successfully; *dehaḥ*—my material body; *adya*—today; *eva*—indeed; *arthaḥ*—the goal of life; *adhigataḥ*—is experienced; *prabho*—O Lord; *tvat*—Your; *pāda*—the lotus feet; *bhājaḥ*—those who serve; *bhagavan*—O Supreme Personality; *avāpuḥ*—have achieved; *pāram*—the state of transcendence; *adhvanaḥ*—of the path (of material existence).

### TRANSLATION

**Śrī Varuṇa said: Now my body has fulfilled its function. Indeed, now the goal of my life is achieved, O Lord. Those who accept Your lotus feet, O Personality of Godhead, can transcend the path of material existence.**

### PURPORT

Varuṇa ecstatically exclaims here that since he has now seen the infinitely gorgeous body of Lord Kṛṣṇa, the trouble of assuming a material body has now been supremely justified. Indeed, the *artha,* the goal or real value of Varuṇa's life, has now been achieved. Because Lord Kṛṣṇa's form is transcendental, those who accept His lotus feet go beyond the boundary of material existence, and thus only the spiritually unaware would presume that the Lord's lotus feet are material.

## TEXT 6

नमस्तुभ्यं भगवते ब्रह्मणे परमात्मने ।
न यत्र श्रूयते माया लोकसृष्टिविकल्पना ॥६॥

*namas tubhyaṁ bhagavate*
*brahmaṇe paramātmane*
*na yatra śrūyate māyā*
*loka-sṛṣṭi-vikalpanā*

*namaḥ*—obeisances; *tubhyam*—unto You; *bhagavate*—unto the Supreme Personality of Godhead; *brahmaṇe*—the Absolute Truth; *parama-ātmane*—the Supreme Soul; *na*—not; *yatra*—in whom; *śrūyate*—is heard of; *māyā*—the illusory, material energy; *loka*—of this world; *sṛṣṭi*—the creation; *vikalpanā*—which arranges.

## TRANSLATION

**My obeisances unto You, the Supreme Personality of Godhead, the Absolute Truth, the Supreme Soul, within whom there is no trace of the illusory energy, which orchestrates the creation of this world.**

## PURPORT

The word *śrūyate* is significant here. *Śruti,* or Vedic literature, consists of authorized statements made by the Lord Himself or His enlightened representatives. Thus neither the Lord nor recognized spiritual authorities would ever say that within the Absolute Truth, the Personality of Godhead, there is the fault of illusion. Śrīla Śrīdhara Svāmī points out that the word *brahmaṇe* here indicates the Lord is full in Himself, and that the term *paramātmane* indicates He is the controller of all living entities.

Thus within the supreme being, complete in Himself and omnipotent, we do not find any jurisdiction of the material, illusory energy.

## TEXT 7

अजानता मामकेन मूढेनाकार्यवेदिना ।
आनीतोऽयं तव पिता तद् भवान् क्षन्तुमर्हति ॥७॥

*ajānatā māmakena*
*mūḍhenākārya-vedinā*
*ānīto 'yaṁ tava pitā*
*tad bhavān kṣantum arhati*

*ajānatā*—by one who was ignorant; *māmakena*—by my servant; *mūḍhena*—foolish; *akārya-vedinā*—not knowing his proper duty; *ānītaḥ*—was brought; *ayam*—this person; *tava*—Your; *pitā*—father; *tat*—that; *bhavān*—Your good self; *kṣantum arhati*—should please forgive.

## TRANSLATION

**Your father, who is sitting here, was brought to me by a foolish, ignorant servant of mine, who did not understand his proper duty. Therefore, please forgive us.**

## PURPORT

The word *ayam,* "this one here," clearly indicates that Kṛṣṇa's father, Nanda Mahārāja, was present as Varuṇa was speaking. In fact, Viśvanātha Cakravartī Ṭhākura states that Varuṇa had seated Śrī Nanda on a jeweled throne and had personally worshiped him out of respect.

Technically, Nanda Mahārāja was correct in entering the water just before sunrise. The following explanation is given by Śrīla Jīva Gosvāmī in his commentary on the first verse of this chapter: After an especially short Ekādaśī, measuring only eighteen hours, about six hours of the lunar day in which the fast had to be broken, namely the Dvādaśī, had already expired before the dawn. Since at sunrise the proper time for breaking the fast would have passed, Nanda Mahārāja decided to enter the water at an otherwise inauspicious time.

Of course, Varuṇa's servant should have been aware of these technical details, which are meant for strict followers of the Vedic rituals. Above and beyond that, Nanda Mahārāja was acting as the Supreme Lord's father and was therefore a most sacred person, beyond the touch of insignificant cosmic bureaucrats like the foolish servant of Varuṇa.

## TEXT 8

ममाप्यनुग्रहं कृष्ण कर्तुमर्हस्यशेषदृक् ।
गोविन्द नीयतामेष पिता ते पितृवत्सल ॥८॥

*mamāpy anugrahaṁ kṛṣṇa*
*kartum arhasy aśeṣa-dṛk*
*govinda nīyatām eṣa*
*pitā te pitṛ-vatsala*

*mama*—to me; *api*—even; *anugraham*—mercy; *kṛṣṇa*—O Lord Kṛṣṇa; *kartum arhasi*—please do; *aśeṣa*—of everything; *dṛk*—O You who see; *govinda*—O Govinda; *nīyatām*—may he be taken; *eṣaḥ*—this; *pitā*—father; *te*—Your; *pitṛ-vatsala*—O You who are most affectionate to Your parents.

## TRANSLATION

**O Kṛṣṇa, O seer of everything, please give Your mercy even to me. O Govinda, You are most affectionate to Your father. Please take him home.**

## TEXT 9

श्रीशुक उवाच
एवं प्रसादितः कृष्णो भगवानीश्वरेश्वरः ।
आदायागात् स्वपितरं बन्धूनां चावहन्मुदम् ॥९॥

*śrī-śuka uvāca*
*evaṁ prasāditaḥ kṛṣṇo*
*bhagavān īśvareśvaraḥ*
*ādāyāgāt sva-pitaraṁ*
*bandhūnāṁ cāvahan mudam*

*śrī-śukaḥ uvāca*—Śrī Śukadeva Gosvāmī said; *evam*—thus; *prasāditaḥ*—satisfied; *kṛṣṇaḥ*—Lord Kṛṣṇa; *bhagavān*—the Supreme Personality of Godhead; *īśvara*—of all controllers; *īśvaraḥ*—the supreme controller; *ādāya*—taking; *agāt*—went; *sva-pitaram*—His father; *bandhūnām*—to His relatives; *ca*—and; *āvahan*—bringing; *mudam*—pleasure.

## TRANSLATION

**Śukadeva Gosvāmī said: Thus satisfied by Lord Varuṇa, Śrī Kṛṣṇa, the Supreme Personality of Godhead, Lord of lords, took His father and returned home, where their relatives were overjoyed to see them.**

## PURPORT

In this pastime, Lord Kṛṣṇa gives a sublime demonstration of His position as the Supreme Lord of all lords. Varuṇa, the demigod of the seas, is most powerful, yet he was happy to worship even Lord Kṛṣṇa's father, what to speak of Kṛṣṇa Himself.

## TEXT 10

नन्दस्त्वतीन्द्रियं दृष्ट्वा लोकपालमहोदयम् ।
कृष्णे च सन्नतिं तेषां ज्ञातिभ्यो विस्मितोऽब्रवीत् ॥१०॥

*nandas tv atīndriyaṁ dṛṣṭvā*
*loka-pāla-mahodayam*
*kṛṣṇe ca sannatiṁ teṣāṁ*
*jñātibhyo vismito 'bravīt*

*nandaḥ*—Nanda Mahārāja; *tu*—and; *atīndriyam*—not seen before; *dṛṣṭvā*—seeing; *loka-pāla*—of the controlling deity of the (ocean) planet, Varuṇa; *mahā-udayam*—the great opulence; *kṛṣṇe*—unto Kṛṣṇa; *ca*—and; *sannatim*—the offering of obeisances; *teṣām*—by them (Varuṇa and his followers); *jñātibhyaḥ*—to his friends and relatives; *vismitaḥ*—amazed; *abravīt*—spoke.

## TRANSLATION

**Nanda Mahārāja had been astonished to see for the first time the great opulence of Varuṇa, the ruler of the ocean planet, and also to see how Varuṇa and his servants had offered such humble respect to Kṛṣṇa. Nanda described all this to his fellow cowherd men.**

## TEXT 11

ते चौत्सुक्यधियो राजन्मत्वा गोपास्तमीश्वरम् ।
अपि नः स्वगतिं सूक्ष्मामुपाधास्यदधीश्वरः ॥११॥

*te cautsukya-dhiyo rājan*
*matvā gopās tam īśvaram*
*api naḥ sva-gatiṁ sūkṣmām*
*upādhāsyad adhīśvaraḥ*

*te*—they; *ca*—and; *autsukya*—full of eagerness; *dhiyaḥ*—their minds; *rājan*—O King Parīkṣit; *matvā*—thinking; *gopāḥ*—the cowherd men; *tam*—Him; *īśvaram*—the Supreme Lord; *api*—perhaps; *naḥ*—to us; *sva-gatim*—His own abode; *sūkṣmām*—transcendental; *upādhāsyat*—is going to bestow; *adhīśvaraḥ*—the supreme controller.

## TRANSLATION

**[Hearing about Kṛṣṇa's pastimes with Varuṇa,] the cowherd men considered that Kṛṣṇa must be the Supreme Lord, and their minds, O King, were filled with eagerness. They thought, "Will the Supreme Lord bestow upon us His transcendental abode?"**

## PURPORT

The cowherd men were filled with excitement upon hearing how Kṛṣṇa had gone to the abode of Varuṇa to rescue His father. Suddenly realizing that they were in fact dealing with the Supreme Personality of Godhead, they joyfully conjectured among themselves about their auspicious destination after finishing their present life.

### TEXT 12

इति स्वानां स भगवान् विज्ञायाखिलदृक् स्वयम् ।
संकल्पसिद्धये तेषां कृपयैतदचिन्तयत् ॥१२॥

*iti svānāṁ sa bhagavān*
*vijñāyākhila-dṛk svayam*
*saṅkalpa-siddhaye teṣāṁ*
*kṛpayaitad acintayat*

*iti*—such; *svānām*—of His personal devotees; *saḥ*—He; *bhagavān*—the Supreme Personality of Godhead; *vijñāya*—understanding; *akhila-dṛk*—the seer of everything; *svayam*—Himself; *saṅkalpa*—of the imagined desire; *siddhaye*—for the realization; *teṣām*—their; *kṛpayā*—compassionately; *etat*—this (as follows in the next verse); *acintayat*—thought.

### TRANSLATION

**Because He sees everything, Lord Kṛṣṇa, the Supreme Personality of Godhead, automatically understood what the cowherd men were conjecturing. Wanting to show His compassion to them by fulfilling their desires, the Lord thought as follows.**

### TEXT 13

जनो वै लोक एतस्मिन्नविद्याकामकर्मभिः ।
उच्चावचासु गतिषु न वेद स्वां गतिं भ्रमन् ॥१३॥

*jano vai loka etasminn*
*avidyā-kāma-karmabhiḥ*
*uccāvacāsu gatiṣu*
*na veda svāṁ gatiṁ bhraman*

*janaḥ*—people; *vai*—certainly; *loke*—in the world; *etasmin*—this; *avidyā*—without knowledge; *kāma*—because of desires; *karmabhiḥ*—by activities; *ucca*—among superior; *avacāsu*—and inferior; *gatiṣu*—destinations; *na veda*—does not recognize; *svām*—his own; *gatim*—destination; *bhraman*—wandering.

## TRANSLATION

**Certainly people in this world are wandering among higher and lower destinations, which they achieve through activities performed according to their desires and without full knowledge. Thus people do not know their real destination.**

## PURPORT

Śrīla Jīva Gosvāmī has elaborately explained how this verse applies to the eternally liberated residents of Śrī Vṛndāvana, the Lord's abode. One of the fundamental philosophical principles of the *Śrīmad-Bhāgavatam* is the distinction between two types of illusion, Yoga-māyā and Mahā-māyā, the spiritual and material states of existence, respectively. Although Kṛṣṇa is God, the omnipotent, omniscient Supreme Being, His intimate associates in the spiritual world love Him so much that they see Him as their beloved child, friend, lover and so on. So that their ecstatic love can transcend the boundaries of mere reverence, they forget that Kṛṣṇa is the Supreme God of all the universes, and thus their pure, intimate love expands unlimitedly. One may consider their activities of treating Kṛṣṇa as a helpless child, a handsome boyfriend, or a playmate to be a manifestation of *avidyā,* ignorance of Lord Kṛṣṇa's position as God, but the residents of Vṛndāvana are in fact ignoring the secondary majesty of Kṛṣṇa and focusing intensely on His infinite beauty, which is the essence of His existence.

In fact, describing Lord Kṛṣṇa as the supreme controller and God is almost a type of political analysis, referring as it does to a hierarchy of power and control. Such analysis of levels of power and hierarchies of rule is significant in a context in which one entity is not fully surrendered, in love, to a higher entity. In other words, control becomes visible, or is consciously felt as control, when there is resistance to that control. To cite a simple example: A pious, law-abiding citizen sees a policeman as a friend and well-wisher, whereas a criminal sees him as a threatening symbol of punishment. Those who are enthusiastic about government policies feel not that the government is controlling them but rather that it is helping them.

Thus Lord Kṛṣṇa is seen as a "controller," and hence as "the Supreme God," by those who are not fully enchanted by His beauty and pastimes. Those fully in love with Lord Kṛṣṇa focus on His sublime, attractive features and, because of the nature of their relationship with Him, do not much notice His controlling power.

A simple proof that the residents of Vraja have transcended lower states of God consciousness rather than failed to attain them is the fact that throughout the pastimes of the Lord they often "remember" that Kṛṣṇa is God. Usually they are astonished at this remembrance, having been fully absorbed in seeing Kṛṣṇa as their friend, lover and so on.

The word *kāma* is conventionally used to indicate a material desire, or else a spiritual desire so intense that it becomes somehow analogous to intense material desires. Still, the fundamental distinction remains: material desire is selfish and self-gratificatory; spiritual desire is free of selfishness, being wholly for the pleasure of the other, the Lord. Thus the residents of Vṛndāvana executed their daily activities solely for the pleasure of their beloved Kṛṣṇa.

It should be remembered that the entire purpose of Kṛṣṇa's descent into this world is to attract living beings back home, back to Godhead. Two things are required for this: that His pastimes display the beauty of spiritual perfection, and that they somehow seem relevant and hence interesting to the conditioned souls of this world. The *Bhāgavatam* often states that Lord Kṛṣṇa plays just like a youthful actor, and He undoubtedly engages His eternal devotees in the dramatic presentation. Thus Lord Kṛṣṇa here muses to Himself that people in this world certainly do not know their ultimate destination, and with an obvious touch of the facetious He also thinks in this way about His own eternally liberated associates, who were playing in this world like ordinary members of a cowherd village.

Apart from the double meaning obviously present in this verse when it is applied to Kṛṣṇa's liberated associates, Kṛṣṇa here makes an entirely direct and pointedly critical observation about ordinary people. When applied to conditioned souls who are actually wandering throughout the universe, His statement that people are acting out of ignorance and lust is not mitigated by any deeper, spiritual meaning. People in general are simply ignorant, and they do not seriously consider their ultimate destination. As usual, Lord Śrī Kṛṣṇa is able to say many profound and complex things in a few simple words. How fortunate we are that God is not a dry field of energy, a transcendent, effulgent blob, or nothing at all—as various people would have it. In fact, He is the most wonderful Personality of Godhead, full of absolute personal qualities, and certainly whatever we can do, He can do better, as evidenced by His brilliant way of speaking.

### TEXT 14

**इति सञ्चिन्त्य भगवान्महाकारुणिको हरिः ।
दर्शयामास लोकं स्वं गोपानां तमसः परम् ॥१४॥**

*iti sañcintya bhagavān
mahā-kāruṇiko hariḥ
darśayām āsa lokaṁ svaṁ
gopānāṁ tamasaḥ param*

*iti*—in these words; *sañcintya*—considering to Himself; *bhagavān*—the Supreme Personality of Godhead; *mahā-kāruṇikaḥ*—the most merciful; *hariḥ*—Lord Hari; *darśayām āsa*—showed; *lokam*—the planet, Vaikuṇṭha; *svam*—His own; *gopānām*—to the cowherd men; *tamasaḥ*—material darkness; *param*—beyond.

### TRANSLATION

**Thus deeply considering the situation, the all-merciful Supreme Personality of Godhead Hari revealed to the cowherd men His abode, which is beyond material darkness.**

### PURPORT

It is clear from this verse that the Absolute Truth dwells in His own eternal abode. Everyone of us tries to live as comfortably as possible, surrounding ourselves with peace and beauty. How can we, in the name of "logic," begrudge the Supreme Lord, our creator, the supremely beautiful and comfortable abode known by people in general as the kingdom of God?

### TEXT 15

**सत्यं ज्ञानमनन्तं यद् ब्रह्मज्योतिः सनातनम् ।
यद्धि पश्यन्ति मुनयो गुणापाये समाहिताः ॥१५॥**

*satyaṁ jñānam anantaṁ yad
brahma-jyotiḥ sanātanam*

*yad dhi paśyanti munayo*
*guṇāpāye samāhitāḥ*

*satyam*—indestructible; *jñānam*—knowledge; *anantam*—unlimited; *yat*—which; *brahma*—the absolute; *jyotiḥ*—effulgence; *sanātanam*—eternal; *yat*—which; *hi*—indeed; *paśyanti*—see; *munayaḥ*—sages; *guṇa*—the modes of material nature; *apāye*—when they subside; *samāhitāḥ*—absorbed in trance.

## TRANSLATION

**Lord Kṛṣṇa revealed the indestructible spiritual effulgence, which is unlimited, conscious and eternal. Sages see that spiritual existence in trance, when their consciousness is free of the modes of material nature.**

## PURPORT

In Text 14 Lord Kṛṣṇa revealed to the residents of Vṛndāvana His own abode, the spiritual planet of Kṛṣṇaloka. This and innumerable other Vaikuṇṭha planets float in an infinite ocean of spiritual light called the *brahmajyoti.* That spiritual light is in fact the spiritual sky, which Kṛṣṇa also, quite naturally, revealed to the residents of Vṛndāvana. For example, if we want to show the moon to a child, we say, "Look up in the sky. See the moon over there in the sky." Similarly, Lord Kṛṣṇa revealed the vast spiritual sky to the residents of Vṛndāvana, but as emphasized in Text 14 and in the following text, 16, the actual destination of the Lord's associates was His own spiritual planet.

## TEXT 16

ते तु ब्रह्महृदं नीता मग्नाः कृष्णेन चोद्धृताः ।
ददृशुर्ब्रह्मणो लोकं यत्राक्रूरोऽध्यगात् पुरा ॥१६॥

*te tu brahma-hradaṁ nītā*
*magnāḥ kṛṣṇena coddhṛtāḥ*
*dadṛśur brahmaṇo lokaṁ*
*yatrākrūro 'dhyagāt purā*

*te*—they; *tu*—and; *brahma-hradam*—to the lake known as Brahma-hrada; *nītāḥ*—brought; *magnāḥ*—submerged; *kṛṣṇena*—by Kṛṣṇa; *ca*—and; *uddhṛtāḥ*—lifted out; *dadṛśuḥ*—they saw; *brahmaṇaḥ*—of the Absolute Truth; *lokam*—the transcendental planet; *yatra*—where; *akrūraḥ*—Akrūra; *adhyagāt*—saw; *purā*—previously.

## TRANSLATION

**The cowherd men were brought by Lord Kṛṣṇa to the Brahma-hrada, made to submerge in the water, and then lifted up. From the same vantage point that Akrūra saw the spiritual world, the cowherd men saw the planet of the Absolute Truth.**

## PURPORT

The unlimited extension of spiritual light, called the *brahmajyoti* in Text 15, is compared to a lake called Brahma-hrada. Lord Kṛṣṇa submerged the cowherd men in that lake in the sense that He submerged them in the awareness of the impersonal Brahman. But then, as indicated by the word *uddhṛtāḥ,* He lifted them up to a higher understanding, that of the Personality of Godhead in His own planet. As clearly stated here, *dadṛśur brahmaṇo lokam:* They saw, just as Akrūra did, the transcendental abode of the Absolute Truth.

The evolution of consciousness may be briefly summarized as follows: In ordinary consciousness we perceive and are attracted to the variety of material things. Rising to the first stage of spiritual consciousness, we transcend material variety and focus instead on the undifferentiated One, which lies behind and gives existence to the many. Finally, rising to Kṛṣṇa consciousness, we find that the absolute, spiritual One contains its own eternal variety. In fact, since this world is a mere shadow of eternal existence, we would expect to find spiritual variety within the One, and indeed we do find it in the sacred text of *Śrīmad-Bhāgavatam.*

Astute readers may note that the pastime involving Akrūra takes place later in the *Bhāgavatam,* after the present affair with the cowherd men. The reason Śukadeva Gosvāmī says Akrūra saw Vaikuṇṭha *purā,* "previously," is that all these incidents took place many years before the conversation between Śukadeva Gosvāmī and Mahārāja Parīkṣit.

## TEXT 17

नन्दादयस्तु तं दृष्ट्वा परमानन्दनिवृताः ।
कृष्णं च तत्र च्छन्दोभिः स्तूयमानं सुविस्मिताः ॥१७॥

*nandādayas tu taṁ dṛṣṭvā*
*paramānanda-nivṛtāḥ*
*kṛṣṇaṁ ca tatra cchandobhiḥ*
*stūyamānaṁ su-vismitāḥ*

*nanda-ādayaḥ*—the cowherd men headed by Nanda Mahārāja; *tu*—and; *tam*—that; *dṛṣṭvā*—seeing; *parama*—supreme; *ānanda*—by ecstasy; *nivṛtāḥ*—overwhelmed with joy; *kṛṣṇam*—Lord Kṛṣṇa; *ca*—and; *tatra*—there; *chandobhiḥ*—by the Vedic hymns; *stūyamānam*—being praised; *su*—very much; *vismitāḥ*—surprised.

## TRANSLATION

**Nanda Mahārāja and the other cowherd men felt the greatest happiness when they saw that transcendental abode. They were especially amazed to see Kṛṣṇa Himself there, surrounded by the personified *Vedas*, who were offering Him prayers.**

## PURPORT

Although the residents of Vṛndāvana considered themselves ordinary persons, Lord Kṛṣṇa wanted them to know of their extraordinary good fortune. Thus, within a lake in the Yamunā River the Lord showed them His personal abode. The cowherd men were amazed to see that the kingdom of God had exactly the same spiritual atmosphere as their own earthly Vṛndāvana and that, just as in their Vṛndāvana Lord Kṛṣṇa was personally present, in their unique vision He was present as the Lord of the spiritual world.

As Śrīla Bhaktisiddhānta Sarasvatī Ṭhākura points out, these verses emphasize that Lord Kṛṣṇa did not merely show the cowherd men a sample Vaikuṇṭha planet but that He specifically revealed His Kṛṣṇaloka, the greatest of eternal abodes and the natural home of the residents of Vṛndāvana, who loved Kṛṣṇa more than anyone else did.

*Thus end the purports of the humble servant of His Divine Grace A. C. Bhaktivedanta Swami Prabhupāda to the Tenth Canto, Twenty-eighth Chapter, of the* Śrīmad-Bhāgavatam, *entitled "Kṛṣṇa Rescues Nanda Mahārāja from the Abode of Varuṇa."*

# Appendixes

# The Author

His Divine Grace Śrīla Hridayananda dāsa Goswami Ācāryadeva is one of the foremost spiritual leaders of the International Society for Krishna Consciousness. He enjoys the rare status of being among the first Western-born members of the authorized chain of disciplic succession descending from the Supreme Lord, Kṛṣṇa. In modern times, the most essential task of Kṛṣṇa conscious spiritual masters has been to translate the Vedic scriptures of ancient India into modern languages and distribute them widely throughout the world. Śrīla Ācāryadeva has made this mission his life and soul.

Śrīla Ācāryadeva appeared in this world on November 5, 1948, in Los Angeles, California. As an academically gifted student at the University of California, Berkeley, he attended a talk given by His Divine Grace A. C. Bhaktivedanta Swami Prabhupāda, the founder and spiritual master of the Kṛṣṇa consciousness movement. Impressed by Śrīla Prabhupāda's scholarship and saintliness, Śrīla Ācāryadeva became a member of the Kṛṣṇa consciousness community in Berkeley and, shortly thereafter, on February 8, 1970, was initiated as Śrīla Prabhupāda's disciple.

From the beginning, Śrīla Ācāryadeva distinguished himself by his oratorical skills, his spiritual dedication and his devotion to studying the writings of his spiritual master, through which he acquired a deep knowledge of Sanskrit. He quickly gained recognition from Śrīla Prabhupāda himself, who marked him as "a literary man" and in 1970 sent him to Boston to accept responsibilities with ISKCON's publishing activities there. Later, Śrīla Ācāryadeva served as president in ISKCON's centers in Gainesville, Florida, and Houston, Texas, and made a significant contribution to the rapid expansion of the Kṛṣṇa consciousness movement there in the early 1970s. In 1972, he adopted the renounced order (*sannyāsa*) in order to fully dedicate himself to serving the mission of his spiritual master: the propagation of the Kṛṣṇa consciousness movement throughout the world. For the next two years he traveled widely, speaking at colleges and universities throughout the United States.

In 1974, Śrīla Ācāryadeva was appointed to the Governing Body Commission of ISKCON and entrusted with the development of the Kṛṣṇa consciousness movement in Latin America. Over the following three years, he established twenty-five centers of the Society and attracted thousands of Latin Americans to the movement, as predicted by Śrīla Prabhupāda himself. In the course of his travels he met with numerous heads of state, government ministers and high religious leaders, conversing with them in fluent Spanish and Portuguese. He also founded the Spanish- and Portuguese-language divisions of the Bhaktivedanta Book Trust for the translation and publication of Śrīla Prabhupāda's books. At present, more than 20 million books in these two languages have been distributed throughout Latin America and abroad.

Shortly before his departure from this world in November, 1977, His Divine Grace Śrīla Prabhupāda chose Śrīla Ācāryadeva, along with ten other senior disciples, to accept the role of spiritual master and to initiate disciples. Currently, Śrīla Ācāryadeva serves as the Governing Body Commissioner for Brazil and the state of Florida and as one of the initiating spiritual masters for Latin America and the southern United States. His most challenging assignment came, however, in 1979, when the leaders of ISKCON, in recognition of his devotional scholarship, commissioned him to complete Śrīla Prabhupāda's monumental translation of and commentary on the *Śrīmad-Bhāgavatam*. For thousands of years in India, great spiritual masters have presented commentaries on the *Bhāgavatam* to make its urgent message clear to the people of their times. Śrīla Ācāryadeva is the first Westerner to be entrusted with this demanding task, and his success in communicating the essence of India's spiritual heritage to modern readers has already been noted by scholars and religionists around the world.

# His Divine Grace
# A. C. Bhaktivedanta Swami Prabhupāda

His Divine Grace A.C. Bhaktivedanta Swami Prabhupāda appeared in this world in 1896 in Calcutta, India. He first met his spiritual master, Śrīla Bhaktisiddhānta Sarasvatī Gosvāmī, in Calcutta in 1922. Bhaktisiddhānta Sarasvatī, a prominent religious scholar and the founder of sixty-four Gauḍīya Maṭhas (Vedic institutes), liked this educated young man and convinced him to dedicate his life to teaching Vedic knowledge. Śrīla Prabhupāda became his student, and eleven years later (1933) at Allahabad he became his formally initiated disciple.

At their first meeting, in 1922, Śrīla Bhaktisiddhānta Sarasvatī Ṭhākura requested Śrīla Prabhupāda to broadcast Vedic knowledge through the English language. In the years that followed, Śrīla Prabhupāda wrote a commentary on the *Bhagavad-gītā,* assisted the Gauḍīya Maṭha in its work and, in 1944, started *Back to Godhead,* an English fortnightly magazine. Maintaining the publication was a struggle. Singlehandedly, Śrīla Prabhupāda edited it, typed the manuscripts, checked the galley proofs, and even distributed the individual copies. Once begun, the magazine never stopped; it is now being continued by his disciples in the West and is published in over thirty languages.

Recognizing Śrīla Prabhupāda's philosophical learning and devotion, the Gauḍīya Vaiṣṇava Society honored him in 1947 with the title "Bhaktivedanta." In 1950, at the age of fifty-four, Śrīla Prabhupāda retired from married life, adopting the *vānaprastha* (retired) order to devote more time to his studies and writing. Śrīla Prabhupāda traveled to the holy city of Vṛndāvana, where he lived in very humble circumstances in the historic medieval temple of Rādhā-Dāmodara. There he engaged for several years in deep study and writing. He accepted the renounced order of life (*sannyāsa*) in 1959. At Rādhā-Dāmodara, Śrīla Prabhupāda began work on his life's masterpiece: a multivolume translation of and commentary on the eighteen-thousand-verse *Śrīmad-Bhāgavatam* (*Bhāgavata Purāṇa*). He also wrote *Easy Journey to Other Planets.*

After publishing three volumes of the *Bhāgavatam,* Śrīla Prabhupāda came to the United States, in September 1965, to fulfill the mission of his spiritual master. Subsequently, His Divine Grace wrote more than sixty volumes of authoritative translations, commentaries and summary studies of the philosophical and religious classics of India.

When he first arrived by freighter in New York City, Śrīla Prabhupāda was practically penniless. Only after almost a year of great difficulty did he establish the International Society for Krishna Consciousness, in July of 1966. Before his passing away on November 14, 1977, he guided the Society and saw it grow to a worldwide confederation of more than one hundred *āśramas*, schools, temples, institutes and farm communities.

In 1968, Śrīla Prabhupāda created New Vrindaban, an experimental Vedic community in the hills of West Virginia. Inspired by the success of New Vrindaban, now a thriving farm community of more than two thousand acres, his students have since founded several similar communities in the United States and abroad.

In 1972, His Divine Grace introduced the Vedic system of primary and secondary education in the West by founding the Gurukula school in Dallas, Texas. Since then, under his supervision, his disciples have established children's schools throughout the United States and the rest of the world, with the principal educational center now located in Vṛndāvana, India.

Śrīla Prabhupāda also inspired the construction of several large international cultural centers in India. The center at Śrīdhāma Māyāpur in West Bengal is the site for a planned spiritual city, an ambitious project for which construction will extend over the next decade. In Vṛndāvana, India, are the magnificent Kṛṣṇa-Balarāma Temple and International Guesthouse, and Śrīla Prabhupāda Memorial and Museum. There is also a major cultural and educational center in Bombay. Other centers are planned in a dozen important locations on the Indian subcontinent.

Śrīla Prabhupāda's most significant contribution, however, is his books. Highly respected by the academic community for their authority, depth and clarity, they are used as standard textbooks in numerous college courses. His writings have been translated into over fifty languages. The Bhaktivedanta Book Trust, established in 1972 to publish the works of His Divine Grace, has thus become the world's largest publisher of books in the field of Indian religion and philosophy.

In just twelve years, in spite of his advanced age, Śrīla Prabhupāda circled the globe fourteen times on lecture tours that took him to six continents. In spite of such a vigorous schedule, Śrīla Prabhupāda continued to write prolifically. His writings constitute a veritable library of Vedic philosophy, religion, literature and culture.

# References

The purports of *Śrīmad-Bhāgavatam* are all confirmed by standard Vedic authorities. The following authentic scriptures are specifically cited in this volume. For specific page references, consult the general index.

*Bhagavad-gītā*

*Brahma-saṁhitā*

*Bṛhad-viṣṇu Purāṇa*

*Caitanya-caritāmṛta*

*Hari-vaṁśa*

*Kṛṣṇa, the Supreme Personality of Godhead*

*Nārada-pañcarātra*

*Śrīmad-Bhāgavatam*

*Viṣṇu Purāṇa*

# Glossary

## A

**Ācārya**—a spiritual master who teaches by example.

## B

**Bakāsura**—a demon in the shape of a huge crane who was killed by Lord Kṛṣṇa.

**Brahmā**—the first created being in the universe. He is the subcreator under the supervision of the Supreme Lord.

**Brāhmaṇa**—a person wise in Vedic knowledge, fixed in goodness, and knowledgeable of Brahman, the Absolute Truth; a member of the first Vedic social order.

## C

**Caitanya Mahāprabhu**—Lord Kṛṣṇa in the role of His own devotee. He appeared five hundred years ago in Bengal, India, to teach love of God through the chanting of the Hare Kṛṣṇa *mantra.*

## D

**Daśārha**—the founder of one branch of the Yadu clan.

**Dvādaśī**—the twelfth day after both the full and the new moon.

**Durgā**—*See:* Kātyāyanī.

## E

**Ekādaśī**—the eleventh day after both the full and the new moon. On this day devotees of Kṛṣṇa fast and increase their remembrance of Him.

## G

**Gandharvas**—demigod singers and musicians.

**Garga Muni**—the family priest of the Yadu dynasty, in which Lord Kṛṣṇa appeared.

**Gopīs**—Lord Kṛṣṇa's cowherd girlfriends in Vṛndāvana. They are His most surrendered and confidential devotees.

## H

**Hiraṇyakaśipu**—a powerful demon who tormented his son Prahlāda, a great devotee, and was slain by Lord Nṛsiṁhadeva.

**Hiraṇyākṣa**—a powerful demon who challenged Lord Varāha and was slain by Him.

## I

**Indra**—the demigod who is the King of heaven. He controls the weather.

## K

**Kaṁsa**—a powerful demon who was an uncle of Lord Kṛṣṇa. He tried to kill the Lord in many ways but was ultimately slain by Him.

**Kātyāyanī**—the material energy personified. She is also known as Durgā and Kālī and by many other names.

**Kṛṣṇa-līlā**—Lord Kṛṣṇa's pastimes.

**Kṣatriyas**—the administrative and protective class; the second of the Vedic social orders.

## N

**Nārāyaṇa, Lord**—the Supreme Lord in His majestic, four-armed form. He is an expansion of Kṛṣṇa.

## P

**Pañcarātra**—Vedic supplementary literatures describing the process of Deity worship.

## R

**Rūpa Gosvāmī**—the chief of the six Gosvāmīs of Vṛndāvana, Vaiṣṇava spiritual masters who directly followed Lord Caitanya and systematically presented His teachings. He wrote many Sanskrit poetic and philosophical works on Kṛṣṇa consciousness.

## S

**Sāṅkhya**—the philosophical analysis of matter and spirit and the controller of both.

**Sautrāmaṇi**—a particular Vedic fire sacrifice offered to Lord Indra.

**Siddhas**—persons who have attained mystic powers by practicing *yoga.*

**Śiva**—the demigod in charge of the mode of ignorance and the destruction of the material manifestation. He is a special expansion of the Supreme Lord.

## T

**Tulasī**—Lord Kṛṣṇa's favorite plant.

## V

**Vaijayantī**—a garland made of five differently colored flowers and reaching down to the knees; often worn by Lord Kṛṣṇa.

**Vaikuṇṭha**—the spiritual realm, which is without (*vi*) anxiety (*kuṇṭha*).

**Vaiśyas**—farmers and merchants; the third Vedic social order.

**Viṣṇu, Lord**—a plenary expansion of Kṛṣṇa who creates and maintains the material universes.

**Yoga**—any one of several processes for linking one's consciousness with the Supreme.

# Sanskrit Pronunciation Guide

Throughout the centuries, the Sanskrit language has been written in a variety of alphabets. The mode of writing most widely used throughout India, however, is called *devanāgarī*, which means, literally, the writing used in "the cities of the demigods." The *devanāgarī* alphabet consists of forty-eight characters: thirteen vowels and thirty-five consonants. Ancient Sanskrit grammarians arranged this alphabet according to practical linguistic principles, and this order has been accepted by all Western scholars. The system of transliteration used in this book conforms to a system that scholars in the last fifty years have accepted to indicate the pronunciation of each Sanskrit sound.

**Vowels**

अ a आ ā इ i ई ī उ u ऊ ū ऋ ṛ

ॠ ṝ ऌ ḷ ए e ऐ ai ओ o औ au

**Consonants**

| | | | | | |
|---|---|---|---|---|---|
| Gutturals: | क ka | ख kha | ग ga | घ gha | ङ ṅa |
| Palatals: | च ca | छ cha | ज ja | झ jha | ञ ña |
| Cerebrals: | ट ṭa | ठ ṭha | ड ḍa | ढ ḍha | ण ṇa |
| Dentals: | त ta | थ tha | द da | ध dha | न na |
| Labials: | प pa | फ pha | ब ba | भ bha | म ma |
| Semivowels: | य ya | र ra | ल la | व va | |
| Sibilants: | श śa | ष ṣa | स sa | | |
| Aspirate: | ह ha | Anusvāra: ं ṁ | Visarga: ः ḥ | | |

## Numerals

० -0 १-1 २-2 ३-3 ४-4 ५-5 ६-6 ७-7 ८-8 ९-9

The vowels are written as follows after a consonant:

ा ā ि i ी ī ु u ू ū ृ ṛ ॄ ṝ े e ै ai ो o ौ au

For example: क ka का kā कि ki की kī कु ku कू kū

कृ kṛ कॄ kṝ के ke कै kai को ko कौ kau

Generally two or more consonants in conjunction are written together in a special form, as for example: क्ष kṣa त्र tra

The vowel "**a**" is implied after a consonant with no vowel symbol.

The symbol virāma ( ् ) indicates that there is no final vowel: क्

### The vowels are pronounced as follows:

**a** — as in but
**ā** — as in far but held twice as long as **a**
**ai** — as in **ai**sle
**au** — as in h**ow**
**e** — as in th**ey**
**i** — as in p**i**n
**ī** — as in p**i**que but held twice as long as **i**
**ḷ** — as in **lree**
**o** — as in **go**
**ṛ** — as in **ri**m
**ṝ** — as in **ree**d but held twice as long as **ṛ**
**u** — as in p**u**sh
**ū** — as in r**u**le but held twice as long as **u**

### The consonants are pronounced as follows:

**Gutturals**
**(pronounced from the throat)**
**k** — as in **k**ite
**kh** — as in Ec**kh**art
**g** — as in **g**ive
**gh** — as in di**g-h**ard
**ṅ** — as in si**ng**

**Labials**
**(pronounced with the lips)**
**p** — as in **p**ine
**ph** — as in u**p-h**ill (not **f**)
**b** — as in **b**ird
**bh** — as in ru**b-h**ard
**m** — as in **m**other

**Cerebrals**
**(pronounced with tip of tongue against roof of mouth)**
ṭ — as in **t**ub
ṭh — as in ligh**t-h**eart
ḍ — as in **d**ove
ḍh — as in re**d-h**ot
ṇ — as in si**n**g

**Dentals**
**(pronounced as cerebrals but with tongue against teeth)**
t — as in **t**ub
th — as in ligh**t-h**eart
d — as in **d**ove
dh — as in re**d-h**ot
n — as in **n**ut

**Aspirate**
h — as in **h**ome

**Anusvāra**
ṁ — a resonant nasal sound like in the French word *bon*

**Palatals**
**(pronounced with middle of tongue against palate)**
c — as in **ch**air
ch — as in staun**ch-h**eart
j — as in **j**oy
jh — as in he**dgeh**og
ñ — as in ca**ny**on

**Semivowels**
y — as in **y**es
r — as in **r**un
l — as in **l**ight
v — as in **v**ine, except when preceded in the same syllable by a consonant, then like in s**w**an

**Sibilants**
ś — as in the German word *sprechen*
ṣ — as in **sh**ine
s — as in **s**un

**Visarga**
ḥ — a final **h**-sound: **aḥ** is pronounced like **aha**; **iḥ** like **ihi**

There is no strong accentuation of syllables in Sanskrit, or pausing between words in a line, only a flowing of short and long (twice as long as the short) syllables. A long syllable is one whose vowel is long (**ā, ai, au, e, ī, o, ṝ, ū**) or whose short vowel is followed by more than one consonant (including **ḥ** and **ṁ**). Aspirated consonants (consonants followed by an **h**) count as single consonants.

# Index of Sanskrit Verses

This index constitutes a complete listing of the first and third lines of each of the Sanskrit poetry verses of this volume of *Śrīmad-Bhāgavatam*, arranged in English alphabetical order. The first column gives the Sanskrit transliteration, and the second and third columns, respectively, list the chapter-verse reference and page number for each verse.

## C



## D



## E



## G

# General Index

Numerals in boldface type indicate references to translations of the verses of *Śrīmad-Bhāgavatam*.


## A

*Abhava* defined, 196
Aborigine girls in Vṛndāvana, **18–19**
Absolute Truth
all existence resting on, 187
ignorance about, as debilitating, 90
illusion absent in, **218–19**
Kṛṣṇa as, 43, 45, 64, **68,** 95, 129, 187
pervasiveness of, 129
*Abudha-liṅga-bhāvah* defined, 190
*Ācārya(s). See:* Spiritual master(s); *specific spiritual masters*
Activities & knowledge, **106**
Acyuta, Lord. *See:* Kṛṣṇa
Aditi, **207**
*Agrahaṇa* defined, 188
*Ahaitukī* defined, 78
Airāvata
as Indra's elephant, **141**
Kṛṣṇa bathed by, **207**
Airplanes of demigods, **13–14**
*Ajānatā māmakena mūḍhena*
quoted, 215
*Ajñam* defined, 139
Akrūra, **228**
*Ambā* defined, 16
Aṁśu, **54**
Analogies
barleycorns burned and cooked & devotees' desires, **50**
birds & sages, 15
boats & sacrifices (fruitive), **138**
child & Kṛṣṇa, **182**
elephant & Kṛṣṇa, **166**
government & Kṛṣṇa, 224
hunger & attacks by Indra, 146
hungry person & Vṛndāvana residents, 146

Analogies (*continued*)
illicit lover & Indra, 119
lake & *brahmajyoti,* **228**
lotus flower & Govardhana, **166**
mushroom & Govardhana, **182**
new sprouts & desire (material), **50**
ocean & material existence, **138**
policeman & Kṛṣṇa, 224
rivers & wives of *brāhmaṇas,* **73**
rose-colored glasses & conditioned soul's perception, 68
sea & Kṛṣṇa, **73**
sprouts & desire (material), **50**
unfaithful woman & Vṛndāvana residents, 119
*Anayā su-labho jñeyā*
verse quoted, 29
*Anekārtha-varga* dictionary, quotation from on *śaraṇam's* definition, 150
Anger & modes of nature, **190**
*Annasya kṣuditaṁ pātram*
quoted, 65
Annihilation of universe, **121–22**
*Anurāga* defined, 173
*Arghya,* 20
Arjuna (cowherd boy), **54**
*Arjuna* trees, **169**
*Artha* defined, 218
*Asat* defined, 149
*Asyā āvarikā-śaktir*
verse quoted, 29
"As you sow, so shall you reap," 112
*Ataḥ sākhyam abhūt tasya*
verse quoted, 11
Atheism & Karma-mīmāṁsā philosophy, 112
188-189
*Avabhṛtha-snāna* defined, 33

## J



## K

Material nature
compared with spiritual world, 113
laws of. *See:* Laws of nature
mechanistic explanation of, **121–22**
*See also:* Material world
Material world
Māyā ruler of, 30
as shadow of eternal existence, 228
*See also:* Material nature
Mathurā, 154
Māyā
internal potencies of Kṛṣṇa &, 30
Mahā-, 30
Yoga-. *See:* Yogamāyā
*See also:* Illusion
*Mayaiva vihitān hi tān*
quoted, 116
"Me generation," 137
Mental speculation, 78
Milk products for Govardhana-pūjā, **124**
Mind & flute-playing of Kṛṣṇa, **6**
Modern society
fighting in, 193
pursuits of, 66-67
"scientific" approach to life in, 127
*See also:* Kali-yuga
Modes of nature
birth-death cycle via, 188, 190-91
causes for, **190**
conditioned souls contaminated by, 190
flow of, 188
freedom from, 188
goodness. *See:* Goodness, mode of
ignorance. *See:* Ignorance, mode of
Kṛṣṇa transcendental to, **186,** 188
passion. *See:* Passion, mode of
piety &, 188
Sāṅkhya philosophy's perception of, **121–22**
stupidity &, 188
time &, 188
type of material body &, 190
Moon compared with Kṛṣṇaloka, 227
*Muhūrtād deva-devasya*
verse quoted, 29
*Mūṅg dāl*, 27
*Mūrti* defined, 198
Music & demigods, 15-16

## N

Nanda Mahārāja
assembly hall of, 165
bathing in Yamunā, **214**–15, 216, 219
in *brāhmaṇas'* (ritualistic) village, 102
cowherd men instructed by, **174–80**
cowherd men question, about Kṛṣṇa, **165–74**
cowherd men told Varuṇa pastime by, **222**
cowherd men worship, **180**–81
Dvādaśī observed by, **214,** 215
Ekādaśī observed by, **214,** 215
Garga Muni quoted by, **175–79**
Indra sacrifice prepared for by, 102
as king of Vṛndāvana, **174**
Kṛṣṇa as perceived by, **180**
Kṛṣṇa blessed by, **159**
Kṛṣṇa debating with, about sacrifices, **107–27**
Kṛṣṇa explained by, to cowherd men, **174–80**
Kṛṣṇa inquiring from, about sacrifice preparations, **103–07**
Kṛṣṇa instructs, about Karma-mīmāṁsā, **111–19**
Kṛṣṇa recovers, from Varuṇa, **216–21**
Kṛṣṇa's arguments accepted by, **128**
Kṛṣṇa son of, **103, 105,** 106
parental role of, 105, 106
spiritual status of, 220
Varuṇa returns, to Kṛṣṇa, **219–20**
Varuṇa's servant arrests, **214–15**
Varuṇa worships, 219
Vṛndāvana residents worship, **180, 181**
Yamunā bathed in by, **214–215,** 216, 219
Yamunā River bathed in by, 219
Yaśodā wife of, 11
Nanda Mahārāja quoted
on Indra, **107–10**
on Kṛṣṇa, nature of, **174–80**
on sacrifice to Indra, **107–10**
Nārada Muni, **208**
*Nārada-pañcarātra,* quotation from
on energies of Kṛṣṇa, various, 29-30
Nārāyaṇa, Lord
compared with Kṛṣṇa, 105, **179**

Vṛndāvana residents (*continued*)
Kṛṣṇa leads, in worshiping Govardhana, **131–**32
Kṛṣṇa protects, **149–56**
Kṛṣṇa shelter for, **144–54**
Kṛṣṇa's pastimes puzzle, **164–74**
Kṛṣṇa's relationships with (various), 158
love for Kṛṣṇa by, 129, 131, **173,** 230
perception about Kṛṣṇa by, **222,** 224–25
pray to Kṛṣṇa for protection, **145**
prosperity of, 140–41
protection of, by Kṛṣṇa, **149–56**
relationship with, to Govardhana Hill, **122–**23
status of, spiritual, 129
wives of *brāhmaṇas* associating with, 83, 93
Yogamāyā &, 224
*See also:* Cowherd boys; Cowherd men; *Gopīs; specific residents*
Vṛṣabha, **54**
Vṛṣabhānu, 33

## W

Welfare activities
as duty, **56**
by trees, **54–56**
Western countries, democracy in, 193
Wind-gods, **141, 143**
Wives of *brāhmaṇas* (ritualistic)
compared to rivers, **73**
compared with *gopīs,* 77, 81, 86, 98–99
compared with husbands (their), 91–92, 98–99
compared with sages, **76**
conjugal feelings of, toward Kṛṣṇa, 73
cowherd boys &, **70–72**
detention of one, **87**
as devotees, **70**
ecstatic symptoms of, 92
vs. husbands, **74,** 77, 83
husbands of. *See: Brāhmaṇas* (ritualistic)
husbands reunited with, **86**
Wives of *brāhmaṇas* (ritualistic) (*continued*)
Kṛṣṇa addressed by, **81–82**
Kṛṣṇa addresses, **77–80,** 81–82, **84–85**
Kṛṣṇa embraced by, within hearts, **76**
Kṛṣṇa instructs, **78–79, 84–85**
Kṛṣṇa met by, on Yamunā bank, **74–86**
Kṛṣṇa requests, to return to husbands, **80, 84–85**
Kṛṣṇa's assurance to, **84–85**
Kṛṣṇa sends cowherd boys to, **70**
Kṛṣṇa's understanding of, **77**
Kṛṣṇa welcomes, **77**
love for Kṛṣṇa by, **76,** 77
material body of one, given up, **87**
praised by *brāhmaṇas* (ritualistic), **91–93**
prayers to Kṛṣṇa by, **81–82**
relatives of, **74,** 83, **84**
separation from Kṛṣṇa advised for, **84–85**
spiritual training lacked by, **93**
status of, spiritual, **76,** 89
surrender to Kṛṣṇa by, **72–74, 76, 80–82,** 83
*tulasī* leaves &, **81–**82
Vṛndāvana residents' association with, 83, 93
Wives of demigods. *See:* Demigod(s), wives of
Women
etiquette for, 42
Kṛṣṇa's attractiveness for, **13**
Work
defined, 118
worship to, **117–18**
Workers (*śūdras*), 119
Worship
to demigod(s)
compared with worship to Kṛṣṇa, 116–17
devotees &, 30–31
discouraged, 116
by *gopīs,* **27–31,** 38, 42
Kṛṣṇa angered by, 119
to duty, **117**